SON OF A GAMBLING MAN

SON OF A GAMBLING MAN

*My Journey from a Casino Family
to the Governor's Mansion*

GOVERNOR BOB MILLER

with a Foreword by President Bill Clinton

THOMAS DUNNE BOOKS
St. Martin's Press
New York

THOMAS DUNNE BOOKS.
An imprint of St. Martin's Press.

SON OF A GAMBLING MAN. Copyright © 2013 by Bob Miller. Foreword
copyright © 2013 by Bill Clinton. All rights reserved. Printed in the
United States of America. For information, address St. Martin's
Press, 175 Fifth Avenue, New York, N.Y. 10010.

www.thomasdunnebooks.com
www.stmartins.com

Design by Kathryn Parise

Library of Congress Cataloging-in-Publication Data

Miller, Bob, 1945–
   Son of a gambling man : my journey from a casino family to the governor's mansion /
Governor Bob Miller. — First Edition.
       pages cm
   ISBN 978-0-312-59181-6 (hardcover)
   ISBN 978-1-250-01246-3 (e-book)
   1. Miller, Bob, 1945–   2. Nevada—Politics and government—20th century.   3. Las Vegas
(Nev.)—History—20th century.   4. Gambling—Nevada—Las Vegas—History—20th
century.   5. Casinos—Nevada—Las Vegas—History—20th century.   6. Governors—
Nevada—Biography.   7. Las Vegas (Nev.)—Biography.   8. Nevada—Biography.   I. Title.
   F845.25.M45A3 2013
   979.3'033092—dc23
   [B]

2012042077

St. Martin's Press books may be purchased for educational, business, or promotional use.
For information on bulk purchases, please contact Macmillan Corporate and Premium
Sales Department at 1-800-221-7945 extension 5442 or write
specialmarkets@macmillan.com.

First Edition: March 2013

10   9   8   7   6   5   4   3   2   1

To Billy V

In the void of paternal guidance, few people are fortunate enough to have someone in their life that can simultaneously fulfill the role of counselor, soothsayer, and friend. Regrettably, my dad died early in my professional career. Fortunately, I have had Billy Vassiliadis to depend upon for honest and objective advice. In a front-page story, the *New York Times* once characterized Billy V as "the Pied Piper of Las Vegas" and perhaps the most powerful Nevadan, noting his "perfect pitch" talent for spinning "sand into pure gold." The Grey Lady understates his value. He has been with me for innumerable decisions, from the cutthroat state budget resolutions affecting all Nevadans to the comparatively trivial family dynamics involving our annual Christmas card photo. If a man can be judged by the quality of his family and friends, then I am so humbled and proud. My dear friend Billy V is without equal, a reliable personal oracle who, incidentally, played such a meaningful, yet typical unassuming, role in retelling my life's tale.

Contents

Acknowledgments   ix

Author's Note   xi

Foreword   xiii

Prologue   1

Part 1
Growing Up in the Shadow of the Mob
7

1 The Chicago Years   9

2 An Offer He Couldn't Refuse   17

3 Adjusting to Las Vegas   23

4 Ross Miller, Casino Big Shot   31

5 The Millers Begin Living the Vegas Life   37

6 Ross Miller Gets Connected in Vegas   49

7 Bob Miller Gets Launched into the World   55

Contents

Part II
Maturing in the Shadow of a Changing Las Vegas
61

8 Leaving Las Vegas—For a Time 63

9 My Brush with History 73

10 Ross Miller and the Great Ringmaster Join Hands 79

11 Law School Grooms Bob Miller for Law Enforcement 85

12 A Klutz Woos a Blond Beauty 93

13 Bob Miller's Political Career Begins 95

14 From the Bench to DA, and Ross Miller's Ghost Appears
for the First Time 101

15 Being District Attorney—Carl Thomas and Vegas Stereotypes 111

16 Crushing Tony the Ant 119

17 Becoming Dick Bryan's Lieutenant 127

18 Sticking It Back to Chic 141

Part III
Governing in the Shadow of an Exploding State
149

19 Acting as Governor, a Role I Never Imagined I Would Fill 151

20 Becoming Governor Proves to Be No Mirage 165

21 A Vegas Visionary 173

22 Controlling a Riot 181

23 A Question of Eligibility 195

24 The Campaign for Governor—A Worthy Opponent 203

25 Taking on the Gaming Industry 215

26 Your Excellency? 221

27 The End of My Political Career, the Beginning of a New Life 229

Epilogue 241

Index 243

Acknowledgments

The following people generously contributed stories and details, insights, and other useful input into the book:

Patty Becker, Rex Bell Jr., Keith Copher, Scott Craigie, Drake Delanoy, Ralph Denton, Shecky Greene, R. J. Heher, Charlotte Hill, Stan Hunterton, Jan Jones, Howard Klein, Ralph Lamb, Bruce Layne, Catherine Cortez Masto, Jim Mulhall, Ann Nelson, Kent Oram, Maria Radeva, Frank Schreck, Ellie Shattuck, David Sheppard, Jeff Silver, Tom Tait, Tito Tiberti, Perry Thomas, Richard Urey, Billy Vassiliadis, Don Wadsworth, Bob Walsh, Angelo Webster, Helen Weimer, and Claudine Williams.

I must also thank my wife, Sandy, and our children, Ross, Corrine, and Megan, who have shared my life and whose encouragement and support made this book possible.

History professor Michael Green of the College of Southern Nevada, retired state archivist Guy Rocha, and UNLV professor Sue DiBella all assisted me in gathering thoughts and data.

My assistants Kay Finfrock and Karlette Adams-Dixon helped keep me on track. Mike Sion provided guidance in the early formation of the book. Jack Sheehan provided some background information. Sara Hinckley and Joseph DiDomizio of the Hudson Group guided me to a publisher.

Acknowledgments

And of course the team of Thomas Dunne Books made this possible. Brendan Deenan provided the editorial expertise necessary to finish the book, while Nicole Sohl of Thomas Dunne Books helped guide me in the necessary procedures. Rachel Howard and Laura Clark coordinated marketing. My sincerest appreciation goes to Thomas Dunne, who took a personal interest in this book and gave me the encouragement and guidance to make my story worthy to be a part of his collection.

Importantly, I also thank my friend Jon Ralston. I have interacted with a good number of journalists, yet perhaps none as skilled as Jon Ralston. His work ethic is unparalleled, his search for the truth is nobler than anyone I've encountered, and his dogged pursuit of the facts is relentless. We have not always agreed, but such is the nature of our professions. I am so honored that Jon agreed to help me in this endeavor. He provided immense help in shaping my unrefined vision of the parallels between my life's progression and that of Nevada. He played an invaluable role in transforming a very raw draft into my life story. I deeply appreciate his help—he is an extraordinary journalist, one who has not only witnessed Nevada's development, but has in fact influenced it through his relentless determination to fairly uncover the truth. I certainly owe him thanks for his instrumental assistance in the pages that follow, but as a Nevadan, I also thank him for dedicating his career to our community.

Author's Note

This is not a typical autobiography. When I first began, I wrote what now seem as universal details of my life, including stories about my incomparable wife and terrific children as well as vignettes about my life's adventures. But along the way, I realized there was a different, more important story to tell. That story, of the son of a Chicago bookmaker with ties to the Outfit who became Nevada's longest-serving governor, parallels the metamorphosis of Las Vegas and Nevada, from a place run by the mob to one where some of the most successful, sophisticated corporations on Earth reside. This is a story of a boy born into the gambling world, who grew into a man who oversaw a gambling world that grew along with him. This is a tale that could not have happened in any other state or in any other city, which I watched—and I hope, assisted—turn from a dusty little railroad stop into the Entertainment Capital of the World. I could not have done any of this without my family and with countless people who have helped me along the way. I couldn't begin to name all the people who have been important to me on my journey—if I did so, this book would be the length of a Russian novel. Instead, I want to give you the signposts of a life that made me what I am as I witnessed and participated in what made Las Vegas and Nevada what they have become. It has been quite the ride, and that is what I want to share here.

Foreword

Las Vegas is one of the most fascinating cities in America. Like so many others, I'll never forget the first time I pulled into town—the city lights glowing across the desert on a warm night in 1966. It's a city that has always treated me well, and I've never tired of hearing tales of its spectacular rise.

What one hundred years ago was just a tiny, dusty stop on the railroad is now the most recognized tourist destination in the world. It is the only city whose population doubled in every decade of the twentieth century, and with that growth came remarkable changes in the community. Bob Miller has had a front-row seat for many of those changes, and he captures them marvelously in the pages that follow.

When I first met Bob in late 1988, he was about to become the twenty-sixth governor of Nevada. He would be the first—and is still the only—governor in state and national history to come from a family with a background in casino gaming. Bob's father was a colorful character that only a gambling town could produce (and I should know, having encountered several of them during my youth in Hot Springs, Arkansas). His generation of Nevadans brought gaming from its illicit roots to the licensed industry we know today. But while Bob has no shortage of stories about that rough-and-tumble era of casinos, he chose a career in law enforcement, which ultimately led into politics.

In the quarter century that I've known Bob and his wife, Sandy, I've learned just why he earned the respect of Nevadans without regard to his family history. He is a man of integrity who cares deeply about the issues facing his state and nation, and who has always been willing to put aside differences to solve problems. That's why his fellow governors selected him to chair the National Governors Association, just as the nation's prosecutors had earlier chosen him as president of the National District Attorneys Association.

Bob's journey could only have happened in Nevada. His memoir gives us all a unique, entertaining, and thought-provoking glimpse of how Las Vegas evolved from its outcast roots to the modern metropolis nicknamed "the All-American City."

—Bill Clinton

Its inhabitants are, as the man once said, "whores, pimps, gamblers, and sons of bitches," by which he meant Everybody. Had the man looked through another peephole he might have said, "Saints and angels and martyrs and holy men," and he would have meant the same thing. —John Steinbeck, *Cannery Row*

SON OF A GAMBLING MAN

Prologue

Looking back, I suppose it was the call I was expecting my entire political life. My past—or should I say my dad's past—had come into the present to threaten my ascension to the pinnacle of Nevada politics.

My dad had been an issue before, but never like this and never with so much at stake. The headline was even worse than I imagined it might be: "Nevada Official Vouched for Man Linked to Mobsters."

The date was September 18, 1988. The headline was in, of all strange places, the *San Jose Mercury News*. I don't know to this day why a Washington, D.C.–based reporter from a northern California newspaper would have done what I saw as a hit piece on a lieutenant governor from Nevada.

But when you'd been in politics as long as I had, you knew there was no such thing as a coincidence. Ironically, the context had nothing to do with any race I was in. But Dick Bryan, the governor who had asked me to run for lieutenant governor a couple of years previously, was running for the U.S. Senate. And his opponent, Sen. Chic Hecht, had no bullets left to fire. He was behind and he needed a new issue. So he loaded me into his gun; I would become governor if Bryan was elected in less than two months.

"The man who could become Nevada's governor next year wrote a confidential character reference for a political supporter and close family friend who had ties to organized crime and was convicted of skimming casino proceeds, federal records show," the story began.

My interview with the reporter is blurry almost a quarter century later. I had written the letter five years earlier, but I was perplexed by the call. I would later realize I had not handled it well at all.

For a guy who had been in politics since 1975, I made a rookie error—I denied something easily proven and then had to concede it was true. Here's what happened:

My father, Ross Miller, had come to Las Vegas in the mid-1950s after a career as an illegal bookmaker in Chicago. One of his close friends was a man named Carl Thomas, whom Dad had taken on as a business partner. He was close to my parents and I knew him as well. After my father died in 1975, Thomas visited my mother almost every day.

My father had been a classic example of what Vegas gaming executives were back in those days—someone with what journalists like to call a colorful past, who had been involved in illegal activities somewhere else but who came to the State of Second Chances to start over. But Thomas was different—he was held out by some of the gaming authorities, even then-Gov. Bob List, as the type of individual they wanted to be involved in Nevada gaming. He was well educated, a self-made man, well spoken, well groomed. On the surface he appeared to be a person who was a forerunner to the type of licensees we have now.

So imagine my shock when Thomas was indicted in 1981 of skimming money from Las Vegas casinos. I was in my first term as the district attorney of Clark County, and all I knew of Thomas was that he was a reliable, caring family friend. After Thomas was convicted, I had a decision to make as he awaited sentencing.

I don't recall who asked me to write a letter on his behalf. But I talked to my friend and close political adviser, Billy Vassiliadis, before I did it. He was unequivocal. He told me not to do it.

"You're going to get hit," he said. "Why would you do this?"

I knew his political advice was sound. I had just been reelected as district attorney. I didn't anticipate running for lieutenant governor or governor, but I thought I might run for DA again. I knew the letter potentially would be used against me. I just decided that I would live with that.

The letter to Kansas City federal judge Joseph E. Stevens was dated July 28, 1983. It was three and a half pages and I was as honest as I could be about where I had come from. I identified my dad as "an illegal bookmaker in Chicago," but I explained to the judge that the "gaming industry in our state was in its early evolution, and experienced gamers could only be found by drawing upon the resources of illegal operators in other states."

My dad was one of those resources and, I explained to the judge, Carl Thomas was one of his friends. I endeavored to tell only of the Thomas I knew, a man who provided my mother "with friendship and compassion" after my father died. I talked about his other positive character traits and even tried to "distinguish him from my father" in his "docile, nonviolent nature."

I neither downplayed Thomas's mistakes, nor did I recommend a sentence. But Vassiliadis was right that it would live on, and the day of reckoning arrived just over five years later on September 18, 1988.

Most political insiders knew when Bryan ran for reelection as governor in 1986 that he would almost certainly take on Hecht in two years, leaving a vacancy for me to fill if he, as most speculated, defeated the weak incumbent.

Bryan seemed to have the race won, but a series of unfortunate events had made the race closer than he would have liked. And now this serendipitous *Mercury News* story had given Hecht one last chance to make up ground less than two months before the election.

The piece rehashed a lot of painful history. My dad had been indicted, like Thomas, for skimming. But the charges later were dropped. The reporter brought up infamous Kansas City wiretaps in which Thomas and another mob-tainted man, Allen Dorfman, were bragging to high-level Mafia types about their relationship with me. They were merely puffing, but it sounded as if I could be, in the parlance, gotten to.

The story quoted one of the tapes:

"The kid's very strong now," Thomas said during the recording. *". . . Super kid. I raised all the money for him. . . . He's been on my payroll (at the Slots-A-Fun) since he quit his job."*

Another one had Dorfman calling Thomas and suggesting my father's friend get me to help mob killer Tony Spilotro get a "fair judge." According to a transcript of the tape, Dorfman said: *"Personally, I have no apprehensions of going to him on this at all. Not for one second. I know the . . . kid since he was born . . . You know our friend, young, young Bobby? I want you to reach out for him and have him call me."*

So there it was: My name mentioned in proximity to an infamous Mafia hit man, Tony "the Ant" Spilotro, who would later be immortalized in Martin Scorsese's *Casino*. Civella and Dorfman also were well-known names in mob lore—and now mentioned in the same breath as the elected district attorney of Sin City.

To say this looked bad would be like saying Charles Manson was not a nice man. Some of this stuff had been used in bits and pieces before and been knocked down in lower-profile campaigns. But it had never been synthesized and laid bare in a national newspaper, and the letter had never before been made public. I believed the writer omitted what I considered important facts, even though this was written by future Pulitzer Prize winner David Wildman.

The story was potentially very damaging—to Bryan's race and to my future. I knew we had to do something.

The local media were all over the story and Hecht pretended he had just walked in on Louis Renault's gambling joint: The senator claimed there was a "cloud of suspicion" surrounding me, raising questions whether I was fit to take over for Bryan should he win.

The Bryan campaign knew he had to respond, and I realized my future was at risk, too. Bryan's lead had slipped, the Democratic presidential nominee—Michael Dukakis—was a drag, and the governor essentially was playing not to lose. In the meantime my credibility was being hammered constantly in a forum where I was not the primary focus.

The story had to be stopped dead in its tracks. And there was only one way to do it.

With Billy Vassiliadis's help, we assembled an array of law enforcement people to vouch for me. I made phone calls, believing people in law enforcement would support me.

We had the top law enforcement representatives from Las Vegas and Reno and past federal officials, too.

The news conference occurred a few weeks after the *Mercury* story had run. Each participant testified to my honesty and integrity. Clark County sheriff John Moran had the most memorable quote: "You can rest assured that Bob Miller is no more an associate of organized crime than the pope."

Vassiliadis told me that would be the headline—Moran's quote about the pope—and he was right.

But it meant even more to me that Stan Hunterton, a lawyer who had once been head of the federal Organized Crime Strike Force in Las Vegas and subsequently was the deputy chief counsel to the president's commission on organized crime during 1984–85, assured reporters the implication from the Hecht campaign was nonsense.

Years later, I saw Hecht's campaign manager, Ken Rietz, on an airplane. He told me that the response press conference had cost Hecht the election—he lost by four points that November to Bryan, and I became acting governor, just ninety days after I had essentially been accused of being a mob plant in Las Vegas government.

Shortly after the election, much to my surprise, another national reporter, this one from *The Washington Post,* was interested in interviewing me. His story appeared on January 2, the day before I assumed the governorship.

I cringed as I read the beginning:

Even before Marlon Brando and Al Pacino in the film *The Godfather* discussed putting a Mafia son into a governor's chair, paperback novelists and conspiracy theorists fretted over the political potential of organized crime.

So what are they to make of Robert (Bob) Miller, who is both the next governor of Nevada and the son of casino owner and former illegal bookmaker Ross Miller, a man who before his death had friends linked to organized crime and was once indicted (but not prosecuted) for alleged skimming of gambling profits?

One of the subheads was not great, either: "Bookmaker's Son to be Nevada Governor."

But the headline, over a story that got better after those sensational first two paragraphs, struck a chord with me: "Son of a Gambling Man."

That's who I am, and I wear the label with pride. I come from a family whose patriarch was involved in illicit activity and who migrated to Las Vegas and became a respectable, successful businessman. I grew up in a city and state that was built by such men, who came here to escape their colorful pasts, and who helped reshape and modernize Las Vegas and Nevada. Eventually, I became the longest-serving governor in state history, presiding over a Nevada where men named Steve Wynn built iconic palaces and where publicly traded corporations did what Ross Miller could never have imagined on the Las Vegas Strip.

This is my story.

Part I

Growing Up in the Shadow of the Mob

1

The Chicago Years

I was eight years old, and we were frolicking in Wonder Lake, just outside of Chicago, where all good mob stories begin, when it happened. My friends and I were playing in the water not far from shore. Suddenly, my father was charging into the lake toward us, clutching a piece of wood above his head. As we stared, eyes wide, he began thrashing violently at the surface around us. In the next instant, we understood. Amazed, we watched as he hoisted an enormous water snake into the air and carried it ashore.

Ross Miller's face betrayed no fear, uncertainty, or hesitation—only determination. The snake never had a chance. He draped its lifeless six-foot length over the cabin fence and left us to our child's play.

That is one of the few, albeit telling and vivid, memories I have of my father, a man of few words and decisive action who, I would later learn, was an illegal bookmaker who consorted with underworld associates. My father was not in the mob, but he was *of* the mob, and it is part of my heritage that I neither shun nor embrace. It simply is. My father was a mysterious figure to me when I was a child...and, indeed, would remain so to most of the people around him for the better part of his life.

Ross Miller was born in 1908 in the tiny town of Equality in southeastern Illinois, the third of five children—four sons and a daughter. My grandfather was a coal miner who died when my father was a young child. Neither my dad nor any of my uncles would follow his dangerous career path. In fact, my father had to drop out of high school to help support the family. He had to become a man too young, but he was chronologically—and temperamentally, perhaps—still a teenager.

One night, he and my Uncle Herschel snuck into a factory after hours and started goofing around with the equipment. At some point, my dad placed his hand in one of the machines. In a stroke of horrible luck, Herschel happened to flip a switch that started the equipment running. My father's right hand was terribly mangled. His ring finger was chopped off about two-thirds the way down, and his index and middle finger were broken. Ever-intrepid, he and Herschel found the missing finger and ran all the way home with it.

In those days, surgical reattachment was unheard of, but that didn't stop my grandmother from hoping. She pickled her son's severed digit and kept it in a jar in the kitchen for many years to come. Perhaps she prayed that modern medicine would prevail and the finger could be reunited with the others on her son's hand. Or maybe she just wanted to preserve the floating finger as a lesson for her sons to avoid foolish behavior in the future.

My father was forced to live the rest of his life with a stub instead of a fourth finger, and the other two damaged fingers were bent at odd angles. He must have adapted well enough because many years later he became a very accurate marksman in the U.S. Army during World War II. He never got to use the skill in battle, though. Perhaps his sharp-shooting ability brought attention to his hand, for it wasn't long after he scored high in target shooting that he was honorably discharged because of the disfigurement.

In their late teens or early twenties, my father and Uncle Herschel drifted between Detroit and Chicago. What they did to get by in that period, I don't know. He never talked about it. But he eventually earned his high school equivalency diploma. At one point he worked as a clerk in a Chicago law office, on his way to becoming a lawyer. But he didn't carry through. Perhaps the time commitment was too great and the wages too meager.

He expressed regret to me, in his later years, that he wasn't able to continue long enough in that law office to become a lawyer. I'm sure this is one reason why one day he would so strongly encourage me to go to law school. He always made it clear that I was not to follow him into the casino business. I rarely questioned what was behind my father's advice; I just always knew that if he said it was not right for me, he did so for good reasons.

Sometime after Prohibition ended in 1933, my father and Uncle Herschel, now in their late twenties, came to own a north Chicago bar. The Silver Palm was a combination burlesque club and bookie joint. To one side of the bar was a door with a secret buzzer that led to the betting operation in back. Down the other side was a stage for the strippers. The Silver Palm was on Wilson Avenue under an elevated ("El") subway station. Today the bar is gone, but the building houses a large pawnshop. The neighborhood hasn't changed much.

One way or another, the Silver Palm seems to have done good business. Dad was a go-getter, a real hustler, with a strong work ethic. Besides the bar, he managed prizefighters, which would eventually change his life and make mine.

In 1943, when Dad went to a Chicago club one night after a boxing card he'd promoted, he was struck by the beauty of a young dancer in the chorus line. Her name: Coletta Jane Doyle, known as "the Irish Songbird," although she was more a dancer than a singer. She had light-brown hair, stood five-foot-two, was twenty-one years old, and had been dancing professionally since her late teens. She was talented; she'd even performed in a show with a rising young comedian named Danny Thomas (who went on to become one of America's most celebrated TV entertainers), and she and the other dancers sometimes attended Mass with him on Sunday mornings. Her parents and three brothers had immigrated to America from the area of the port city of Drogheda, Ireland,* in 1920. Coletta was

---

* My wife and daughters and I took a trip to Ireland and drove to Drogheda. We found all of the locations where my grandfather and uncles had lived, except the street where my grandfather was born. We knew it was named Crooked Street and we went to a church to ask directions.

born the following year. Her father supported the family as a house painter. Her brothers were thirteen to fifteen years older than she, and protective of their baby sister. After she and Ross Miller began going out together, one of her brothers always chaperoned. Of course, the fact that my dad owned a bar might have made that duty less onerous.

Eventually it was apparent that this was a serious courtship. My father and Coletta Doyle dated for a year. One of the few stories about my father that my mother told me in later years, after Ross Miller had died, concerned a time when a couple of wise guys, whom she described as Mafia-connected hoodlums, made some inappropriate comments about her. My father decided they had gone too far. In the ensuing brawl, two of them proved to be no match for one of him. But Ross Miller knew that might not be the end of it; they were the sort of weasels who could be tempted to shoot him in the back. He phoned Uncle Herschel at the Silver Palm to bring him a pistol, just in case. My mother said my father had no regard for Mafia thugs, and did not associate with them.

My father wasn't a gangster, but because of the nature of his business, he moved in their world. He could handle it; he was a tough guy. Having grown up hard, he knew how to use his fists. When I was older, I learned from Uncle Hersch, as I and others usually called him, that when he and my father ran the Silver Palm, they never bothered hiring bouncers. The Miller brothers were quite capable of handling whatever problems came up. Uncle Hersch wasn't as intimidating as my dad, but he was a bit larger and burlier. Later, after they sold the bar in Chicago, Uncle Hersch moved on to Hot Springs, Arkansas, where the authorities tended to look the other way. Eventually he came to Las Vegas, and what little I learned about my father's background, I mostly learned from Uncle Hersch in his later years, when we golfed together. My uncle, although fairly tight-lipped like Dad had been, would occasionally tell me a story about the old days in Chicago.

Finding no one in the church we went next door to a pub to ask the bartender. One of three men sitting at a table looked up and said, "I wouldn't be knowin' where Crooked Street is, but when I leave this pub every street is Crooked Street." We never did find it.

One anecdote speaks volumes to me about my father's character. When Ross Miller and Coletta Doyle married in 1944, it was in a Catholic church. Dad was not Catholic. He was Protestant (though nonobservant). Yet when the priest who married them asked Dad to promise that he would raise his children Catholic, Dad gave his word. And true to his nature, he kept it.

He may have moved around in a rough world, but Ross Miller lived by certain unwavering principles. And paramount among those was that if you said it, you did it. Your word was your bond. In the world of illegal gambling, written contracts had little or no place. The ethic of keeping one's word was deeply ingrained in Ross Miller. And it extended into all areas of his life, no matter who he was keeping company with.

Of all of my dad's qualities, this one may have been most ingrained in his son. Later, when I would go into politics, I would try to keep all the promises I made. And I learned not to make promises I couldn't keep. I might not have realized it contemporaneously with my campaigning or serving, but the spirit of Ross Miller was guiding me in how I conducted myself. People have said a lot of things about my father and about me, but those who knew us would say we were men of our word.

I was born on March 30, 1945, and from the time I was of age, in keeping with Dad's promise, I was sent to Catholic schools.

Even though my father worked odd hours and I didn't see much of him, it was far from a lonely existence for my mom and me. There were always aunts, uncles, and cousins around. Usually they were the relatives on Mom's side, although my aunt Louise, Dad's sister, had a daughter, Ethel, about my age, and so I spent a lot of time with her.

My uncle Hersch dropped by once in a while. My uncle Joseph, Dad's youngest brother, lived in Chicago, and we occasionally saw him and his three children, who were a bit younger than me. He sold ads for the Yellow Pages of the phone book. Dad's oldest brother, Eugene, drifted in and out of our lives. Uncle Gene was a character. He was smaller than his brothers and didn't share their naturally macho nature. He compensated with an exaggerated image of himself. He sported a large mustache and considered himself debonair. He was a theatrical booking agent in Detroit, a wheeler-dealer type. He was the talker in the family.

My father, as I said, was stoic. To him, business was business, and these matters weren't discussed with the wife or children. Ross Miller's world was black and white. He did business with a word and a firm handshake, and that meant the deal was sealed and not to be broken. He expected those he dealt with to abide by this creed, as well. I admired Dad's integrity, and strove to follow suit. I never wanted to disappoint him. I wanted to be a standup guy, like him. I also knew from a very young age that I wasn't cut from the same tough cloth as he and Uncle Hersch. I didn't have their personalities. Whatever it was I'd end up doing for a living when I grew up, I knew I wouldn't be following Dad's career path, of which I had only a vague idea at the time, anyway. He made sure of that, too. If there was one cardinal rule in our house, it was that there was to be no gambling of any kind, or even the instruments of gambling. No dice. No deck of cards. Not even for a game of gin rummy.

It was understood that I would graduate high school and go to college, even though neither of my parents nor any of their siblings had done so. The Millers were a family that aimed to get ahead. Ross and Coletta Miller recognized that education was the route to upward mobility, and respectability. And so they sheltered me from what Dad did for a living. Mom seldom brought me to the Silver Palm. When she did, it was in daytime when the club was empty. I never saw the back room that was a bookie joint. But one time when we showed up to get him, I walked down the other side of the room to where the stage was in back. What grabbed my attention was the drum kit. I sat at it and banged on the skins. Fortunately, no strippers were around to come out and shock me.

I had no clue what took place on this empty stage during performances at night. And no one was about to tell me.

Our little apartment was on the second floor of a three-story brownstone, about eight blocks from Lakeshore Drive, set among other brownstones. All the other kids in our neighborhood lived in the same sort of small apartments, dressed in similar clothes, walked to the same schools. Mine, St. Gertrude's, was a half block away. One luxury item our family had that most of our neighbors didn't was a television set. It was in a big wood frame with a tiny screen, and sat in the living room. I was a regular viewer of *The Howdy Doody Show.**

On a typical Saturday, each of the kids in the neighborhood would be given a quarter by their parents and walk to one of the two nearby movie theaters, where a dime got you in and fifteen cents paid for popcorn and a Coke. You could spend hours there, watching the serials such as *Flash Gordon,* whose plots carried over week to week, followed by a feature film. Another destination was Lachman's candy store, a couple long blocks from our building, where a penny bought you gumdrops, jelly beans, little dots, or a piece of licorice shaped like a record player; a nickel got you a fountain soda.

The brownstone buildings in our neighborhood were a good playground for the games of childhood: cowboys and Indians, cops and robbers. There were little passageways, like tunnels, in and out of the apartment complexes. Alleys ran between the buildings. For some reason, when we played cops and robbers, I always chose to be sheriff. I was on the good guys' side. Maybe we're born with such a predisposition. I idolized Hopalong Cassidy, the clean-cut cowboy hero of Saturday movie matinees and a TV series, and whose likeness was re-created on lunch boxes. I played the part proudly. I carried two toy guns on either side of my belt, and a toy rifle. Sometimes I'd lead my posse through the neighborhood, trying to rescue the little girl who played the heroine in distress. Other times I'd try to hunt down Robbie Russell, who was a loner in the neighborhood and liked to play the bad guy.

---

* In the 1950s this was a show named after a puppet and was perhaps the forerunner to the Muppets.

I had no idea what my father really did for a living, but it's fair to say my childhood was fairly typical. I played with my friends, watched movies, and, of course, discovered the joys (and obvious sorrows) of the Cubs—Ernie Banks and Ralph Kiner were the stars of the era. It was a typical Midwestern childhood, or so I thought. Until 1955, that is, when my life would change as my father's did, as his world I knew so little about put him on a path to the place where my character would be hewn and I started down a road that could not have been more different.

2

An Offer He Couldn't Refuse

Paul "Red" Dorfman ran labor unions for the mob, advised underworld boss Tony "Big Tuna" Accardo, and facilitated Teamsters chief Jimmy Hoffa's rise to power in exchange for the Mafia's access to the pension fund that would finance casinos on the Las Vegas Strip. He also was a friend of Ross Miller and likely had a role in putting his family on the road to Las Vegas in 1955.

I remember meeting Dorfman when I was a kid. I can't help but chuckle now that I thought then he was in the insurance business. I recall him as a pleasant man who seemed to like children. But he also, I would later discover, liked the mob and was a key player. He also probably had a hand in my dad's illegal bookmaking business.

The U.S. Senate Select Committee on Improper Activities in the Labor or Management Field deemed Dorfman in the 1950s to be "a major figure in the Chicago underworld." Federal investigators said that Dorfman was the man who had introduced Hoffa to key figures in the Chicago Syndicate, and that in return, Hoffa had channeled sizable union insurance-fund contracts to Dorfman's adopted stepson, Allen, who raked in hefty commissions. The Teamsters' Central States Pension Fund was the largest bankroller of hotel-casinos in Las Vegas as the city grew into a gambling mecca.

In 1955, my father would be offered an opportunity, either by Dorfman or someone close to him, to buy into the ninth resort and the first high-rise on the Las Vegas Strip, the Riviera. The hotel had opened on April 20th thanks to an investment group from Miami (Accardo, though, was said to be the real owner) that included Harpo and Gummo Marx. But, as Steve Fischer wrote in *When the Mob Ran Vegas: Stories of Money, Mayhem and Murder* and later summarized in the *Las Vegas Sun*: the Riviera, which opened in 1955, had lost money consistently for three months. Accardo, the de facto owner, knew that if a casino loses money for ninety straight days something more than bad luck is going on.

He gave the official on-site owners fifteen minutes to leave. Then Accardo asked Gus Greenbaum, retired president of the Flamingo, who was living in Scottsdale, Arizona, to return to Las Vegas and save the Riviera. Greenbaum declined.

A few nights later, Greenbaum's sister-in-law was murdered in her bed. Gus changed his mind and came to Las Vegas to work for Accardo, Fischer wrote.

(Greenbaum initially was an associate of Meyer Lansky, a member of the Chicago mob and a syndicate accountant for Las Vegas casino operations. After Bugsy Siegel's death, Greenbaum helped run the Flamingo. With a $1 million loan from the Chicago mob, Greenbaum soon turned the casino's fortunes around, according to Ed Reid and Ovid Demaris in *The Green Felt Jungle*.)

On December 3, 1958, a maid found the bodies of Gus and Shirley Greenbaum in their Phoenix home.

This was my father's world, a world he successfully kept hidden from me. Greenbaum was among those who were part of the second round of investors in the Riviera, along with Ross Miller. I do not know exactly how Dad was availed the opportunity to buy five points* in the

---

* In those days, casino owners sold "points" rather than percentages of a property so that there

Riviera. It's possible—maybe even likely—he'd heard about the investment through Paul Dorfman. It's also easy to imagine why my father reached for the opportunity. The potential to be realized from a large, legal (and posh) gambling resort in small but booming Las Vegas was astronomically higher than that of a small-time bookie joint tucked under an El station in Chicago.

The thirteen partners Dad was joining, with his sliver of ownership in the Riviera, included people whose names were already prominent in the budding Vegas casino world: Davie Berman, who'd been a partner with the late Benjamin "Bugsy" Siegel in the Flamingo and reputedly had been a cold-blooded killer who'd risen up the ranks of organized crime as a gambler and bootlegger in Minneapolis; Charlie Rich, who would open the Dunes later that year with his son, George Duckworth; and Greenbaum, whose guiding hand had brought the Flamingo into solvency following Siegel's death at the hand of a mob assassin's bullet, and who had interests in other Vegas casinos.

My father had occasionally taken trips to Las Vegas, but I never thought much of it until one day my mother told me that we might be moving there. That was a shock. Like any kid, I didn't want to move anywhere.

"Where's Las Vegas?" I asked.

"Out west," she said.

Out west?! This alarmed me even more.

My concept of that part of the country had been shaped by Westerns on television and in the movies, men in cowboy hats with six-shooters on their hips, and dusty streets lined with wood-framed structures. Saloons with tinkling pianos and swinging doors, horses, tumbleweeds, certainly not…casinos. I doubt I even knew what a casino was.

Why would we want to leave Chicago for some tiny backward town far, far away?

Mom explained that Dad and Uncle Hersch were selling the bar because

---

would be no limit of 100 percent on raising capital. When they sold points they would value them by dividing from the total.

Dad was now one of the owners of a hotel in Las Vegas. She didn't go into details. It would have been beyond the understanding of a ten-year-old anyway.

Before my father uprooted us, he had to check out the situation first-hand. So he'd moved by himself, staying in the Algiers motel next door to the Riviera. After a month as a pit boss, he'd decided it was a go. The opportunity to own a piece of the Riviera excited him. And he obviously had every confidence the state's regulators, the Gaming Control Board, would approve his group's licenses. He told Mom to pack up and to make the move.

It was late summer, and I was out of school. Mom opted to travel by train. Although my father had flown to Vegas, she didn't like the idea of making such a long journey by air.

After our train left Chicago and the landscape soon changed to wide-open spaces, I stared out the windows, imagining I was traveling backward in time. I half expected to see cowboys and Indians out on the plains. I had a couple of toy cap guns with me, which helped me pretend I was heading out to the Wild West. As far as the friends I'd left behind in Chicago were concerned, that's where I was going: "Out west." It was where the whistling ricochets of bullets echoed amid rigid cacti, and coyotes howled at the moon.

In truth, I didn't know what to expect in Las Vegas. All I knew was that I had been pulled out of a large urban environment and was going to be plunked down in a desert, in the middle of nowhere, as if being transported to another planet.

The train ride took three nights and two days. We arrived in downtown Vegas at a small wooden building, the Union Pacific depot. Dad was waiting for us. We stepped out into the dry heat of a September morning in the eastern Mojave Desert.

The depot stood at the corner of Fremont and Main streets. As Dad drove us, I stared out the car window at the jumble of casinos: the Golden Nugget Gambling Hall, the Lucky Strike Club, the Boulder Club. The Horseshoe Club was on the ground floor of a three-story brick building topped by a sign reading HOTEL APACHE. The signage on the first-story overhang of the Horseshoe Club included the picture of a horse's head; the lettering spelled GAMBLING SALOON & RESTAURANT. Rising like a giant above a sign in front of the Pioneer Club was a neon cowboy in blue jeans, yellow-checkered shirt, and red bandana, an arm rising and lowering in a "Howdy Podner" greeting. He was known as Vegas Vic.

3

Adjusting to Las Vegas

The Las Vegas the Millers alighted in more than a half century ago bears virtually no resemblance to the city of today. The Strip in 1955 could not have been more different from the glittering gambling places that now dot Las Vegas Boulevard South. Except for my father's new place of employment, the Riviera, they were all ranch-style, one-story properties that were one-dimensional compared to the three-dimensional spectacles that would sprout from that same ground decades later. You could have purchased property on the Strip for next to nothing because the Flamingo was the farthest out and it was well past others.

The city that would become a sprawling metropolis of more than two million was a dusty, desert-dominated small town of 50,000 when the Millers arrived. The airport was just off the Strip, a single-story building where planes landed outside a wire fence. There were no gates; this was your grandfather's McCarran International Airport.

I remember walking home from a movie and a windstorm blew so much sand that I had to lie on the ground facedown for over thirty minutes. Desert didn't just surround the small town; it was interspersed throughout. There was no air-conditioning, just swamp coolers. Mass at St. Anne's was so crowded many had to wait outside; some wore bathing attire. The priest insisted parishioners made certain their bathing suits were covered when they took Communion.

Las Vegas was a small, Western burgh where Helldorado was the festival of the year and people dressed in cowboy garb in what would one day be Glitter Gulch. The hotels were not really hotels, but casinos with cottages in the back. The casinos were right in the middle, not separated as are to-day's modern ones. The outside portions would be restaurants, showrooms, and a lounge. Shows were popular entertainers with an opening dance line (generally not topless in the early or dinner show and topless in the midnight show) followed by an opening act (Barbra Streisand opened for Liberace in her first Las Vegas appearance) and then the main act. It was not until the '60s when Lido de Paris and then Folies Bergere opened that shows were without a headliner but rather novelty acts interspersed with dancers and topless showgirls. Bally's has the only remaining such show. Dinner shows were $7.50 including the meal and at midnight, $5 including drinks.

Because Las Vegas was small there was a great sense of community, and many celebrations were centered around Western themes. Helldorado Days was the biggest. The parade on Fremont Street had elaborate floats, and each hotel would try to outdo the other with showgirls and sometimes entertainers atop many. The local high school bands would march—and there were only a few of them. Las Vegas High was the only public one in Las Vegas. Bishop Gorman was the only private high school. Rancho High School was in adjoining North Las Vegas.

Downtown was full of people in Western gear and if you did not wear such garments downtown during the celebration, you were thrown into a make-believe jail cell until you bought a button. Maybe one reason the community was so close is that outside of here no one else had legal gaming, no other state had quickie divorces (although Reno actually was more famous for that) or legalized prostitution. No other city, I'm sure, had gathering places where prominent politicians consorted with low-level and high-level criminals from other places who had come west to the one place where they could reinvent themselves as community leaders and philanthropists. But just as after you came to Nevada, you might be perceived differently, when residents left the state, they had to put up with stereotypes, too ("Do you live in a hotel? Do you gamble all the time?"). That, I must say, still happens today.

Chicago was all buildings bunched together, as in our neighborhood of brownstone apartments. But Las Vegas spread out like boiling water on a flat surface, the streets almost swallowed by the desert. We drove from the train depot downtown into neighborhoods of single-story homes.

My father had bought half of a duplex on the edge of town, in an area known as Francisco Park. The corner street, San Francisco Street (soon to be renamed Sahara Boulevard), marked the city limits. Our duplex was brick and had a carport with two spots, one for the neighbor, and one for us. Swamp coolers were set up in windows to temper the heat, which in summer could swelter to nearly 120 degrees. Modern air-conditioning didn't exist. Our half of the duplex had three bedrooms, a real upgrade over the apartment in Chicago; it meant I could have my own bedroom. Space was a luxury I never appreciated before our move to Nevada.

But we quickly found that the desert contained visitors that liked to crawl into our place. Along with the heat and dust that penetrated the duplex came ants and, occasionally, scorpions, which were most efficiently eliminated with the whack of a stick.

The wind outside frequently kicked up to howling fury, and the sand blew so fiercely it left little pit marks on your face and body. The nights, however, chilled considerably. The desert environment was harsh, too. A pet dog belonging to a family across the street wandered about a mile into the sand and brush, and was killed by a rattlesnake.

There, on the edge of town, getting adjusted to my new home, I sat and stared at the expanse of desert behind our duplex and felt infinitely small. The Mojave seemed to stretch to the ends of the earth, for miles and miles and miles. It was a void of stark, ancient wilderness, dunes, bluffs, and jagged ridges, against which the new city streets seemed an insignificant and impermanent intrusion.

When we arrived in 1955, Las Vegas already was undergoing what would become the many growth spurts it would experience during the next several decades. Forces at work were attracting newcomers by the droves. The new casinos opening up drew those who wanted to fill the employee ranks, and people who had run small-time gambling operations illegally outside Nevada. Those newcomers now jumped at the chance to operate legally, and among them were people such as my dad who wanted to buy a piece of the action. Then there was the general trend of Easterners and Midwesterners simply moving west for the sunnier climate. They saw that Las Vegas's economy was prospering, not only due to the burgeoning clubs, but also the growth of Nellis Air Force Base and the Nevada Test Site north of town. The population of Greater Las Vegas doubled every decade during the 1900s.

In 1940, nine years after gambling was legalized in 1931, the population in the Las Vegas Valley had been only 8,400. By 1950 it was nearly 25,000. Now, in 1955, the metropolitan area numbered about 80,000. That year, trying to deal with school overcrowding and widely varying standards in about two hundred small school districts scattered throughout the state, the legislature reformed the school system to create a countywide school district in each of Nevada's seventeen counties. Las Vegas was hard-pressed to keep up with the exploding student population.

I felt the effects of this immediately. I was very lonely the first couple weeks, out there on the edge of this Western desert town, waiting to start school. Making good on his promise to the priest, my father intended to hold me out of school until there was an opening at a Catholic school. That lasted until a truant officer found out that I was not attending classes, and said I had to enroll at a public school, John C. Fremont, until I could transfer to a Catholic school. But Fremont had just been built and had yet to open, so instead I went to John S. Parks Elementary for half days until Fremont opened.

Finally, there was room for me at St. Anne's Grade School, which had grades one through five and would be adding a new grade each year up to eighth grade. From the fifth grade on I would always be in the oldest class in grammar school. St. Anne's was within walking distance of our home.

I soon found that, unlike in Chicago, Dad wasn't the only parent working nights. It wasn't uncommon in Vegas for parents to work night shifts, because a fair number of them were employed in the casinos. That was true for a few of my classmates.

Every Sunday night, our family dined at the Riviera's Hickory Room. It was a time set aside exclusively for the Millers. Rarely did anyone else join us. It was our special time to be together as a family. In fact, pretty much our only time.

Our meals were a mixed blessing for me. It was great to see my father, even though it forced me to head out of the house instead of savoring the last part of the weekend before school. Ross Miller made use of these dinners to address every issue my mother would have brought up to him from the previous week.

"OK!" he'd begin, then run down the list of transgressions. "Don't do this again," and, "Don't do that again." He may not have been physically present in our house every night, but it was obvious who ruled the roost.

It was the only time each week that we would spend any real time together. I might see him for a minute or two as he left for work before dinner. He would return after I was asleep. I somehow always knew my father loved me—my mother's constant presence helped and I'm sure she reassured me how much my father cared. Occasionally, a friend of my father would tell me how proudly Ross Miller talked of his son, and I was elated to hear it. But I couldn't help but wish he would say it to me, as any kid would. I am sure this is why I try to tell my own children I love them as often as I can. Unlike my father, I tried to be there for their special events. In this way—as in many others I would only come to realize later—Ross Miller influenced me, not just in what I would do but what I wouldn't. I don't resent my father for not being around more; I just accept that he was from a different life experience than my own and in his world, family interaction was mostly about laying down the rules. He demanded results—as he would from an employee—but he was not so great at the pats on the back we all need sometimes.

So there in our booth in the Hickory Room, my father would grill me about my progress in school. That was paramount: He expected good grades. I always felt the pressure in the classroom. But if there was one break I could count on, it was that he wasn't pushing his son to excel athletically. My father neither encouraged nor discouraged me in sports. It was obvious to everyone, including him, how uncoordinated I was. Sure, I was tall, but I was skinny and clumsy. My father wasn't very optimistic that I'd blossom into a jock. I desperately wanted to, but I was no great shakes playing baseball or football on the school playground or in pickup games. (And I hadn't really discovered basketball yet.)

My lack of finesse was one more way in which I differed from my father. He was a pretty fair athlete himself. His game was golf, and when he was awake in the daytime with a few hours before going in to work, he'd often spend his time on the links. He was a founding member of the Las Vegas Country Club. In fact, he became such an avid and proficient golfer that he ended up playing in the Bing Crosby National Pro-Am in Pebble Beach, California, and competed in another pro-am, the Bob Hope Desert Classic, every year since its inception in 1960 (as the Palm Springs Desert Golf Classic) until his death. He always encouraged me to take up the game but I never did so until after his passing. I don't know if I would have been able to play with him had I learned earlier. But I regret that I may have missed an opportunity to spend more time with him.

Even though Ross Miller fit perfectly into the Las Vegas environment, that didn't mean my father would be immediately accepted by those who regulated the casino industry. Indeed, shortly after we arrived, the Gaming Control Board cast a critical eye on the fourteen applicants from the Riviera during a casino licensing hearing in September 1955. The board decided that more information and review was needed on six of the investment group's applicants, and action on their license applications would be deferred. The remaining eight, including Ross Miller, were approved, but not before board member William V. Sennett made this statement on the record:

"This is a difficult case to resolve. It is symptomatic of both the financial situation in Las Vegas and the criminal activities and the notoriousness some of these people have. On this license some of these men have police records dating pretty far back into the twenties and the thirties. To offset this, they have been in Nevada for many years and their records here have been without official blemish, as nearly as we can determine, with the exception of one technical violation. They have been previous licensees, passed by the tax commission. They have work cards and will work in the club.

"I will vote on this one with reluctance on the basis of the financial situation at the hotel and because of the financial aspect in Las Vegas. In addition to that, I don't think we can abruptly change our method of procedure or our standards for acceptance without giving some notice as to what that will be. I won't vote on the same basis again. I think that this constitutes notice to anybody who might come up.

"I would like to point out that the obligation of the members of the industry to the state is very great. Nevada has been very good to them. It gave them sanctuary, a chance at respectability, and acceptance into the community here. In the future, I think that the industry members, Gus Greenbaum included, should be aware of the great obligation when the state accepted them and be guided by this in the future in their choice of associates. Much greater demands will be made upon them in the future."

The new ownership group officially took over the Riviera. Gus Greenbaum was chairman of the board. Ross Miller was at the bottom of the totem pole. He was starting as a pit boss, supervising blackjack and craps dealers. But he had a game plan. At every chance when points became available, he would exercise his option to buy stock in the Riviera.

4

Ross Miller, Casino Big Shot

Looking back, I realize that my father's smooth rise to success was mirrored in those early Vegas years by my awkwardness. My father was becoming a real player at the Riviera while his son was cruelly nicknamed "Boob" Miller because I seemed to be breaking a different bone every year. While I was having the typical gawky teen's rough time of it in high school, my father had discovered the ideal environment in which a man like himself could prosper. He was perfectly suited to managing a casino floor in 1950s Las Vegas, an era when hands-on treatment was required.

Ross Miller had the personal touch characteristic of his generation of gambling entrepreneurs, who had come up through small independent operations. They had developed their business abilities in close and constant contact with the people in their establishments. In my father's case, running the Silver Palm in Chicago meant greeting, charming, or cajoling (and occasionally intimidating) bar patrons and bartenders, gamblers, and dancers. Ross Miller also was required to play the diplomat with cops walking the beat, and prove himself trustworthy among the kind of men who ended up financing casinos in Nevada. In this way, he had honed keen interpersonal skills, not to mention a savvy business sense. He kept an eye on the big picture, but was practiced in thinking quickly on his feet.

31

All this was typical of casino men in that pioneering era in Vegas. They possessed sharp instincts, and had effective ways of handling people one on one. When it came, for example, to approving an increase in credit for a high roller, my father would be out there on the casino floor, talking with the player, then making his decision right there, based on his gut feeling. No bank or credit check, no computer records. He just relied on experience and intuition to gauge whether the gambler was good for another marker.

As Valley Bank president, E. Parry Thomas, who had arranged the loans for the Riviera's owners and my father's partners (the first financial institution in Nevada to do so), says, "Ross Miller was as good a casino man as there was in Las Vegas in those days. I'd rank him up there with Carl Cohen at the Sands in his ability to run a tight ship." (Cohen was the guy who punched Frank Sinatra and knocked out his teeth when the singer was misbehaving one night at the Sands.)

"The thing I admired most about Ross," Thomas adds, "was that he was one hundred percent honest. He was a man of great integrity, very practical, with good common sense. He rode very tall in the saddle in my book, and I liked him tremendously."

In that pre-corporate era, the casino business was all about taking care of the good customers and making sure they kept playing, and kept coming back. The hotel rooms and restaurants, shows and shops were all loss leaders, designed to keep the gamblers in the house. Lounge shows were free, and featured popular entertainers such as Louis Prima and Keely Smith, Don Rickles and Shecky Greene. Here, too, Dad had his hands full with tricky management calls. Some of the performers proved to be a handful. My dad groused about the singer Johnny Rivers asking to bring his motorcycle into the hotel. My father told him he had to park it out at the loading dock. "One of these days I'll have them throw his motorcycle away," Ross Miller grumbled.

Shecky Greene was perhaps the most difficult. He was arguably the most talented comedian of that era, an extraordinary mimic and impressionist who could improvise an entire set. But he also was constantly having issues with alcohol, gambling, and other personal problems.

Greene later admitted that although in those years he was packing the lounge at the Riviera, and was regarded as the comedian that all other comedians in town looked up to for his timing and improvisational skills, his relationship with Dad was anything but harmonious.

"Ross Miller developed a hatred for me," he says, "and I have to say the feeling was mutual. I was drinking then and had some bad habits, so he had his reasons."

Greene recalls that there were several factions with ownership in the Riviera in those years, and "they all hated each other." He says that one day Sidney Korshak, the attorney who represented the "silent partners" in the hotel, called him and my father to a meeting in the coffee shop.

Korshak was no ordinary attorney. He had risen from his days reputed to be in Al Capone's Chicago outfit to become a classic fixer in Hollywood, with one FBI agent, William Roemer, telling the *Los Angeles Times* after he died in 1996 that he was the "primary link between big business and organized crime." It should be noted that Korshak was never charged, much less convicted, of any crime, although he'd been subject to multiple investigations.

Korshak was one of many men with links to La Cosa Nostra that my father dealt with, unbeknownst to his son—I was more concerned with girls than godfathers.

"Korshak demanded that we shake hands and bury the hatchet," Greene remembers. "But Ross refused to shake my hand. Korshak then said, 'Either you shake his hand, Ross, or you're leaving this place.' So Ross stuck out the hand with only three fingers ... I got only half a hand."

My father was starting to look the part, too. He still wore turtlenecks from time to time, but I remember him often in a black suit and black shirt with a very thin white tie. He looked straight out of Damon Runyon's *Guys and Dolls*. But that was the norm in Las Vegas at that time. My dad was dressed like so many others, it seemed ordinary to me.

In his trademark outfit, my father was always roaming the casino floor, strolling through the restaurants and showrooms, and greeting guests, often by first name. In those days, bosses made sure their guests felt comfortable. They knew how to go the extra mile. Las Vegas public-relations firm owner Ellie Shattuck remembers when she was out on her second date with Frank Shattuck, the man she would marry in 1961. Ellie had grown up in town and in the 1950s was one of the first female cub reporters at the *Las Vegas Review-Journal*. Frank at that time was an administrative assistant to Nevada Gov. Grant Sawyer. Frank had connections on the Strip and called my father about getting good seats to the late show in the Riv's showroom, where Liberace or Peggy Lee was performing.

Ross Miller arranged for Frank and Ellie to be seated at a table front and center. After-dinner cocktails were customary then, and the couple ordered B&Bs. When the waitress brought the drinks, she leaned over the table to hand a glass to Ellie, and tipped over Frank's drink, spilling the brown sugary liqueur all over his silk tie. The liqueur would have stiffened and ruined the tie. As my father was making the rounds, he noticed the mishap, hurried over, and said, "Oh, Frank, give me your tie." He left the room, and returned ten minutes later with a brand-new narrow tie. Frank and Ellie were amazed. But that was characteristic of my father, and of Vegas casino operators back then.

Ellie Shattuck still thinks fondly of that generation of casino chiefs. "I refer to them as the 'Damon Runyon characters.' They belonged on Broadway. Pinky rings. Slick suits. They were always extremely well groomed, and they were always gentlemen. They never addressed anyone in a bad manner, and they were just really great people." Of my dad, she says, "Ross Miller was a gentle giant, and a man of perfection."

I suppose I thought of my father that way, too. But he certainly consorted with some imperfect men, as I would learn later. And he was the kind of man who would dismiss such descriptions of himself—or anyone else. My father was someone who shunned attention. He wanted only to provide a life for his family that was better than the one he had lived. He had been raised the hard way, without a father and with little schooling, and he was determined that I gain as much education as possible and choose a different career path. I always knew that I was expected to study and go on to college and beyond. It was what my father wanted, and I wanted to live up to his expectations.

My father may not have expected his employees to be perfect, but he did demand they be aboveboard. He was fair and loyal to those who were faithful. He'd privately help those with hospital bills, never wanting to draw attention to his benevolence.

Fellow casino owners recognized this trait in him. "He did a lot of good for the people he helped. He was a very generous man, a very charming man," says Claudine Williams, who with her husband co-owned the Silver Slipper casino on the Strip and would become the first woman to achieve glittering stature in an industry dominated by men.

But Ross Miller also, like many of the outwardly charming casino bosses of that era, had another side. I didn't see it when I was young, but I would later learn about what my father was capable of doing.

These were not scenes from a movie such as *GoodFellas*. This was really what it was like in the 1950s in Las Vegas.

One time my father caught wind that one of the card dealers was "chip-munking," adroitly slipping gambling chips into his mouth during the play, hiding them in his cheeks so he could take them into the break room later and stow them out of sight. Dad came up behind and slapped the embezzler on the back, and the chips spewed out. I'm not sure what became of the cheating dealer. But I'm certain he never worked in the clubs again.

Ross Miller didn't have to get physical with another dealer who similarly aroused a suspicion of stealing chips. He merely stood at a bank of slot machines, a short ways from the table, and fixed his stony stare on the dealer. The man finally realized he was being watched. It spooked him so badly that, in the middle of his shift, he suddenly took off running, out the front doors, and never came back.

Personnel problems such as employee theft were dealt with differently, partly because casino operators were less constrained by lawsuits. The fleeing dealer surely was afraid of facing whatever disciplinary or punitive actions my father or the other bosses had in mind.

I never heard that my father used violence on any transgressing dealers, although he valued loyalty so much, I am sure he thought about it.

Once he was accused of assault and battery by two dealers who had been stealing and he whispered to his lawyer, Drake DeLanoy (as DeLanoy later recalled): "You know, this wouldn't happen down in Hot Springs. They'd just move their fingers a little bit."

He'd explained that in Hot Springs, Arkansas, a town with a substantial presence of illegal casinos, employees caught cheating would have their fingers wrenched as a painful reminder not to repeat such transgressions against the house.

By that time, in the mid-sixties, Vegas had become more civilized. Ross Miller's years of being his own bouncer were past, but the intimidation that undoubtedly helped control unduly rowdy customers in Chicago remained. He had a stern, no-nonsense look on his face most of the time. I would see it when he was unhappy with me. A look was enough to scare his son or a wayward employee or customer. But in Las Vegas, his inner charm, thoughtfulness, and generosity were evident, too. At the time I knew virtually nothing of the backgrounds of those he associated with but I did know that he was respected at work and in the community.

5

The Millers Begin Living
the Vegas Life

As the 1960s arrived, the Millers moved to a house on the Desert Inn golf course, a place that no longer exists and is now in the shadow of the Wynn hotel. But back then it was an exclusive address and I knew we were moving up in the world. My father built his ranch-style dream house on a quarter-acre lot along the fifth fairway that cost the princely sum of $3,500—the price of a night at a fancy Strip suite these days.

Ross Miller seldom did business at our new, swanky home. But my father still maintained close connections to his Chicago associates, including the Dorfmans, and I do remember one weekend visitor to the country club home, one Jimmy Hoffa, the president of the International Brotherhood of Teamsters. I'd met him briefly once or twice before, but the fact that such a famous person was at our house impressed me. My father drove him over. Hoffa didn't have a bodyguard with him, and when I greeted him, he was very nice and easy to talk to. I didn't stay for lunch, though. He and my father had business to discuss. I definitely wasn't invited.

It seems strange looking back that it was only a few years later that Hoffa would go to prison and only a decade or so before he would disappear, thought to have been executed by the mob for his activities in Las Vegas. He helped facilitate millions of dollars in loans that helped build the modern Strip. In the city's early history, conventional financing sources such as banks did not want to provide loans. As a result most of the casinos received seed money from the Teamsters Union Pension Fund. Thus, Hoffa was a frequent visitor to Las Vegas and was treated much like you would a landlord. I would like to tell you that I hid and eavesdropped that day on Hoffa's conversation with my father so I could relate it to you today. But I would never have taken that chance, never having wanted to feel my father's wrath—not to mention Hoffa's—if he'd caught me.

My father's hard work and dedication at the Riv moved him up the ladder. He bought more and more stock in the resort, and worked his way up to casino manager. Some of the partners he had when he'd first bought in simply moved on to other investments. But the departure of Gus Greenbaum, who came to the Riv as chairman of the board, was more dramatic.

It wasn't until I was into my adulthood that I learned about the reputations of the likes of Greenbaum and fellow Riviera investor Davie Berman. Berman reputedly had been a cold-blooded killer who'd risen up the ranks of organized crime as a gambler and bootlegger in Minneapolis, Minnesota; after World War II he'd partnered with Bugsy Siegel in the Flamingo. Berman had died, some said under suspicious circumstances, on the operating table in 1957.[*]

Greenbaum, meanwhile, as part of "the Chicago Outfit," had been sent by the syndicate to Las Vegas as the accountant for casino operations, and

---

[*] Berman's daughter, Susan, authored the memoir *Easy Street* about her father, who died when she was twelve. She also wrote a documentary about Las Vegas, which appeared on the A&E network, excerpts of which still appear on the History Channel and others including portions of interviews with me.

Susan's murder on Christmas Eve of 2000 has been the subject of TV crime stories. Much of the focus is on a bizarre set of circumstances involving a college friend of hers named Robert Durst, whose wife mysteriously disappeared in 1982. Susan had been his spokeswoman.

Durst, who it turned out had paid Susan $50,000 in the months prior to her death, later turned up in Galveston, Texas, where he had been disguised as an old woman. His next-door neighbors' body turned up in the neighboring bay. He was later charged, but pled self-defense and was acquitted. Police considered him a person of interest in Susan's death because the investigation of Durst's missing wife had recently been reopened. No one was ever charged with Susan's murder.

had been directed to take over running the Flamingo after Siegel's murder. Later, he was assigned to chair the board at the Riv.

Greenbaum evidently wasn't suited to the post. Historians have recorded that he abused drugs, womanized, and gambled excessively. His vices led to financial straits, and he began skimming from the casino. This didn't please certain interested parties in Chicago or elsewhere. In December 1958, Greenbaum's and his wife's bodies were discovered in their home in Phoenix, Arizona, their throats slashed. The murders remain unsolved to this day, but it is suspected that it was a mob hit. As Bugsy Siegel once told an investigative reporter looking into mob dealings, "You don't have to worry about getting knocked off. In our world, we only kill each other."

At that time, I was thirteen. About all I remember when the news surfaced about Mr. and Mrs. Greenbaum's murders was that Dad was concerned. One of the major partners at the Riv had been killed. As a child, I thought no more of it. For all I knew, the man and his wife had been slain by someone burglarizing their home.

Ross Miller knew a lot of people, and a lot of people knew him. Dad never mixed his business life with his family life. But it was clear to me that he had some powerful friends. Although by nature he kept a low profile outside of work, he maintained clear boundaries between what happened at the Riviera and what happened in the Miller household. He never bothered introducing me to Liberace, or Harry Belafonte, or the other celebrities playing the Riv. He didn't want me hanging around the hotel, for starters; he also didn't want me being starstruck. To him, these entertainers were simply contracted workers at the hotel. The attitude that no one person is more important than another did rub off on me. Famous people never have taken my breath away. I don't care if you're the guy sweeping the floor, parking the car, cooking the dinner, running the casino, owning the casino, or entertaining on the main stage, or a diplomat or president or monarch. Those are just jobs.

But there was one instance when my father couldn't resist showing off a bit to his family. The comedian Richard Dawson was married to a budding movie star, Diana Dors, a curvy, blond Englishwoman in the mold of Jayne Mansfield and Marilyn Monroe. Dad invited them to lunch at our house. Dors was hyped to be Hollywood's next great femme fatale. Ironically, Dawson would turn out to gain much more fame than Dors, whom he eventually divorced. He became the emcee in the 1970s of TV's *Family Feud*, where his trademark was kissing all the female contestants. But there, in the early 1960s, I was a lot prouder of having Diana Dors eat at our table. An anecdote about her went a long way with my school pals.

Despite my father's new status, people told Ross Miller he was crazy to live that far out, in the middle of the Strip, because our house would be infested with rattlesnakes and other desert vermin.

But my parents knew our new residence wasn't destined to be on the outskirts for long. Las Vegas's population was continuing to grow at a fast clip, and so was its tourist economy. In the four years since our arrival, growth was obvious. Before our move to the Desert Inn Country Club, even the stark desert around our duplex, in what had been an extreme end of the valley, suddenly was filled with construction activity as homes rose and the streets expanded. Maryland Parkway, a main arterial, was continually being extended farther south. The town's first mall, the Boulevard Mall, was being built on Maryland Parkway. The resorts on the Strip, including the Riviera, were doing brisk business. Our family's fortunes were rising with it. Dad, four years into his career at the Riv, was now casino manager as well as part owner.

Our new house was commensurate with dad's new status. The DI Country Club was one of the two nicest sections of Las Vegas. The other was Rancho Circle, toward the center of town, a neighborhood of large upscale homes. Our house had a carport with a basketball hoop attached to the front of it. There was just enough room on the sloping driveway for playing short one-on-one or two-on-two games. In back was a swimming pool, a little cactus garden, and a bit of grass in a yard large enough for playing Wiffle ball. I wasn't particularly good at any sport, perhaps in part because I most frequently played with my friend Bruce Layne, who made varsity in all major sports by our sophomore year, but it was there I devel-

oped my competitiveness since I hated to lose and would constantly practice to get better.

Dad wanted Uncle Herschel to buy the lot next door. Uncle Hersch
had moved to Las Vegas in 1956. After he and Dad sold the Silver Palm,
my uncle first had gone to Hot Springs, Arkansas, and worked in the underground but tacitly permitted gambling joints for a year. Then he came
to Vegas and got a job as a pit boss on the graveyard shift at the Riv. He
later divorced, and spent a lot of his off-work hours on the golf course.
He'd finish work at 8 A.M., eat breakfast, and be off to the golf course,
sleeping in the late afternoon and evening before starting work again near
midnight.

Unfortunately, the $3,500 for the lot at the Desert Inn Country Club
was too steep for Uncle Hersch. Las Vegas clothing-store owner Jacob
"Chic" Hecht (later a U.S. senator whose reelection campaign would be
pivotal to my political career), who owned a women's clothing store downtown, ended up buying the land. He never developed it; it remained
empty dirt. (Steve Wynn bought the lot in 2004 to build on it as a part of
the Wynn Las Vegas Resort.)

Dad had our house built in a Southwestern-ranch style. The roof had a
gentle slope and was covered with tiny pebbles. To save on paying contractors, Dad had engineers from the Riv out to help with the construction. (That's something you couldn't do today.) It was common to see Riv
engineers or maintenance crews working on the house even after construction was completed. The hotels and casinos were private companies
and owners felt as if the hotel employees worked for them personally, not
the company per se. Las Vegas was still a far cry from the corporate America that it would mirror later.

The casinos, though, were off-limits for Ross Miller's son. It was part
of his walling off his personal and private lives—and, perhaps, wanting a
different kind of life for his son. "I better not hear about you hanging
around the casinos at all," my father would say. He didn't need to elaborate. He'd find out pretty quickly, through the grapevine, if his son was
messing around in the clubs. Las Vegas was a small town, and it seemed

everyone knew everyone else's business. There weren't many hotels then, and they weren't places in which you could easily hide in a crowd. Besides lodging, most hotel-casinos contained a buffet and nice restaurant, as well as a coffee shop. The showroom was open only at night, and there was an entertainment bar or lounge, generally open nights, also. Nearly all the other space in a Vegas hotel property was occupied by slot machines or gaming tables. The casinos had no elaborate designs or corners to turn, unlike now. They consisted of just one big open area where everyone in the place was visible. And no one would ever have had trouble spying a tall gangly boy, most likely wearing a cast.

I ventured into the casinos, however, when it was time to look for my first summer job.

The summer after my sophomore year at Bishop Gorman High School, when I was sixteen, I landed a busboy job at the Stardust Resort & Casino, a newer, upscale hotel. The Stardust had opened on the Strip in 1958, three years after the Riviera, and immediately made a national splash with its giant "Big Dipper" swimming pool, a drive-in theater, and the state's largest casino (16,500 square feet). The Stardust also boasted the largest sign in the world; it was an array of stars brilliantly lit by 11,000 bulbs that could be seen sixty miles away. The Stardust was just at a different level from its competitors. Its interior décor was posh, accented in deep reds and browns.

A busboy job at the Stardust was a great gig. I worked room service, which meant zipping around on a cart. The Stardust, like most hotels in Vegas then, had guest rooms in the back, not like today's towers. There were two-story buildings behind the Stardust, and I would retrieve meal trays.

I didn't last long, though. One day I came to work very tired. I said as much, and one of the waiters said, "Ah, go around the corner and take a catnap." I'd seen waiters grabbing shut-eye when business was slow. It sounded good to me. So I curled up in a corner of the kitchen, out of sight, and dozed off.

A loud voice awakened me. I opened my eyes to see, staring down at me, the chairman of the board of the Stardust: Al Benedict. He was not a tall man, and he was of slender build, but his demeanor left no doubt he was the boss. He was a serious man. Just my luck, there he was touring the kitchen that afternoon. The sight of me incensed him.

"You're fired," he said.

To this day I don't know whether I was set up. I suppose I was just a naïve kid and a perfect mark for the waiters. Maybe they resented the fact that my dad was a boss at the casino across the street. Or maybe they were just having some cruel fun at my expense. I can imagine now that one of them picked up a phone right after I'd nodded off and told a manager, "Guess what this kid's doing?"

I turned in my bow tie and jacket. I was a nervous wreck. Dad was going to kill me. This was surely my last day on Earth.

He certainly was displeased when I told him.

"You've embarrassed me," he said. "I can't believe you did something that stupid."

Those words crushed me. I knew I had no excuses to make. I'd deserved to be fired. Worse, I had let my dad down. I was not a stand-up guy; I was a sleeping boy.

I would not be out of work long, courtesy of my father's' upward trajectory. Thanks to him, I landed a plum job working as a lifeguard at the Riviera pool, although he told the head lifeguard to keep an eye on me, to make sure I wasn't sloughing off.

I ended up keeping the lifeguard job for four summers. Like any job that involved dealing with people, it was an education in itself. In some ways, it would prepare me for what turned out to be a career in public office. I was shy by nature but the job put me into a position where I would have to chitchat with guests, and it wasn't unusual for out-of-towners to ask me whether I lived in the hotel. Tourists couldn't believe people actually resided in regular homes in Vegas. To most visitors, our city was just the Strip and downtown's Glitter Gulch, surrounded by cactus-studded desert wilderness. They were unaware of the neighborhoods of ranch-style houses, or the parks and ball fields, the churches and schools. They just saw Sin City. People stayed up all night. There were no clocks in the hotels or natural lighting in the casinos, for obvious reasons. The city never slept, and it didn't want its customers to, either.

Las Vegas, though, was quite a conservative town then. There were various taboos in the early 1960s that have since fallen by the wayside, as in the rest of the country. African-American guests were not made to feel welcome in the resorts on the Strip or downtown, even though blacks worked as laborers and, of course, as top-notch entertainers in the show-rooms and lounges. Desegregation was slowly taking hold, as Vegas wrestled with the nickname "the Mississippi of the West," a derogatory label slapped on it by civil-rights activists. I heard some unbelievable conversations between guests and the staff at the pool. Some segregationist-minded whites maintained that if blacks were allowed to enjoy the pool, whites would quit going there, or would demand the pool be drained and refilled.

The bosses who ran the Strip and downtown casinos believed that gamblers from the South would not want to visit a place different from the society in which they lived, and most of these casino chiefs were not exactly racially progressive themselves. But even if they were sympathetic toward civil rights, they wouldn't allow such sentiments to interfere with the bottom line. It's shocking to reflect that in the years I was a lifeguard there were no black hotel guests at the Riv or any of the downtown or Strip properties, nor did blacks work as dealers or waitresses there. Even the black entertainers stayed at the only lodging available to them, in an area of town then referred to as the Westside. Through the efforts of Gov. Grant Sawyer, and a welfare mom named Ruby Duncan, who led protest marches, the resorts finally were desegregated.* At least,

---

* In 2008, Ruby Duncan was awarded the National Association of Secretaries of State's Margaret Chase Smith American Democracy Award, beating out the likes of Al Gore. My son had nominated her.

in theory. Sawyer, whose two terms as governor ran from 1959–67, wanted to do for Nevada what U.S. Sen. Hubert Humphrey of Minnesota urged the country to do in 1948: walk into the bright sunshine of civil rights. Sawyer got an Equal Rights Commission through the Nevada Legislature, which gave it everything but money for a budget and the power to do anything.

Racial mixing wasn't the only taboo at the Riv. Public displays of affection that would be considered G-rated today were considered racy in Las Vegas in 1963. The stage was one thing, with its risqué (for its time) topless shows and scantily clad showgirls. Public behavior was another matter.

In summer 1963, we lifeguards were concerned by two young newlyweds embracing in the pool. The woman was well built and happened to be a singer opening for Liberace in the Riv's showroom. Her curly-haired husband, a fledgling actor of some sort, had a thick mat of chest hair. Both were from Brooklyn, strong-minded and brassy, and didn't seem to care what people made of them kissing passionately. We lifeguards had to go in the water and ask them to stop, saying, "Look, there are kids around here and if you're going to get romantic, could you please go back to your room?"

It turned out that wasn't the only friction this pair would cause.

A day or so later, the woman phoned down to the pool from her room. She gave me her name and room number and said, "I would like a longue."

"Certainly," I said. "Do you know where around the pool you would like to lounge? I'll set it up for you whenever you come down."

"No," she said, rather curtly. "I want this longue in my room on the patio."

As politely as I could, I said, "Well, the longues are for the pool area, but I would be glad to set it up down here anywhere you like."

She hung up.

Soon after, I got a call at the pool from one of the hotel owners. "Who just spoke to Miss Streisand?" he asked. I told him that I had, and I related the conversation.

"OK, I understand," he said. "But would you take her a chaise longue?"

So I did, carting it up the elevator to the third floor, down the hall, through her bedroom, and outside so that she could be the only guest having a chaise longue on her patio. In return, I received no tip, or even a thank you.

It was only a few years later that this woman became a major international star, and a celebrity of such stature that the public knew her by her first name only, Barbra. There at the Riv's pool, I'd encountered Barbra Streisand, who in 1963 was a brash twenty-one-year-old. Her twenty-four-year-old husband, by the way, was actor Elliott Gould.

Dad kept an eye on me at the pool. He'd usually get to work around 5 or 6 P.M., and I'd usually get off work at 7. I'd glance up and there he'd be in his dark suit, standing there watching, maybe making sure I wasn't sleeping on the job again. Of course, I wasn't supposed to hang around the hotel after work; he'd made that clear enough

Las Vegas already was different from any other city in the world. An ocean of multicolored neon bathed the Strip. Marquees advertised the names of the country's greatest entertainers. By the 1960s, Las Vegas had usurped Broadway as the live-entertainment capital of the nation. The Great White Way couldn't compete with the Strip in terms of paying power to performers. The casino bosses wanted the best in the business so they could draw the most customers and the highest rollers, and they had the cash to spend. At the same time, the admission prices to the showrooms were bargain rates.

The Riv alone featured such luminaries as Liberace, Sid Caesar, Imogene Coca, Harry Belafonte, and Red Skelton. Elsewhere on the Strip, any one of the clique of entertainers the media dubbed "the Rat Pack" might be performing. When Frank Sinatra, Dean Martin, Sammy Davis Jr., Joey Bishop, and Peter Lawford held their legendary "Summit" in the Sands' Copa Room over a three-week period in 1960, during their filming of *Ocean's Eleven*, Dad used his connections to get me in, twice.

The lounge shows, of course, were free, and who knew what future star might be appearing. Wayne Newton, for example, got his start as a high-pitched teenager in Vegas's lounges, performing with his older brother Jerry. One of the favorite lounge acts at the time was the Check-mates, a soul group that featured vocalists Sonny Charles and Sweet Louie, and that later on scored big on the charts with an R&B hit, "Black Pearl."

One night, after an evening at the drive-in with my date, it was still early. She insisted we return to the Riv. She was a hotel guest I had met at the pool and going to a drive-in was not her idea of seeing Las Vegas. I kept protesting, but she wanted to get into the lounge show. I resisted but finally relented. Neither of us was of legal age, but that didn't keep a lot of young people from making their way into the lounges. I really couldn't think of a compelling reason not to try, except that Dad might find out. But I never told any of my dates who my dad was, so I couldn't use that as an excuse for why we should avoid the lounge.

So we gave it a whirl. To my relief, there was a long line outside. I was able to convince the girl that we probably couldn't get in. But as we were making our way out, I made a small logistical error: We walked past the maître d'. He spotted me.

"Oh, Bob! How great to see you! Would you like to see the show?"

"Well, you look pretty crowded..." I began.

"No problem! Stand right here. Just give me a minute!"

He came back a few moments later carrying a little round table, fol-lowed by an usher carting two chairs. "OK, follow me," the maître d' said.

He walked down to the middle of the room and stopped right in front of the stage, adjusted some other tables out of the way, and put ours down. As he seated us, he said, "I hope you enjoy the show."

The cocktail waitress was waiting nearby. She greeted me by name and took our drink orders.

My date was so impressed she barely knew what to make of the VIP treatment. Eyes wide, she gasped, "Do they treat all the lifeguards here like this?"

6

Ross Miller Gets Connected
in Vegas

Las Vegas still was a small enough town in the 1950s and '60s where the key players of public life were on a first-name basis. Clark County sheriff Butch Leypoldt knew the people running the hotels. After all, he had to make sure there was good communication so he could preserve the integrity of the primary industry, gaming, and keep the town safe. In fact, casino security guards in those days were deputized by the sheriff and carried guns. This practice eventually was banned, because of legal concerns about casino employees doubling as peace officers, but it worked fine at that time. The casino guards, hired because they were well experienced in the gambling business, knew what crimes to watch for, such as cheaters "spooning" the old one-armed bandit slot machines, rigging them to pay out. The guards also would watch for petty criminals such as pickpockets, purse-snatchers, or chip grabbers, who, once apprehended, would be discouraged not only from repeating the error of their ways, but from setting foot in the casino again. Meanwhile, more severe crimes, such as armed robbery, were beyond imagination in those days. Ralph Lamb, who served as sheriff from 1960 to 1978, says, "We didn't even visualize a casino ever being stuck up."

My father and Sheriff Leypoldt got to be friends. Later, after Lamb, the colorful cowboy sheriff, took office, he and Dad became close friends. Dad was not a person who warmed up quickly to people. After becoming sheriff, Lamb paid a get-acquainted visit to my dad, shook hands, and chatted for a spell. He broke through Ross Miller's stony façade after it became apparent they understood each other. Dad wanted his operation to run smoothly, and intended to play by the local rules. For his part, Lamb didn't cotton to casino operators who'd come from out of town and handled personnel matters on the sly. The sheriff's office, increasingly cooperating with the FBI, always was on the lookout for wise guys with extensive rap sheets skulking around gambling operations or worming their way onto the casino payroll. All hotel casino employees had to obtain work cards from the sheriff's office.

Lamb explains, "We tried to keep it as clean as we could keep it, because the federal government was always looking. They looked at everybody in Las Vegas like it was the end of the world out here. We were trying to show them that with the work card law, that we had control."

Operators like my dad knew the stakes and the rules. Clear and open contact with the sheriff's office was key. If a card dealer with a lot of gambling experience but a shaky record from out of state was offered employment at the Riv, Dad or one of his partners might put in a good word for him with the sheriff. Lamb understood the game as well as anyone. In his down-home mind-set, investors bought a casino, hired people, and naturally wanted their friends around them. Lamb kept an open mind when a casino operator asked him, "Listen, can this guy go to work?" If the guy looked all right to Lamb, the sheriff might give him a six-month work card; if that period passed with no misbehavior, he might get a twelve-month card. Vegas, in maintaining an ethos of the Old West, was all about second chances. Or as Lamb puts it, in his folksy drawl, "We kind of straightened some guys out that way."

My dad, having developed in Chicago his appreciation for the political realities of a city, cooperated well with the sheriff's office. Dad was upfront with his needs. Says Lamb, "He just talked straight and forward to me. If he wanted something, he just came out and told you about it, and didn't send people to see you. I kind of liked that."

Lamb says the communication line ran both ways. "If my people saw someone in the casino that they knew was in the Black Book, they'd go to Ross Miller and tell him, and the guy would be ejected immediately. He never would try to circumvent anything like that." Lamb as sheriff wasn't concerned about shenanigans going on secretly at the Riviera. Of greater worry to him were casinos such as the Dunes, where the ownership was bought out and a new group came in with whom he wasn't familiar. The Dunes changed ownership several times. "It took a while to get acquainted around, see who is who, who was hanging around, why is this guy there. With Miller and them at the Riviera, you knew all of their people, and everything was up and aboveboard."

Las Vegas was then truly the land of second opportunities. Lamb and others cared less about what you had done and more about what you were doing now. Las Vegas would never be what it is today unless there was tolerance in the early days for executives with "colorful backgrounds." In those days the only men with experience in running a gambling operation had learned their trade elsewhere—where it was illegal.

As befit a high-profile businessman in his new town and new life, Dad also was well connected with Nevada politicians. One in particular whom he befriended was Grant Sawyer.

Sawyer was a Democrat who'd begun his political rise by getting elected district attorney in rural Elko County. When Grant was running for governor in 1958 against two-term Republican incumbent Charles Russell, my uncle Gene, who'd moved to Vegas, volunteered for the campaign and drove Sawyer around on part of his swing through the rural counties north of Las Vegas. Sawyer's political stances were hardly backward. He was so progressive for his time, on issues ranging from education to the environment to race relations, that many powerful people in the state regarded him as radical. Indeed, after his election he pushed hard to desegregate the casinos. He also backed legislation during the first of his two terms that put sharper teeth into the state's regulation of casinos. A state gaming commission that regulated the industry better than the old state tax commission had, and the creation of the Black Book. Nevertheless, in the early 1960s, the gaming industry faced a wave of bad national and international publicity that went beyond sensationalized media accounts.

U.S. Attorney Gen. Robert Kennedy, the president's brother, wanted to deputize a group of state officials under his command so that he could conduct a raid on all of the casinos. As historians would later note, Gov. Sawyer had to contact Bobby's big brother in the White House to get it called off. But that didn't stop Bobby or FBI director J. Edgar Hoover from illegally wiretapping Las Vegas casinos and their executives.

As it happened, Sawyer became the first governor in the Western states to endorse the presidential campaign of an underdog candidate from Massachusetts named John F. Kennedy. A couple interesting stories about Dad emerged from this period, courtesy of Ralph Denton, a longtime Democratic Party activist in Nevada, who knew my dad.

Ralph, a native of rural Caliente, was a protégé of longtime Nevada U.S. Sen. Pat McCarran, who'd helped Ralph transition out of working on ranches and mines into a job in Washington, D.C., in the Senate. Ralph went to law school and began practicing in Vegas in 1954. He was an ardent Democrat and coordinated the southern Nevada gubernatorial campaign for Grant Sawyer. That's when he first met Ross Miller.

As Ralph Denton tells it, a Chicago lawyer named Hy Raskin, who had worked on the presidential campaigns for Democratic nominee Adlai Stevenson, had come to Nevada to raise money to get Sawyer elected. The idea was that a Democratic governor in Nevada could prove helpful to winning delegates from the state for the incipient presidential candidacy of U.S. Sen. John F. Kennedy, who would be running in 1960. Raskin had connections with Dad from his Chicago days, evidently, and introduced him to Ralph.

"Ross Miller gave us $1,300 cash," Ralph says. "That was the first money given to Sawyer to run for governor by a gambler in southern Nevada."

In those days in Nevada, there weren't campaign-disclosure laws. There were no limitations. Frankly, everyone in Las Vegas lived by cash.

A hotel executive typically had a wad of $100 bills in his pocket, wrapped with a rubber band. (I don't know if any of them bothered buying a money clip.) Political candidates would go hotel to hotel, in hopes that a casino operator might reach into his pocket, roll off the rubber band, and say, "Here's a few hundred dollars."

The gist of a second story Ralph shares about Dad is that you can take the bookie out of Chicago, but you can't take Chicago out of the bookie. This is to say that old-fashioned, off-the-books bets were still accepted by Vegas casinos in the 1950s and early '60s.

In 1960, Ralph was Nevada state coordinator for Kennedy's presidential run. Nationally, the race between Kennedy and Republican vice president Richard Nixon was extremely tight. According to Ralph, on the eve of Election Day, November 8, John Kennedy's youngest brother, Ted, called Ralph to ask the spread. While it was illegal for casinos to take bets on elections, Ralph called Ross Miller, who told him the odds were 6–5, pick 'em. In other words, a bettor could gamble $6 to win $5 on either candidate. Ted told Ralph, "Get me $5,000 down on Jack." Ralph relayed the bet to Dad, who told Ralph, "You got it."

Even though wagers such as these were off the books, they could be made in confidence. That points up a virtue of the old-time gamblers: Their word was their bond. Denton puts it this way: "I've always said that the most trustworthy man in the world is a bookmaker, because he can't stay in business if his word isn't good. If Ross Miller told me he was going to do something, he would do it."

A little later, Ted Kennedy called Ralph again and asked him to get another $5,000 down on his brother John. Ralph called Dad to see if he could double the bet, and Dad told him, again, "You got it."

Now Ralph was on the string to Dad for $10,000.

"On election night," Ralph recalls, "I'm as nervous as a whore in church. I knew that if Kennedy lost, the next morning, Ross would be there for this ten grand."

That is, if Nixon won, Ralph would have to find a way to come up with $10,000 on the spot until Ted Kennedy could pay him back.

It was late on the morning of November 9 that word finally came that JFK had been elected.

"That morning, without any problem, I had that money delivered to me," Ralph remembers. "Ross sent it with somebody. They paid off immediately."

7

Bob Miller Gets Launched into the World

I still was inching up toward my full height of six-foot-five, and remained as awkward as ever on gangly legs. The coaches weren't too high on me. But as I eyed my senior year, I determined to work extra hard. I practiced basketball endlessly on my own in the off-season. To my delight, that summer out of school I could feel myself improving. I was finally growing into my body, moving with greater agility and confidence. During tryouts that fall, I made varsity. I had high hopes for a successful season, but to my great disappointment I found myself mostly sitting on the bench as the season got underway. The coach's opinions of me seemed to have carried over from the past.

After the first few games, I was thoroughly upset. I'd worked so doggedly to improve my game that I yearned for a chance to show what I could do. Finally, I decided during one game that if the coach didn't put me in, I was quitting. Sure enough, I rode the pine the entire game. I turned in my uniform and joined a city-league team, along with some other students from Gorman and from Las Vegas High.

I ended up leading that league in scoring while my team captured the championship. It was exciting, but not the same as high school sports. In retrospect, I wish I'd stuck it out on the Bishop Gorman squad and fought my way into the lineup. But my competitive nature wouldn't allow me to accept a role as just a practice player.

I had much more success in the classroom than I did on the basketball court. I was earning good grades, and indeed would graduate with honors. Along with my friends, I also became interested in another competitive venue—politics, which at this level meant student government. My friend Tito Tiberti wanted to be student-body president. But he was not alone.

I aimed to toss my hat into the ring, too. I'd already gotten a taste of politics, having run at the beginning of the year for junior-year homeroom representative. I'd earnestly handed out fliers promoting my candidacy. Probably too earnestly. My classmates decided "Boob" Miller was at it again: making a spectacle of himself in an overserious quest to achieve. It became a joke to them, which, of course, guaranteed a punch line at my expense. A day before the election, David Reeves, a classmate who was a bit of a loner, piped up, "I have an idea, this will be funny. Let's just elect me!"

To my chagrin, David won! The taste of defeat was very bitter. But after I'd digested the experience, I felt a surging hunger to win the next time I ran. I would just have to be smarter about it .

As senior year approached, I analyzed the options. Student-body president seemed too lofty a goal; I set my sights on vice president. For his part, Tito was a heavy underdog. I was in the same spot in my race, clearly a dark horse. Two popular kids, a football player and the captain of the drill team, were running for vice president. But the same dynamics at play in public elections existed in school races. If there was one thing I could count on, it was a cross-section of support from the different grades. I was dating a freshman, knew many sophomores, and I had a fair number of friends among my fellow juniors. They campaigned for me among their classmates. The race culminated in a decisive event: a required speech in front of the entire student body. Here, too, I was in luck. I'd thought through what I was going to say, and when it came time, I kept my comments brief and to the point about what I'd accomplish as vice president. That was in keeping with the "KISS" rule of public speaking: Keep It Short, Stupid. Although I'd never done any public speaking, I must have intuitively understood that principle.

For whatever reason, I also felt comfortable speaking in front of the hundreds of kids. My remarks went over well. The school principal, Father Anson, told me later that I'd captured more than 50 percent of the vote among the four candidates.

Tito took his race, too. It was no accident; once he'd decided to run, he'd organized his campaign and gotten out there to win votes. His popular, heavily favored foe, R. J. Heher, committed two classic mistakes in politics: (1) underestimating his opponent because his opponent was a first-time candidate, and (2) relying on his own historical popularity among the junior class. What Tito did was campaign among the much larger freshmen and sophomore class—Tito, quite simply, got out the vote.

These political lessons sunk in deeply for me. So did the subsequent experience during senior year of running student government. I have to say that Tito proved to be an able president: he understood immediately how to put his subordinates to work. To this day, he jokes that he made me everything I am, because he constantly delegated duties to me as vice president. I was the one who had to do the grunt work of organizing the Homecoming Dance, and so on. Thus I learned how to be an effective governmental representative. It boiled down to one thing: putting in the long hours of work.

Another indelible truth I absorbed was that as an office holder you need to surround yourself with capable people, then let them do their jobs. Tito was great at that. But if an ultimate decision was required on a matter, it was his to make, since he was at the top of the ladder, and he made it decisively.

I took note of this, and would end up employing this administrative model myself years later, when I held public office.

To my amazement, as I stood on stage during the commencement exercises with my fellow class of 1963 graduates of Bishop Gorman High School, I saw Dad stride to the front row with a camera. This was completely out of character for the stoic, reserved Ross Miller. Beaming with pride, he snapped my photograph.

That moment spoke volumes to me. He had never attended the high school basketball games or other events I participated in, leaving it to my mother to represent the family. Now he was not just present but noticeably happy. My various graduations were repeats of this side of my dad but this was the first and just his attendance was a surprise to me. The man who never told his son, in words, that he loved him, was clearly brimming with emotion. The son had passed a major milestone on the way to adulthood, and, indeed, gone further in formal education than he, the father, a self-taught man. The Millers were moving up in the world.

As for myself, I was probably feeling more like an adult than I deserved to. I'd be off to college in the fall, to the University of Santa Clara, five hundred miles away. I could feel the parental leash loosening. I'd already been giving it some steady tugs.

There was a tradition among the high school students in Las Vegas in the '60s to invite the student-body officers of the various schools to the other schools' graduation parties. The week before commencement, my buddies and I from Bishop Gorman partook wholeheartedly of the schools' festivities, imbibing of the refreshments and carousing. We stayed out late several nights in a row, and in the process I violated a cardinal rule of the Miller household. Mom had set a midnight curfew for me on weekends, but the true deadline, not to be flouted, for being home and in bed, was before Dad got home. "You've gotta be home before your dad," Mom would say. That usually meant about 2 A.M., and I knew my health would be in jeopardy if I didn't beat the deadline.

But now that I was eighteen, I figured that if my friends stayed out into the wee hours on weekends, why shouldn't I? So I started getting home later and later. Either Dad hadn't noticed, or he'd chosen to ignore my indiscretions. On graduation night, I stayed up all night with my friends and didn't get home until the next morning. Not much happened; my parents cut me the slack.

That summer I was working again as a lifeguard at the Riviera. One day my friend John Garber, who stayed out late all the time, suggested we hit the town that night. Sounded good to me. I figured there'd be no repercussions at home. And even if there were, I was an adult now. I could stand up for myself.

I came in the front door around 4 A.M. and went to my bedroom. A moment later, Dad walked into my room. My parents' bedroom was just across the hall. He'd been listening for me.

"Where the hell you been?" he growled.

"I was out with my friends," I said, matter-of-factly.

His voice rose. "What makes you think you can stay out till this hour?"

My voice rose. "I'm eighteen; I can do what I want."

It was the first time I'd ever talked back to him. Dad's face flushed. But I wasn't going to back down.

The words started flying back and forth. Dad, however, never was interested in debate.

He moved directly to his closing argument:

"If you don't shut up, I'm going to hit you with a closed fist."

He'd cuffed me with an open hand a few times over the years, to get my attention. But I was an adult now and I towered over him.

I laughed.

I saw it coming, and started to duck. Too late.

Smack on the side of my head. I stumbled back as a bell clanged once, sharply.

"That's it," he said. "You think you're such a big shot. You're on your own!"

He stalked out.

I shut my door, gingerly fingering my stinging ear. Just like that, I'd been booted from the roost. Tossed out into the world to find a roof over my own head.

I felt a stroke of panic. What would I do for money? Dad's word had gotten me the lifeguard job at the Riviera. Now he was chairman of the board at the Riv. So I'd just run afoul of the top guy at my workplace.

I pulled the covers up around me and went to sleep for what would be my last night in my bedroom, in the comfort of the family house.

The next morning, Mom shook me awake.

"Get going. You're late for work!"

"What?" I said. "Where were you last night?"

"What do you mean?"

"Well, Dad kicked me out of the family. He told me I'm on my own now. I'm trying to figure out where to go."

"Oh," she said, laughing it off, "he's over all that. Just get to work!"

I did. And I stayed out of Dad's way for a day or two. The buzzing in my ear lasted three days. He really packed a wallop. Guests at the pool would come up and ask me for a lounge chair, and I'd have to turn my good ear toward them to hear.

It wasn't uncommon back then for a father to strike an unruly son. Some of my friends were literally getting into fistfights with their fathers. So in that context, my spat with my father was not much to talk about. Of course, that was then and this is now. I have never struck my children, nor can I imagine ever doing so. But my dad had a different life experience where he had in Chicago, and perhaps earlier, needed to use his fists.

And looking back, he was right to administer an attitude adjustment. I was being a smartass eighteen-year-old, and thought that I didn't need to pay attention to my parents anymore. He convinced me otherwise.

And, I suppose, I would be paying attention to Ross Miller long after I left home and long after he was gone.

Part II

Maturing in the Shadow of a Changing Las Vegas

8

Leaving Las Vegas— For a Time

In 1963, the mob was in full flower in Las Vegas. The Chicago Outfit had infiltrated nearly every casino on the Strip, from the Aladdin to the Dunes to the Flamingo and, yes, to the Riviera, where Ross Miller was a prominent figure. The state was still small—only 337,000 people—and Clark County only had about 20,000 hotel rooms, one seventh of today's total. But it was a gold mine for the mob and an attorney general by the name of Robert F. Kennedy had been sniffing around. When a bug was discovered at the Sands—and then others were discovered—Gov. Grant Sawyer, who had been trying to make gaming respectable, was outraged. He had already traveled to Washington two years earlier to confront both of the Kennedys—he had heard RFK was planning raids, but he got no satisfaction from him or his brother, the president. Las Vegas and its mob connections were on the federal government's radar, and Ross Miller was a blip on that screen.

That was the Las Vegas I left behind as Ross Miller's son arrived on the campus of Santa Clara University, the small Jesuit school in northern California in the fall of 1963. My first roommate, the product of a Jesuit upbringing in Omaha, saw me as a godless heathen from Las Vegas—we weren't roommates long. But others were more accepting of the supposed interloper, expressing curiosity and not hostility. Indeed, another student from the same school as my first roommate, Dave Hickey, didn't see me as the devil incarnate because I hailed from Sin City. Hickey was a good sport, and he was present at one of the funniest incidents of my college days. It happened during a school break during my sophomore year, when I brought home with me Dave and another of our buddies who was from Nebraska.

These wholesome young men from Omaha were excited to be visiting racy Las Vegas so I suggested we go to one of the afternoon topless revues, despite the fact that we were underage. Naturally, I chose a club other than the Riviera, given Dad's feelings about my not hanging around the casinos. As the usher seated us near the front of the stage, my Midwestern friends were thrilled; I played it cool, the worldly Las Vegan. We were enjoying the entertainment when the emcee's booming voice announced: "And now, the featured entertainer of our show . . . the lovely Francine!"

Francine strode out: a tall, beautiful brunette. Nonchalantly, I told the others, "That was my date to the senior ball."

They shot me skeptical smirks. "Yeah, right!" they said. I couldn't blame them. Up there on stage, serenely topless, Francine looked twenty-five years old. Not to mention, out of our league.

Suddenly, the stage lighting changed just enough to illuminate our table. Francine looked down in the middle of her number, noticed me, and exclaimed, "Oh, Bobby, hi!" She was as shocked to see me as I had been to see her. But neither of us were as shocked as my two friends.

Of course, it was more the coincidence than anything that surprised me. In a city such as Las Vegas, a certain number of girls you go to school with inevitably end up working as dancers, just as a certain number of guys become card dealers or pit bosses. Casinos are the prime employers. In those days, in that smaller Las Vegas, it was common to see the showgirls off-hours at the grocery store or cleaners, going about normal daily life as if they were housewifes in Des Moines (only wearing a lot more makeup, and with false eyelashes as large as tarantulas).

Francine joined us after the show for a drink. That kind of validation . . . well, it just doesn't come along every day.

Unlike high school, I did not begin my college career on a track to be an honor student. At freshman orientation, I had no notion of what I should select as a major. One of the presenters mentioned the concept of an economics major in the College of Liberal Arts, which he suggested offered the best of both worlds. I imagined myself as a successful business-man at a cocktail reception discussing the arts, perhaps in French. It sounded good at first but my academics would suffer from this decision, plus the distraction of living away from home and my parents' watchful eyes for the first time. What finally turned around my mediocre marks was switching majors between my junior and senior years. I'd earned good grades in my poli sci but not as good in my economic courses; the con-cepts were easy enough for me to grasp, although I wasn't contemplating a career in politics. What's more, I could finish out a poli-sci degree in four years with the credits I'd accumulated. That was probably my deciding point. I did not want to have to face my father and tell him I needed a fifth year of college to earn my bachelor's degree. I'm sure he would have po-nied up the extra tuition after grumbling, but I didn't want to come across as a failure to him. His respect meant the world to me. I wanted both my parents to be pleased with their son. I knew how much they sacrificed so that I could get an education and make something of myself. They had high expectations. (To this day, even though they've been dead for several decades, I want my parents to be proud of me. A child's love doesn't end when his parents are gone.)

By my sophomore year the "hippie movement" had started taking root, especially in nearby San Francisco. I went there occasionally on weekends and checked out the scene. I felt no animosity toward the growing number of long-haired young people on the streets, but I knew this was not me. I didn't fit in. And I knew my parents would never accept my trying to do so. Like the protestors, I didn't agree with everything about the Vietnam War—but I didn't believe everything was wrong, either.

The summer between my junior and senior years I was able to con-vince my dad to let me join my friend Tito Tiberti on a trip to Europe. We traveled throughout for most of the summer using a book called *Europe on*

$5 a Day as our guide. Yes, it was that inexpensive back then, assuming you stayed in hostels or cheap hotels, and hitchhiked or took trains. The most eventful portion of the trip began when we were in Vienna, Austria, and saw a notice through American Express offices to travel to Budapest, Hungary. This was during the height of the Cold War and such a thing seemed unthinkable so, being adventurous, we signed up. A bus took us to the Hungarian border, which had two rows of high barbed-wire fences with gun turrets spaced throughout. There was one hundred yards of no-man's-land in between. A sense of adventure and foreboding engulfed me as we rode through the gates. Once in Hungary we were confronted by heavily armed Russian soldiers and as luck would have it they chose to open my suitcase. It is important to note here that Dad didn't have ordinary business cards. They were imitation $1,000 bills, the size and color of regular U.S. currency. And he had given me stacks of them to hand out all over Europe.

As they opened the suitcase the guards' eyes widened. One guard peeled off a bill and handed it to me with a quizzical look on his face. I took it and then attempted to hand it back, wherein he jumped backward, his head shaking no, no, no. I suddenly grasped the error of this and tore the bill in half and threw it away to show it had no real value. Apparently they then concluded that these were not real bills and let us proceed. If not I suppose the name of this book would be *My Years in a Russian Prison*.

By my senior year, I knew I would be going to law school. A law degree was what Dad wanted for me, and that's what I wanted for myself, and I had no idea what I would do if I didn't continue my education. He wanted to see me go far in a career, and that was my desire, too. Ross Miller wanted a different kind of life for his son than he had led—and was leading.

Shortly before I graduated in 1967, I got a call from my mother. It was May 11. In a shaky voice, she broke the news that Ross Miller had been indicted, along with other executives at the Riviera, on charges of casino skimming.

Federal agents had been targeting Las Vegas resorts for some time, believing that lots of revenue was going unreported, and therefore that the government was missing out on a fortune in uncollected taxes. This was the first foray by the feds into the legalized gaming world, and after a six-month investigation, Ross Miller and six others were indicted by a grand jury. By this time, my father, an original 4 percent investor in the Riviera, was the chairman of the board of directors. In some ways, he was the biggest of the fish the government had ensnared in its net. The others were lesser Riviera executives and current and former investors in the Fremont Hotel downtown. The federal government had used wiretaps for several years to buttress allegations that my father and others were, according to the indictment, part of a scheme to "appropriate, conceal, and skim some of the currency" when the end-of-the-day count was made.

Nevada's new governor at the time, Paul Laxalt, put out a statement revealing the state had "cooperated when requested in the federal grand jury investigation on conduct alleged to have occurred prior to this administration."

In the *New York Times* account, my father, who was fifty-nine at the time, was described as having come to Las Vegas "as a dealer in 1955. The former sponsor of a nightclub in Chicago, he owns 12.3 percent of the $15 million Riviera Hotel."

Beyond my close personal connection to this event, it was a pivotal moment in the history of Las Vegas. As an Associated Press account pointed out at the time, the real question raised by these indictments, which came after Gov. Grant Sawyer's previous administration had concluded there was no skimming, was this: "Can the state effectively control the gambling industry?"

I was shocked and scared at the notion of Dad facing charges from a grand jury investigation, and even prison time, if he was found guilty. I wondered whether to come home immediately. Mom told me to stay put, that she'd keep me informed. Dad wasn't going to say anything about the matter, she said. So I stuck it out on campus, waiting for more news.

The news didn't come until nearly a year later, when two of the men indicted, including Edward Levinson, an officer at the Riviera, pleaded no contest to the skimming charges in March 1968. They were fined a combined $8,000 by federal Judge Roger Foley. In the back-and-forth between the Justice Department and attorneys for my father and the others, all of the charges against the other five defendants were dismissed.

I was, of course, enormously relieved. I surmised, as many Las Vegans did, that it had been overzealous prosecution by the feds. I never discussed the matter with my father. That probably seems a bit strange but I knew that sensitive conversations with my dad were only initiated by him, not by me. He never brought it up. At my college graduation, no one, including me, would notice any evident concern. The ultimate resolution was conveyed to be by my mother, not my father. I knew so little that only in researching for this book did I learn that there were wiretaps. Of course, if I had been older then or had gained my law-enforcement experience, I suspect I might have dared to ask him a question or two, but such was not the case then. I knew only that he had been charged and that the case was dismissed and at the time that was enough for me.

I'd scored well on my Law School Admission Test, but I needed a high GPA within my major, and it wasn't high enough in my economics courses. If I worked hard, I could have a high GPA in poli sci and get into law school, which was my ultimate goal as an undergraduate. I didn't necessarily want to become a lawyer; I still had no idea what career I'd pursue. I just knew that law school provided a fantastic education, and would better my chances in whatever field I ultimately chose. That had been true of some of the big businessmen in Las Vegas, such as Hank Greenspun, publisher of the *Las Vegas Sun*. He'd been a lawyer before plunging into the media industry, coming to own a newspaper, radio station, and television station, followed by a lucrative career in real estate development.

When I graduated from Santa Clara in spring 1967, the commencement speaker was none other than Nevada's new Republican governor. Paul Laxalt had attended Santa Clara for three years before his studies were interrupted by military service in World War II.

Laxalt was forty-four, dark-haired, and handsome. He'd defeated two-term incumbent Sawyer the previous year. Laxalt was polite to me, one of only two Nevadans in the graduating class. And as I recall, he was cordial with my dad; at least I did not notice any tension or snub. Unbeknownst to me, although my father and every other casino executive were paying close attention, that spring Laxalt would be signing into law Nevada's Corporate Gaming Act. The consequences would be far reaching, because the new law opened the gates for huge sums of investment capital to pour into the state's gaming industry. The act removed the requirement for background financial checks previously required of all shareholders of license applicants; with the new law, only a corporation's key executives and stockholders (not every last shareholder) needed to be licensed. This law had been largely constructed and promoted by E. Parry Thomas, the Valley Bank president in Las Vegas, who understood that unless his city matured from an era where figures with questionable backgrounds held ownership in the casinos, into one where corporate control was more the norm, then its future growth would be severely limited. This Corporate Gaming Act was part of Laxalt's strategy to push the mob out of Vegas casinos and attract investors in a league far above what the Teamsters Central States Pension Fund could muster—and at a time when the state was beginning to move away from the founding gamers and the outside scrutiny that accompanied them. But given Nevada casinos' dubious reputation on Wall Street, it would turn out that six more years would pass before the revolution of corporate ownership would truly begin in Vegas, demarcating a break from the era of independent investors from my dad's generation. In 1973, maverick entrepreneur Kirk Kerkorian opened his $106 million MGM Grand Las Vegas, which is presently the Bally's hotel (not the newer MGM) on the Strip, financing the resort by selling his Flamingo and the International Hotel to Hilton Hotels Corp. That marked the first time a publicly owned conglomerate was in charge of a Las Vegas casino.*

---

* By 1976, 63 percent of the Hilton Corporation's earnings came solely from its Las Vegas establishments. Hilton's success spurred the interest of other businesses; soon, Sheraton and Holiday Inn were investing in Las Vegas and buying casinos. The ascendance of corporate ownership marked a sea change in Las Vegas. The crime syndicates simply could not compete with the enormous sums of capital the corporations could invest in hotel-casinos. The corporations began buying up the mob-controlled properties; what's more, since the chief local industry no longer was reliant on mob money, law enforcement began pursuing these undesirables

Sitting there in cap and gown among my fellow members of Santa Clara's Class of '67, my thoughts were far from the major business developments taking place in my hometown. I'd been gone the better part of four years, and now was eyeing another three years away. I'd applied to Loyola Law School, in downtown Los Angeles, and felt good about my prospects of gaining admission. I was satisfied with that, although Dad had harbored grander ideas. When it had come time for me to apply to law schools, he'd asked me where I was sending my transcript. I'd mentioned Loyola and Santa Clara.

"Well, did you apply to Harvard and Stanford?" he asked.

"Dad, I'm not going to get into Harvard and Stanford."

"How do you know that?!"

"Well, my grades aren't high enough…"

"You don't know unless you try!"

I explained to him about the extensive forms and expensive fees for applying to the likes of Stanford, Berkeley, or the Ivy League schools, and that there was no chance I could get accepted.

"Don't worry about sending in the hundreds of dollars," he'd said. "I'll pay the money, son. You fill out the forms. You apply!"

So I applied to Stanford, and to Boalt, but wasn't accepted at either. I knew I wasn't qualified, but to my father, if you didn't try, you never knew. He believed I'd given up shooting for the most prestigious schools only because I was discouraged. And that attitude didn't cut it for him.

But law school—I was accepted at Loyola—would have to wait a year at least, in any regard. My draft board in Las Vegas notified me that there'd be no more deferment for education, and I was likely to be drafted. The Vietnam War was ramping up. So my first order of business was figuring out where I'd be wearing a uniform.

---

more aggressively. By the mid-1970s, the state Gaming Control Board began penalizing and refusing gambling license applications to known mobsters.

I contemplated my options. It was obvious to me that it was better to volunteer than to be subject to the whims of the Selective Service System. I had two years of ROTC under my belt, but some of my friends, such as Dave Hickey, had four years and would go into the military automatically as officers. I thought of myself more as an officer than an enlisted man, but would have to choose the right branch of service with the clearest route to earning a commission. I thought about applying to Officer Candidate School.

Then I learned that my friends Tiberti, Layne, and a couple other friends from high school had enlisted in an Army Reserve unit. They had joined D Battery, a searchlight unit. I learned there was an opening, applied, and was accepted. It was a six-year commitment. Before I could begin law school, I had to serve on active duty for several months.

After two months in Nevada, I went for two months of basic training and two more of advanced training as an infantryman at Fort Dix, New Jersey. The only consolation was that my ROTC experience let me go in as a Private First Class, E-3 in rank, instead of as a buck private. This rank made me a platoon guide, sort of the head grunt.

Although I was Catholic, I hit upon a little scam and mustered the nerve to carry it out. I indicated my religious preference as "Jewish" so that I could get some extra time off duty because of the Jewish High Holy Days of Rosh Hashanah and Yom Kippur. To my chagrin, a sergeant asked me to escort the other Jewish guys in my unit to synagogue; there, I would have had to pretend I knew what I was doing. I was worried that these weekly trips would give me away, but fortunately the rest of the Jewish soldiers persuaded me that we should go to the PX instead each week. I confided in one Jewish friend that should anything happen, he should bring me a priest, not a rabbi for my confession. He kept my secret and even took me to New York City to stay with his family during the High Holy Days.

As I look back, my ploy was both the most risky and perhaps the most stupid thing I ever did. It did, however, give me an enhanced appreciation of bigotry, and helped me develop a strong intolerance for discrimination.

The captain in charge of our company would run alongside of me during advanced infantry training, yelling, "Hurry up, Miller, or we're gonna light up those furnaces!"*

During law school I served in a personnel service company in Southern California. For various reasons, perhaps mainly that we were about as functional as M.A.S.H., I kept getting promoted after law school. The remainder of my military career would be spent back in Nevada. I transferred back to Las Vegas and switched from an Army to an Air Force Reserve unit, based at Nellis Air Force Base. This was a medical unit, and since it had no other ranking enlisted men, I was the de facto enlisted man in charge, the "first sergeant." Some of my friends from Bishop Gorman were in this unit. The U.S. military campaign in Southeast Asia was winding down by then; about the most significant contribution our unit made, as I recall, was that the physicians performed a fair number of vasectomies on the base.

Right before my six-year commitment was up in 1973, the Air Force disbanded our unit. I received an honorable discharge.

---

* When I grew up in Las Vegas, there was a saying that Vegas was a town of Protestants and Catholics, run by Mormons and owned by Jews. This referred to the fact that the population mostly was Christian, many of the bankers, other prominent businessmen and elected officials were Mormon, and many of the hotel owners were Jewish. The diversity meant I hadn't been exposed to much bigotry, except for discrimination against blacks in the hotels.

9

My Brush with History

In the spring of 1968, with law school beginning for me in the fall, I decided to find a temporary job over the summer in Los Angeles. I was taking a speed-reading course in the evenings after work. The site happened to be just across the street from the venerable Ambassador Hotel, on Wilshire Boulevard. So there I was, on Tuesday, June 4, on the same night there was a Bobby Kennedy for President rally at the Ambassador, which was held to culminate his campaigning in California.

I was a registered Democrat. Like most people, I'd joined the party to which my parents belonged. Plus, the Democrats' platform tended toward inclusion of minorities and promotion of civil rights and equal opportunities under the law. These were always core values for me, but I wasn't a big fan of Bobby Kennedy—I remembered what he had tried to do to the casinos in my state. Piecing together from what I'd heard from other casino people in Las Vegas, and reading between my father's lines, it seemed that both the former president and his brother, Bobby, had been ahead of their time in living the present Las Vegas slogan, "What happens here, stays here."

I hadn't made up my mind who I would vote for in my first election (the voting age then was twenty-one), and I was leaning toward Humphrey, even though I was Catholic. But since I was interested in politics in general, and agreed with some of Bobby Kennedy's message, I was curious about the Wilshire rally. So after my speed-reading class was over I went across the street to the Ambassador to watch. There, I ran into a guy I knew named Armijo, who was a private in my Army Reserve unit. He had been hired as a freelance photographer by Kennedy's campaign and was at the rally to take pictures.

Armijo and I ended up having some drinks together in a bar at the Ambassador. The election results that night showed Kennedy nosing out Eugene McCarthy in the California primary. That boosted his chance of winning his party's nomination, and his supporters were excited. Approaching midnight, Armijo and I left the bar to hear Kennedy's victory speech in the hotel ballroom. Armijo snapped photos. As soon as the brief speech was over, I beat it back to the bar.

I was dancing with a girl when Armijo came rushing in, frantic and jabbering excitedly: "They shot him, they killed him. I think he's dead." Bewildered chaos took over the corridor. Everyone was engulfed by a state of shock and its components: a mixture of disbelief, dread, and grief. In what was probably just minutes but seemed like hours, police officers in uniform arrived. We were told we could leave the hotel, but we couldn't take our cars out of the hotel parking area. That stranded Armijo and myself downtown until the curfew was lifted. Police cordoned off the hotel outside.

Armijo and I made it out of the Ambassador and wandered over to an all-night coffee shop. We watched the news coverage on television but didn't say much. There were few details at that point about what appeared to be an assassination. At 6 A.M. we wandered back to the Ambassador. The lot had been opened, we got our cars, and drove off. The atmosphere that night was almost surreal. It felt like you could cut the air with a knife. I was dazed and confused to be in the proximity of such tragedy and chaos. I did learn from the experience that calm and order must prevail when emotions run high. In some ways it set a tone for me in life that when others came to me in a panic I would try to be calm and deliberate. All crises pass but rational thinking must control the decision making at the time.

If Bobby Kennedy's death—and my proximity to it—was a searing moment in my life, 1968 was a pivotal year in my father's life. He had been out of Las Vegas on business, and then later at our family's condominium in Palm Springs, when two of the Riviera's largest shareholders, Charlie Harrison and Lou Miller, announced they were selling out to new owners. They did so without consulting Ross Miller. When my father found out upon returning home, he was irate. To him, this was an unconscionable act of duplicity by close associates.

Charlie Harrison had come to Las Vegas from Detroit, where he had been a bootlegger. His ability to obtain a Nevada gaming license had been in doubt. Ross Miller had provided significant assistance in getting Harrison licensed. They had become best friends thereafter. Harrison moved into a house down the street from us. As for Miller (who was no relation to us), Lou had been encouraged by Dad to come to the Riviera from the Sahara. My father was chairman of the board and, in effect, had hired Lou.

My father's fury and hurt were understandable, since friendship and loyalty were paramount to him.

When he got back to Vegas, my father continued going into his office at the Riviera every day, just as if he were still an owner. He did this for a month, daring to see if anyone would tell him to vacate. Not surprisingly, no one did. No one had the nerve to tell Ross Miller to clear out his desk.

Tito Tiberti remembers a moment from those times: "Ross had always treated me as an equal," he says, "and there were times we had man-to-man talks. I remember around that time driving by the Miller house by the Desert Inn Golf Course, and Ross was standing in the front of the house. He had on red slacks and no shirt. It was summer, so that wasn't unusual. He invited me in for a drink, and he told me that there had been an internal fight over ownership of the Riviera, and that he had been voted out while he was still in the room. He was really troubled by it."

My father finally came to terms with the sale and quit going in. This was the end of a chapter in Ross Miller's career—and in the family's life.

Ross Miller's participation in ownership of the glitzy resort on the Strip had been the predicate for his moving up in the world. The one-time bar owner who'd taken back-room sports bets and handled his own bouncing in Chicago had clambered up the economic ladder, thanks to the Riv. A high school dropout, he'd earned his way into prestigious social circles.

The Riviera today is far different from what it was then. The Riv of Dad's era was one of the finest quality hotels in Las Vegas. Admittedly, quality then was a far cry from the standard of today's Vegas megaresorts, but in those days the Riv competed with the Sands for featuring the most famous entertainers. And it was the Riv that first let hotel guests go up (via elevator) instead of out to their rooms on the Strip. So Dad, from humble beginnings, had risen to be chairman of a hotel of elegance.

The Riviera had afforded our family a comfortable lifestyle. I had slept on a bunk bed in the dining room of a Chicago apartment when I was small, but was able to spend much of my childhood with my own private bedroom in a ranch house on the then-prestigious Desert Inn Golf Course, with our address being just down the street from famous actress Betty Grable. She had two daughters, Victoria and Jessica, through her marriage to bandleader Harry James. For a short while I dated "Jesse James."

My father's success at the Riviera allowed him to partner in building the Seven Lakes Country Club, which featured a small, par 58 golf course, in Palm Springs, California, and he'd bought a condo on the course. I'm sure it bothered my father a lot when he ran into snobbery in Palm Springs, where he was an investor and part-time resident.

Ross Miller had joined the prestigious El Dorado Country Club over the objections of movie actor Randolph Scott, who complained that no Vegas guy should be allowed to become a member. The board members told Scott that he, himself, could resign if he didn't want Ross Miller in his club. My father ended up with a locker close to Bob Hope's.*

---

* After my dad's death, Bob Hope, Hollywood's most famous golfer, played in a tournament

My parents' condo in Palm Springs was on the 10th tee of the Seven Lakes course, and our back window looked out onto the 18th green. The course turned out to be the setting for a scene that was absolute in its contrast to the raging political disaffection running through the ranks of American society in 1968.

Late that year, I decided to drive up from L.A. to the condo for the weekend. My father was in Vegas, and my mother was at the condo. While there, we caught a rumor that President Johnson had flown into Palm Springs after a trip abroad, and was going to meet with former President Eisenhower, who had a home on the grounds of the El Dorado Country Club.

That Sunday, Mom and I kept seeing men in suits with radio cords in their ears strolling around our complex. Sure enough, LBJ and Ike had decided to play a quick round of golf, but didn't want the press following them and so kept the location secret. They'd gone in the front door of Ike's house, then out the back door and zipped over to Seven Lakes. As the present and former presidents golfed for two-and-a-half hours, a group of about fifteen residents, including my mom and me, trailed. It was rather remarkable for us to see, although we weren't close enough to hear their chitchat. As they reached the 10th tee, we went up to our front door, just a yard or two from the tee box.

As President Johnson stood at the tee, he looked over at Mom and did a couple of double takes.

People had told her in the past that she looked like the first lady. Evidently, the president saw the resemblance.

I've always wondered what he—a lame-duck president struggling to manage and somehow push toward conclusion a hugely unpopular war, battered by public-opinion polls, his visions of a "Great Society" apparently shattered along with his legacy in history—was discussing with his predecessor, a man who'd been a national hero in a very different war.

---

that was a memorial for Ross Miller. The anti-Vegas bias wasn't shared by the people who mattered most in Palm Springs.

Unlike Johnson, Eisenhower had been elected to the White House twice in landslides, and had presided over a period of unprecedented prosperity in this country. Here were two leaders from different political parties, who ruled in decidedly different eras. What subjects did they broach? What counsel, if any, was LBJ seeking from Ike? Was it foreign policy? Was it a sharing of ideas on how to quell unrest, mollify the masses, and keep America from tearing apart at the seams?

Or were they simply talking about how to cure a slice and avoid three-putting? I was in awe to be near a president, much less two. Little did I know at the time that I would later meet several U.S. presidents and even dine at the White House.

There was one rather amusing incident with White House staff that occurred at our Palm Springs home a couple years later.

Frank Fitzsimmons had taken over as head of the International Brotherhood of Teamsters in 1964 after Jimmy Hoffa was convicted of attempted bribery of a grand jury and sentenced to fifteen years in prison. Dad formed a friendship with Fitzsimmons, and the two golfed together in Palm Springs when the powerful labor leader flew in on vacation. The Teamsters Union still held financial interests in many Las Vegas hotels.

During one of these trips, a phone call came to our condo. Mom answered. The voice on the other end said, "This is the White House calling for Mr. Fitzsimmons. Is he there?"

"Well, he's just outside," Mom said. "Excuse me for a moment."

She took a couple of steps, then stopped, stunned by what she'd heard. She returned to the phone to make sure she had really heard what she thought she had.

As she picked up the receiver again, still in a state of amazement, all she could think to say was, "What color did you say your house was?"

10

Ross Miller and the Great Ringmaster Join Hands

In the summer of 1968, right before I headed off to law school at Loyola, a short, portly man joined us at our regular Sunday night dinner at the Riviera's Hickory Room. My father never invited people to our family ritual, so this guest piqued my interest. Actually I sat stunned by the mere fact that he was eating dinner with us and even more so as I heard why. I quickly gathered that he was there to pitch Ross Miller on a business proposal. My father was a very busy man, and maybe the only open slot in his schedule was Sunday night, and he wasn't about to cancel dinner with us. So he'd invited this man to eat with us and give his spiel.

Our guest made an instant impression on me, and not necessarily a favorable one. He was in his mid-forties, with a large round head, big jowls, and confident eyes that beamed with impulsive energy. He talked a mile a minute: a world-class con man, I thought. He was a man who proudly proclaimed, "I have a new idea about every twenty-one seconds." He spent much of the time at our dinner complimenting my father as a great casino guy. It was brown-nosing at its finest.

The man was Jay Sarno, who would become one of the iconic figures in Las Vegas history and have a large impact on Ross Miller's career in the gaming industry. Sarno was sometimes referred to as a "front" for the mob and their association with the Teamsters but he would become a transformative figure after he and his business partner, Stanley Mallin, hooked up with two other men my father knew—Allen Dorfman and Jimmy Hoffa. With financing from the Teamsters pension fund, Sarno would buy his way into the Strip and in the mid-1960s would design and build what for many years would be the most famous location in Nevada: Caesars Palace.

It had seemed like an outrageous proposition: a fourteen-story hotel themed on ancient Rome, with classical columns and water fountains out front, and female help in skimpy togas and desk clerks in tunics. Sarno was meticulous in adhering to his theme, even designing the cocktail waitresses' bust-baring costumes and having guest-room doorknob signs that read: Do No Disturbus.

But far from being frivolous, Caesars' design was ingenious. Its shops, showrooms, and restaurants were centered around the casino, feeding the action at the slots and tables. And Caesars' escapist theme worked a special kind of magic. It made guests feel like Caesars and Cleopatras. The result: From the moment it opened in 1966, Caesars was packed. Sarno's over-the-top resort had managed to capture a lot of the high-end gambling market. He clearly understood that the Vegas mystique touched on visitors' wildest escapist fantasies, and he ingeniously integrated a sense of fun and outrageousness into his designs. In many respects it was this concept that set the tone for the theme-oriented hotels that dot the Las Vegas Strip of today.

At the time of our dinner with him in 1968, Sarno was selling Caesars Palace, and the price was yielding him a hefty profit. He'd proved all the naysayers wrong. So, brimming with brainstorms as he was, he had an even more outlandish scheme in mind.

As Jay Sarno explained to my father at our dinner, he wanted to try another themed casino. He gushed grandly about his idea for a casino built around a circus concept. This new place would have elephants, trapezes, and a carnival midway, all designed to appeal to people's childhood fantasy of running away and joining the circus. There would be no need for hotel rooms at this enormous Big Top–shaped casino, because guests would flock there from other hotels on the Strip just to enjoy the many attractions. In fact, he'd charge admission. He'd have the Greatest Show on the Strip. He'd hire the best talent away from the world's circuses. Players could be betting at blackjack tables and look up and see acrobats soaring through the air. There would be a pink-painted elephant circling on a train above. Sarno's eyes danced with excitement as he explained his latest brainstorm.

Yes, this portly gentleman had plenty of big ideas, all of which sounded utterly ridiculous to my ears.

As our family left the restaurant, my father, for one of the only times I can remember, solicited my opinion about business.

"Well, what do you think of that project?" he asked.

My answer was straightforward: "That's the stupidest idea I've ever heard in my life."

Bob Miller, gaming visionary.

Apparently, Ross Miller saw potential that I didn't because a few months later, he partnered with Sarno in building his new resort, across the boulevard from the Riviera. When Circus Circus opened in October 1968, sporting a gigantic, pink-and-white oval circus tent and a casino the size of a football field, it became the first totally themed casino in Las Vegas. It was not the Circus Circus of today, designed mostly to attract families. No, Sarno's idea was an adult version. It included (for a very short while) a slide or fire pole for descending to the main floor; the Midway featured a knock-the-girl-out-of-bed game, and peep shows, both of which used topless women.

Sarno even had a machine in which customers could drop a quarter and a live chicken would dance for them. Only a small fraction of the clientele understood that the poor bird was standing on a hot plate, which would heat up at the drop of a coin.

I recall how my father loved bringing Tanya the elephant into the casino. Tanya's trainer had taught Ross Miller how to command the elephant, and the trainer always stood nearby while my father had her pull a slot-machine handle (there were no buttons in those days on the "one-armed bandits"), or toss a pair of dice with her trunk. It was quite a sight, which I'm certain will never be replicated, as was the huge grin on the normally stony face of Ross Miller.

My father and Sarno were very different, but they became close friends. Both men loved golf and they used to play a lot together, and for sizable sums of money. Golf was one area where my father was not reluctant to wager. One day, as they walked off the course, my father started peeling off $100 bills and handing them to Sarno, who said, "This is too much. We didn't bet this much."

"Yeah, I pressed you," Dad answered. "I doubled the bet on the sixteenth hole."

"Well, I didn't hear you press me," Sarno said.

"I don't give a damn if you heard me or not," Dad said. "I pressed you, and I lost. That's how much I owe you."

"Well, what if I had lost?" Sarno asked.

"You would've paid me," Dad said.

That is one of my favorite stories about my father because it illustrates one of his greatest attributes: integrity. Having come from a background in illegal gambling where there are no written contracts, Ross Miller lived by an unspoken code of ethics shared by many of his generation in the gaming business: He was a man of his word. And he expected others to live up to theirs.

My father remained partners with Sarno for some time, but eventually sold his interest in the property. Sarno and his partner, Mallin, finally leased the casino in 1974 to two experienced operators, Bill Bennett and Bill Pennington, who turned the resort around, bought it out, and created a company that would eventually become a giant on the Strip with the Excalibur, Luxor, and Mandalay Bay.

After parting ways with Sarno, Ross Miller bought half of the little place in front of Circus Circus, called the Slots-A-Fun Casino. With only 17,700 square feet, it was the smallest casino on the Strip and went after the low-end gambler with small betting minimums at the tables. Location meant a lot; Slots-A-Fun profited from the foot traffic of its enormous neighbor.

Ross Miller partnered in the Slots-A-Fun with a younger man whom he had met at the Las Vegas Shrine Club. That man's name was Carl Thomas.

11

Law School Grooms Bob Miller for Law Enforcement

As my father consorted with men who would later be tied to organized crime, I was at Loyola, which would put me on a path, ironically enough, to a law-enforcement career.

I put a great deal of pressure on myself to succeed in law school. If I failed, I wouldn't just be flunking out of law school. I'd be a source of shame to my parents. That would be almost too horrible for me to bear. Informing my father that I'd washed out of law school was a conversation I didn't want to have.

Law school is difficult, and Loyola was a pretty tough school. I understood from the start that there were many students much smarter than I. Therefore, I determined that I would simply have to work harder than they if I was to survive. I'd already had that experience as an undergraduate at Santa Clara. I made up my mind to bear down with dogged discipline. If I ended up failing, it would not be due to a lack of effort. For the first time in my scholastic endeavors, I would set aside as many distractions as possible and I would try my hardest to concentrate virtually all my time on studying.

Every weekday I drove from my apartment to the Loyola campus in downtown Los Angeles for the first class at 9 A.M. After my last class in the afternoon, I stayed on campus, studying in the library, until 9 or 10 P.M.

That was my routine Monday through Friday. Saturday, I drove to the UCLA campus in Westwood for a change of environment, meeting up with a few fellow law students around 10 A.M. We'd study in the library until 3 P.M., then head to the gym and work up a sweat at basketball. That was my big release. I didn't have much of a social life. I rarely had a date. I'd usually go back to my apartment and watch television on Saturday night. On Sunday I'd sleep in, then go back to UCLA and study from noon to 6 or 7 P.M. In some ways this experience would prepare me for the rigorous hours associated with governing a state.

One of the reasons I'd chosen law school at Loyola instead of Santa Clara was that I knew too many people at Santa Clara, and I easily could have gotten distracted trying to date coeds, attending sporting events, or hitting bars. At Loyola I was a stranger with no social connections, and there were very few coeds compared to male students, and so it was simpler for me to lead the scholarly life. Yes, I concentrated very hard on my studies, to the exclusion of almost everything else.

I was elated at the end of the year when I saw the grades posted for three of my classes. Not only had I passed the courses (to my immeasurable relief), but I had registered a high enough grade point average to possibly make the honor roll. Then I received the grade in my torts class. It lowered me off the dean's list by a thin margin. I felt good, though, having nearly made the dean's list. That gave me a comfort cushion with my GPA, allowing me to relax from my anxiety over washing out, disappointing my parents, humiliating myself. I knew then that I had the ability to be successful at difficult challenges if I kept my priorities straight.

Most students in my class sought law-clerk jobs for the summer. These were difficult to find, since firms prefer hiring second- or third-year law students. I didn't have the connections to land that sort of job in L.A., anyway, so I focused on finding something in Las Vegas. Since it seemed more interesting to me to work around the courts instead of in a law firm, I thought about searching for a job with the Clark County Sheriff's Office. The summer after I'd graduated from Santa Clara, while I was serving in the D Battery Army Reserve unit, and before I'd gone to New Jersey for infantry training, I'd worked a couple months as a clerk in the office of the undersheriff in Las Vegas. So I had an in of sorts. I also had my dad in my corner. He was, as I've mentioned, good friends with Sheriff Ralph Lamb.

Ross Miller called up Lamb, who said he didn't have any positions to suit me for the summer, but was glad to help out. Lamb phoned his friend, L.A. County Sheriff Pete Pitches. A job interview was arranged. And as good luck had it, Pitches hired me and assigned me to court services. That's how I became a bailiff in Department 72 of the Superior Court in and for the County of Los Angeles.

This job ended up being more than I'd expected, in the way of excitement.

Bailiffs are sheriff's deputies, and at that time in L.A., they could go to work immediately after being sworn in, until such time as another class was ready to begin at the police academy. Since I was there just for the summer, I'd be missing the police academy schedule. That meant that I was starting immediately as a regular commissioned peace officer in uniform, wearing a badge, and carrying a .38 pistol. It was on-the-job training, with target practice available on the police firing range.

That summer, there was a retrial for one of the defendants, Jimmy Lee Smith, infamous for his role in the "Onion Field" murders. I was assigned to the courtroom next door.

The case was well known.* In 1963, two convicted criminals out on parole and in the midst of a robbery spree were pulled over for a broken taillight by two Los Angeles Police Department officers. The criminal who was driving, Gregory Ulas Powell, pulled his gun on one of the officers, Ian James Campbell, and held it against Campbell's spine, forcing

---

* A best-selling book, *The Onion Field*, by former Los Angeles police officer and best-selling crime novelist Joseph Wambaugh, would be published in 1974, and a motion picture by the same name released in 1979.

Campbell's partner, Karl Hettinger, to give up his gun to the other robber, Smith.

Powell and Smith forced the officers into Powell's car, and Powell drove to an onion field outside Bakersfield. Campbell was shot and killed but Hettinger managed to escape. Hettinger later testified that Powell initially shot Campbell, but that because he was fleeing, he couldn't tell which man, Powell or Smith, had fired four bullets into the chest of the fallen policeman.

Smith drove off in Powell's car, leaving his cohort behind. Law officers caught each man shortly thereafter. Smith and Powell stood trial together and were sentenced to death, but the defendants ended up being retried separately after certain laws changed in the mid-1960s.

I was asked to escort Smith into the courtroom one morning. As I walked him down the hall, he made a comment to me regarding what Hettinger had testified on the witness stand the day before.

"The lying sonofabitch," Smith had said, and went on to correct a sequence of events. What Smith told me was obscure, but seemed to implicate him in Powell's murder. After Smith was seated in the courtroom, I called the prosecutor over and disclosed Smith's statement. It had been given to me voluntarily, and therefore, I believed, was not protected by the Miranda Rights, which require that a suspect in custody be given a warning informing him he has the right to remain silent instead of making potentially incriminating statements to officers of the law.

The prosecutor decided to call me as a witness, and he approached the bench with his request. The judge called a recess to question me in camera, meaning in private. The courtroom was cleared so the jury wouldn't be influenced. The judge had me sworn in and I sat in the witness box. I gave my testimony about what Smith had told me. The prosecutor and defense attorney argued over the admissibility of this information. The judge ended up ruling that the information was too prejudicial. I guessed that he worried about a violation of the Miranda Rights, which the U.S. Supreme Court had mandated three years earlier.

I was hard-pressed to accept the judge's decision in that context, because

Smith had spoken to me of his own volition, and with no prompting from me. Yet I understood that the judge might have been acting pragmatically, foreseeing that admitting the statement could have opened the door to yet another appeal by Smith's lawyer.

In the end, Jimmy Lee Smith remained in prison.

My work in the courts also confirmed to me that criminal law was much more interesting to me than civil law, even if more money was to be made in a career in the civil arena.

My summer as a bailiff also helped me focus my career goals a bit more sharply. I knew that the big bucks in criminal law were earned on the defense side. I hadn't any idea yet what area of the law I'd practice in, or even if I'd practice law at all, but there was one thing I did know: I would never be a criminal-defense lawyer. It didn't fit my personality to argue on behalf of a client whom I suspected had committed a crime, and try to win the case by any legal maneuver possible. Were I to forge a career in criminal law, it would definitely be on the prosecution side.

My second and third years of law school were a bit easier than my first had been. I had spent the summer between my second and third year also as a deputy sheriff but in Las Vegas. My study habits were also well honed by now. But even in my third year, I was unsure what area of the law to pursue after I'd graduated and passed the bar.

My two summers working in the courts had kindled my interest in criminal law. But some of my best grades had been earned in classes on trusts and wills. Meanwhile, my father, who came from a blue-collar background and was friends with high-ranking union officials, talked to me about specializing in labor law. I just didn't know in which direction I'd ultimately head.

Maybe I would be putting my eventual law degree to work outside the law anyway, perhaps in the business world. Las Vegas was a go-to place for entrepreneurs. My dad didn't want me directly involved with gaming, but I saw there were vast fortunes to be made.

Perhaps I'd join a company that would strike it rich with the next big resort. A voice inside me said it didn't require rocket science.

I graduated from Loyola Law School in 1971 and turned my attention to studying for the bar exam in Nevada. I returned to my parents' home in Las Vegas to cram hard, which paid off when I passed the bar. Not long afterward, I was given a new job: as a deputy DA. At the start, newbies in the office were sent to justice court daily to represent the DA's office at arraignments and preliminary hearings of the cases that, if continued, would end up in district court. These cases included felonies ranging up to first-degree murder. We also prosecuted lower-court matters—misdemeanors such as petty theft and disorderly conduct—and eventually would work our way up into handling trials in district court. All this meant on-the-job training. We new hires each had a senior deputy DA to help us along, but after a few days we were expected to solo.

Each day we were handed a stack of dockets involving serious crimes. We had to prepare for preliminary hearings on these cases, arguing that there was probable cause to try a defendant for an alleged crime. Because the court calendars were clogged, the judges often pressured us county prosecutors to work out sensible plea agreements on cases with lesser crimes. Each of us junior attorneys in the criminal division averaged a half-dozen cases a day.

It was a daunting experience at the start. Law school trains you to think in a certain way and research in a certain way. But it doesn't train you specifically how to present a battery, burglary, robbery, or murder case. And all these ended up on our plates my first year in the DA's office. From day one, the work was very time-consuming. It consisted of studying cases, preparing arguments, and arranging witnesses. It required a disciplined lifestyle. I was taking home big files every night to prepare for the following day's cases. But I appreciated that the DA's office was the perfect place to develop prosecutorial skills and accumulate experience in a hurry.

One day I was stunned to see a high school classmate in jail garb awaiting arraignment with others who had been arrested. His name was John Hicks. His father had been an owner of the Thunderbird Hotel, which stood next to the Riviera. My mind drifted back to the many times my father had said to me "don't be going into the hotels like John Hicks and stay away from him." I looked to see the charge. It was murder. The case revolved around Hicks and a friend of his named Murphy banging on the door late at night of a man named Myers who supposedly owed Hicks loan-shark money. As they busted in, Myers shot and killed Murphy. Hicks was charged under a felony murder law, which provided that if someone is killed during the commission of a felony—even though unintended—it constituted murder. Hicks was ultimately set free since the court ruled the felony murder rule did not apply if the co-perpetrator was the victim. But his lifestyle caught up with him in 1973 at age twenty-eight when he was shot in the back of the head while exiting his apartment. The crime went unsolved but it was suspected that the fact that Hicks had an affair with Geri Rosenthal—the wife of reputed mobster Lefty Rosenthal—(portrayed by Sharon Stone in the movie *Casino*) may have been the reason he was killed.

In the end, the intensive workload and accumulation of experience as a deputy DA benefited my career. As I honed my skills in the courts, we took on increasing prosecutorial responsibilities. One of the hot-shot defense lawyers I often faced in court was Oscar Goodman, a man in his early thirties who'd been the chief deputy public defender in Clark County before going into private practice and gaining renown as a tough, shrewd defense attorney. As his reputation grew, in fact, Goodman ended up representing Meyer Lansky, Lefty Rosenthal, and Anthony "Tony the Ant" Spilotro in their cases in federal court. In fact, in the movie *Casino*, Goodman would play himself representing Spilotro, who was played by Joe Pesci.

Goodman, who would later become arguably the most popular mayor in Las Vegas history, was as media savvy as they come, and was very colorful even back when we faced him as a defense attorney representing lesser-known clients. Goodman excelled at raising objections and motions in court. He had an aura of confidence, even arrogance. He also had the reputation for being extremely thorough in his research. That was a credit to his secret weapon: a lawyer in his firm named Annette Quintana, whose mind was brilliant for writing motions and papers. Quintana was an invaluable asset for Goodman behind the scenes.

Her legal brilliance, coupled with his public persona, created a powerful combination. It also didn't hurt his career that he had the intestinal fortitude (if that's what it was) to represent clients whom a lawyer such as myself would be hard-pressed to stomach. I was glad to be on the prosecution side. But I had to prepare extra hard to try cases against Goodman.

12

A Klutz Woos a Blond Beauty

Unlike my father, I did not spot my perfect mate dancing on a stage. There were, of course, dancers performing in the major Las Vegas showrooms but their work hours and mine did not coincide. I did meet and date one briefly (after all, I did live in Las Vegas) but it was impossible to coordinate schedules.

Las Vegas in the early '70s had grown but there were no nightclubs that are so common in hotels now. Most dancing occurred in cowboy bars and I wasn't a great fit there, either, and after-work social gathering holes didn't exist. So meeting women was a challenge. My friend Jeff Silver's sister was a schoolteacher and set him up on a blind date. Jeff asked his date if she had a friend who might like to meet me. She gave me the phone number of Sandy Searles, a teacher of the deaf. In seeing her I was as stunned by her beauty as I was impressed by her intellect. That first date didn't go so well. She confessed later that she didn't like me very much at first. She did decide to give me a second chance and I pursued her with vigor, knowing I would be a fool to not give this my all. We dated a few months (she says fortunately for me between basketball seasons since I was playing constantly). It was, however, during softball season and on the way to a game when she said she loved me. I wasn't going to let her give that a second thought so I asked if she loved me enough to marry me and I got a yes. Hopeless romantic, I obviously am not. But able to recognize the opportunity of a lifetime and act upon it: that I could do.

Like me, Sandy had grown up in Southern Nevada—for her, North Las Vegas was home. Her father was the chief engineer at the Sahara Hotel, so we had some common experiences. Her uncle owned the local dairy, so she had summer jobs handing out ice cream samples. She had been a competitive swimmer in her preteen years and was very social by nature.

We went to tell our parents. My father had met her and I know liked her but of course he was the stoic Ross Miller. I told him I was so excited that I hit four home runs that night. With a blank stare he said, "I hope something better comes out of this marriage than four home runs." It would: three incredible children and five grandchildren to dote on so far. My father did not get to live long enough to meet his grandchildren and my mother died four years later. But I had found a partner who worked tirelessly to support my elections, who has always been there to offer advice and whose passion for public education is unequaled. I highly recommend blind dates, although I would recommend putting some forethought into an actual proposal.

13

Bob Miller's Political Career Begins

In addition to my personal life, 1973 marked a new turn in my professional life as well. Ralph Lamb was as transitional a figure in Las Vegas history as Ross Miller or Jay Sarno. He is the character played by Dennis Quaid in the fall 2012 CBS-TV series called *Vegas*. Lamb was the kind of guy who once dragged a mobster named Johnny Roselli across a table by his tie, took him to jail, and then sent him packing—probably by sundown, like an Old West gunslinger. Lamb once arrested a bunch of troublemaking Hells Angels, loaded their bikes on a truck, drove the bikes to the California border, then after arresting all the bikers he shaved their long hair and saw to it that they, too, got out of town. Lamb was a cowboy overseeing what was still a cow town—part Clint Eastwood and part Rod Steiger.

And in early 1973, Ralph Lamb offered me the job of being the attorney for the sheriff's department. Lamb liked me well enough. He'd known my family for years and had watched me grow up, because he was friends with my dad. As I've said, the sheriff appreciated that the Riviera gave him no cause for concern about unsavory characters or Black Book inductees skulking around the premises. Ross Miller and his colleagues were straight shooters, in Ralph's book. What's more, Ralph was only too happy to help me get my footing on a law-enforcement path, because he saw that my dad was trying to set me on a stable career course.

I was intrigued by Lamb's offer, but I didn't want to leave the DA's office. So I asked my boss, District Attorney Roy Woofter, if I could do each job half time. He agreed, and so did Lamb. So I divided my work hours between the two departments. My office was next to Ralph's, and it was interesting for me to work closely with him.

Several months after I started, the Nevada Legislature combined the Las Vegas Police Department and the Clark County Sheriff's Department, creating the Las Vegas Metropolitan Police Department. However, since Lamb was so well regarded, the elected sheriff was designated to head the LVMPD (the former chief of police became the undersheriff).

I found my work in Metro interesting: I was researching the nuances of search-and-seizure and other laws governing police conduct, and getting the word out via internal bulletins and staff briefings. Meanwhile, in the DA's office, I was assigned to perform all the misdemeanor screenings, deciding from police complaints sent to our office which criminal cases should be prosecuted in our overcrowded courts. It really boiled down to whether, based on evidence, our attorneys could prove a case in court.

I also had a trial load, and occasionally prosecuted cases in district court. After more than two years in the DA's office, I was developing as a trial attorney. However, I spent a good portion of my time in the courts of Justices of the Peace, where most criminal cases were sent to first. The JPs were elected and until then also performed marriages, which was quite lucrative but delayed the criminal courts. Additionally, they were not required to be lawyers. Later both of these permissions were removed in Las Vegas Justice Courts. In 1973, Las Vegas was still a small town, despite the places beginning to dot the Strip to the south and the amount of money coming in.

Worst of all, I noticed some of the JPs had amazingly cavalier approaches from the bench. One stuck out and reinforced what a small town I was still living in, despite a population now above 300,000.

I caught wind that one JP had adopted a habit of turning to the courtroom spectators and asking them to vote on the guilt or innocence of defendants. Since the spectators mostly were defendants awaiting their hearings, and their lawyers, the voice vote would always be "innocent." Apparently, this had been going on for a short period of time.

One day I walked over to this JP's courtroom as a spectator and stood to one side. As usual, the room was full of criminal defendants, their attorneys, and bail bondsmen. Sure enough, the JP was playing to his audience. He would read a summary of a case, then announce that so-and-so (the defendant's name) "is charged with disorderly conduct. What do you think? Guilty or not guilty?"

The response: a loud chorus of "Not guilty!"

It was a carnival atmosphere.

I realized the judge was trying to be funny. It was true that the offenses with which the defendants were charged probably didn't have a lot of merit. In those days, Vegas police regularly arrested people on the Strip or downtown who looked unsavory, and charged them with disorderly conduct or loitering, more or less to clear them off the street. I knew most of these charges were destined for dismissal. But the judge's cavalier attitude made a mockery of the system.

When he asked for a vote on the next case, I yelled, "Guilty!" It was a lone dissenting vote, but my message got through to him loud and clear.

The judge knew that I worked for Metro and the DA. I wasn't about to run and tattle to the newspapers about his little game. I was just making a point about the need for decorum in a court of law. The point was taken. He never called for a vote from the gallery again.

In 1974, a justice of the peace in Las Vegas Township retired before his elected term was up. The Clark County commissioners were to appoint a replacement. I decided this was my chance to bring a fresh mind-set to the bench.

By the time I applied, a prominent attorney, Mahlon Brown III, whose father was a ranking state senator, already had asked several of the commissioners for the job and gotten their commitments. I was candidly told as much by one of the commissioners, Tom Wiesner. Wiesner said he was sorry I hadn't asked him earlier, but he'd given his word. He told me I'd be a strong candidate if another opening arose. I always appreciated Tom's straightforward approach and we remained friends for many years until his passing. It is noteworthy that during many of my election years, Tom was the Republican National Committeeman for Nevada but because he placed friendship above partisan politics he remained neutral in all my elections.

As it turned out, state lawmakers, realizing there was a shortage of justices to handle Clark County's clogged court calendars, authorized two new JP positions for Las Vegas Township during the 1975 Legislature. One post would be temporarily filled by appointment that year, with the job beginning July 1, then be up for election in 1976. The other would be filled in the following election.

I applied for and received the temporary appointment by the Clark County commissioners. I would be running to retain this post the following year. My father was excited that his son was possibly going to be a judge. But, unfortunately, he would never get to see me on the bench.

Ross Miller, as tough a man as I ever knew, had developed esophageal cancer. Surgery in November didn't remove all of the cancerous tissue—the disease was too far advanced—but he resolved to continue living a normal life. In February 1975, he played in the Bob Hope Desert Classic, as he had each of the previous fifteen years. In the next several months he spent most of his time in Palm Springs. His demeanor and actions left the impression, at least to me, that he would win this fight as he had so many others. We did talk more often and he was more and more treating me as an adult and less as a project. I was busy at work in Las Vegas so face-to-face time was still limited. By May he was bed-bound at Sunrise Hospital in Las Vegas. I spent every day for weeks watching him weaken. We would talk occasionally about the prospects of my receiving the judicial appointment. That seemed to bring him some pleasure amid his pain. Often I would wait in the hallway, not knowing what to do or to say. I recall the

NBA playoffs were on TV and would watch for a while but not with my customary interest. Although I did not have as much interaction with my father as I would have liked to have had during his lifetime, he was at the center of my life. I was always trying to find ways to make him proud of me. Now at age thirty I would not know his reaction except from the experiences I had learned up until then. One thing I did know is that he wanted a very different life for me and I was beginning on that journey with only his memory to guide me.

His condition steadily declined. Toward the end, he called me in. We each had tears in our eyes. "I want you to know that I love you and I always have," he said. It was the first time I'd ever heard him utter those words.

The following day, he passed away.

It would only become clear to me later how much Ross Miller has shaped me, even though we had very few in-depth conversations. But he had been a role model for me—his determination, his integrity, and his intensity. Not only would he be a presence in my life through what he instilled in me, his career and his associations with men in organized crime and on the fringes of the mob would have an impact on my political career for decades to come. Ross Miller's shadow would always be with me, but I would spend some of my career trying to step outside the shadow cast by some of his more unsavory associates. It would not take long for my father's apparition to be conjured.

14

From the Bench to DA, and Ross Miller's Ghost Appears for the First Time

My job as a JP paid $30,000 a year. Unlike my predecessor, I couldn't augment my income by marrying couples in court. State lawmakers had done away with that privilege in Clark County, knowing it was abused and created a backlog of cases. I realized that my court reporter was earning approximately three times my salary. But that didn't concern me. I was eager to tackle my new duties. And that included establishing order in the court.

I determined from the start to maintain a formal atmosphere in the courtroom. Meting out justice was a serious responsibility, and demanded professionalism by all the officers of the court, including the defense lawyers, some of whom took punctuality and decorum less seriously.

Having come from the DA's office, I sympathized with crime victims and respected witnesses who came forward. By this time I'd reviewed thousands of cases of criminal activity: batteries and assaults, thefts and worse. There were a lot of people committing crimes out there, and a lot of people being hurt. Every case that wound up in my court for arraignments or preliminary hearings, even the most minor offenses, deserved to be handled with dignity. I would not be lighthearted on the bench like some of the JPs I'd appeared before. Nor would I countenance a lackadaisical approach from the attorneys.

A fair number of attorneys had the habit of showing up late to justice court, or missing scheduled hearings entirely. They'd gotten used to the laxity permitted by other JPs. I recognized why these JPs had fallen into the behavior of cutting lots of slack to the defense lawyers. It was easier to get along with them that way. Day in and day out, justice court was full of defendants and their attorneys. It was more comfortable to establish an air of congeniality than to remain impartial and aloof, or to be perceived as adversarial.

But I reminded myself that my job wasn't to please the defendants and their lawyers, but to serve the citizens who weren't in the courtroom: the victims, the witnesses, and the peace officers also involved in the case. I represented the general public, not the accused. When I donned my black judicial robe and took my place on the bench, I needed to remain dispassionate. So each day I mentally extricated myself from the mood in the courtroom that was weighted toward the defendants. I knew I had to be vigilant to avoid falling into the psychological trap that had ensnared other JPs.

My youthful appearance didn't help me in my quest to establish decorum. At age thirty, I was young compared to the other JPs, and some veteran defense lawyers assumed I would honor the informality in justice court to which they'd become accustomed. But they were in for a surprise. To their dismay, I took the court calendar seriously. If they showed up late, they were admonished. This soon made me very unpopular with a few of them. I think Ross Miller would have been proud.

My first of what would become (even though I had no clue at the time) many political campaigns came in 1976. I enlisted the help of Sig Rogich, a budding advertising/political operative who had started R&R Advertising in the early 1970s. Rogich would later become an adviser to both Presidents Bush and Reagan and work in Bush 41's White House. But back then, he handled candidates of both parties, we had known each other since high school, and he knew I was a novice who needed help. Rogich would fill that role, assisting me with the basics such as campaign logos. He initially provided me with a tri-colored bumper sticker with MI in red,

LL in yellow, and ER in green. I told him great, a perfect fit for the son of the former owner of the Circus Circus. Staring at me incredulously he said, "You are supposed to choose one color, dummy." But it was up to me how I would be listed on the ballot and in the campaign literature. I'd always been known as Bob Miller, and it suited me, but I was a judge and believed that "Robert Miller" sounded more judicial, so that's the name I used when I filed with the county clerk to run for office.

About an hour before the close of filing for candidates, the clerk called me and said, "Well, we have some confusion because we have two Robert Millers running for the justice of the peace."

I scurried back over to the registrar's office. There I learned that another Robert Miller had decided to file toward the end of the very last day of filing, my first of many "Welcome to politics, young man" moments.

I hastily revised my submission to say I was running as Bob Miller. At least that fell in line with an enduring feature of Nevada politics, which is that it is very personal, and candidates are advised not to come across as stuffy. Campaigning as "Bob" would be fine, except that I already had campaign ads on billboards and signs all over town, seeking votes for Robert Miller.

Necessity is the mother of invention. My campaign staff and I had bumper stickers printed that merely said, "Bob." We slapped them on our signs at an angle to attract attention to the name change. I was grateful to have such devoted helpers. And if there was one campaign volunteer I had to admire more than anyone, it was my wife. Sandy not only toted our young son, Ross—named for my father—around town, delivering signs to the people who'd agreed to have them in their yards, but she was the one who went to a T-shirt shop and used a hot-iron press to affix my face onto 2,000 shirts under the lettering, BOB MILLER FOR JUSTICE OF THE PEACE.

The coincidence of two Robert Millers filing for the same office perturbed me, so I did a little informal investigating. I called each of the several Robert Millers listed in the local phonebook and found that not one, but possibly two, of the other candidates for JP had separately called these Robert Millers.

It was obvious to me what had happened. One of these namesakes had agreed to run for the office. And surprise, surprise: He'd never run for office before. This particular Robert Miller happened to be a baggage clerk at McCarran International Airport.

Some of my supporters who were veterans of election campaigns told me I'd been victimized by a very old ploy. We decided to spin it to our favor.

My campaign staff tipped off the media about the name confusion and reporters went to interview the baggage clerk. The reporters learned he had suddenly gone on vacation, I assume with some newfound cash in his pocket. The reporters interviewed people who worked at the airport with Robert Miller, and these coworkers expressed astonishment that he had any aspiration to run for any office. They said he had never mentioned that interest to any of them.

Through the news stories, the public became aware of the situation. At campaign events, people would ask me, "Now are you the good Bob Miller or the bad Bob Miller?"

I'd laugh and say, "Well, I'm the incumbent. You'll have to decide the other part."

Ultimately, the same-name maneuver backfired for my opponents. In a field of fifteen candidates, I captured the most votes in both the primary and general elections.

My first run for public office ended up teaching me indelible truths about political campaigning in America, truths that I'd encounter again and again in subsequent campaigns. One truth was how creative opponents can be in trying to sabotage your run. Another was how the media can be of help under certain circumstances by reporting on negative campaigning, scandals, or unusual developments. Often, however, journalists will just stick to the general facts, reporting responses or accusations from one camp or the other, without saying which side is telling the truth. The public, therefore, gets an unbiased but frequently superficial presentation of the news. So the burden of trying to convince voters of the actual facts falls upon the candidates.

I counted myself fortunate, though, that after my campaign staff alerted local media about two Robert Millers on the JP ballot, journalists seized on the oddity. Their news reports did prove helpful to my campaign by pointing out which Miller was which. In fact, no doubt despite my consternation, it was likely that the media were most instrumental in my election success.

The success tasted sweet not only to me, but to my mother. She knew how proud my dad would be also and told me so. Her face beamed with pride. My accomplishment, as modest as it was, was beyond what she, as a member of a working-class immigrant family, could have imagined. She took great joy in being able to say, "My son is a judge."

This accomplishment was different from financial success. My father, through his indefatigable work ethic at the Riviera, and his side investments, had become a millionaire by his later years. But a judgeship spoke to being a vital part of society, to respectability and dignity. Unlike a casino executive of my father's era, no one would look funny at you when you said you were a judge.

I realized that my career path would be far less lucrative than my father's. Yet, mine probably was the path he would have pursued had he been given the opportunities.

Serving on the bench allowed me to join the Nevada Judges Association, which introduced me to lower-court judges from communities throughout the state. I didn't give it much thought then, but the close connections I made in the NJA would prove fortuitous to me in later years, when I ran for statewide office.

One of the municipal-court judges I got to know at NJA gatherings was a former policeman named Seymore Brown. He'd served on the bench for many years in Las Vegas, in this era before judges were required to have law degrees and pass the state bar exam. Seymore was colorful. When we went into bars, he'd order his favorite drink: "W and W." That stood for "wodka and water."

One time, the judges association met in Winnemucca, in north-central Nevada. After the day's events, a group of us, including Seymore, decided we'd check out the brothels that were tucked away on Baud Street. We were just going to have a drink at a bar in one of these bordellos that were legal in zones in rural counties by voter approval. I'd never seen the inside of a cathouse before. My colleagues made the same claim for themselves.

We were admitted through the gate of one and walked in the door. A working girl in scanty attire was sitting at the bar. She looked up and exclaimed, "Seymore, how are you!"

The rest of us were stunned. She chatted amiably with him.

"Well, she'd been in my courtroom," he later explained. "She's been where I work; I haven't been where she works."

In 1978, after three years as a justice of the peace, my appetite was whetted to run for a higher office. I was now thirty-three. Sandy and I had two young children. Our son, Ross, had been born in 1976, four days short of my thirty-first birthday, and our daughter Corrine had come along eighteen months later. We needed more room, and bought a new house near Tropicana Avenue. It was our first freestanding house. I wanted to push my career ahead.

The office I set my sights on: Clark County District Attorney. I knew I was qualified. I understood the job inside and out. I'd worked as a deputy DA prosecuting cases, and on the other side of the bench as a justice of the peace hearing cases being prosecuted. But moreover, I felt a strong sense of mission. Frankly, I didn't like how the DA's office was being run. I saw far too many cases being plea-bargained in the interest of expedience. I saw that a great many Las Vegans held the DA's office in low regard, perceiving it as being soft on crime. I knew without a doubt I could do better were I in charge. Sandy fully backed my decision to run.

The bigger question was whether I had much of a chance to win.

I anticipated running against the incumbent, George Holt. But to my surprise, Holt passed on seeking a second term in favor of running against his adversary, Ralph Lamb, who was seeking reelection to an unprecedented fifth term as Clark County sheriff. After I filed, I found myself in a field of four candidates in the democratic primary: two former DAs, George Franklin and Roy Woofter; myself; and Bucky Buchanan, a barrister who had flouted my authority as a JP by repeatedly missing scheduled court appearances.

Franklin and Woofter had to be considered the favorites, given their experience. Buchanan, on paper, seemed to be the weakest. But I felt a twinge of foreboding seeing his name in the race.

Buchanan already had waded into Nevada politics, serving on the board of regents of the state's higher-education system. Regent posts were paid very little but often served as a springboard to bigger offices. I wondered, though, why Bucky, a successful defense lawyer, was seeking the Clark County DA's position, the chief prosecutor's office. I entertained the thought that he was doing so out of spite, because he disliked me.

My suspicion soon took on more weight because of a pair of strange developments.

As the date of the primary vote approached, Buchanan suddenly acquired a large sum in campaign donations. It was illogical that he could have raised that kind of money from the usual sources seeking to back a strong candidate, since Buchanan was a heavy underdog, and polls showed him trailing in fourth place. Former DA Roy Woofter was showing strong in the polls and, to me, was the man to beat. Roy had been DA before George Holt, and Roy's name was freshest in the public's mind. In fact it was Roy who had given me my first job after law school.

Then, what raised my concern even more about Buchanan's intentions was that he didn't use his newly flush campaign chest to go after Roy Woofter. Instead, in a nasty twist, Buchanan's people began running political advertisements attacking not only me, but also my mother and my late father.

My mother had inherited Dad's interest in the tiny Slots-A-Fun casino in front of Circus Circus. She had a Nevada gaming license. Buchanan's campaign ads criticized her and, in turn, me, suggesting that I couldn't possibly be an impartial county prosecutor if I was the son of someone in the gaming business. The ad also characterized my mother derogatorily as a "gambler," made light of my father's early gaming connections, and mischaracterized a case I'd heard as JP, suggesting I'd allowed murderers to walk free.

It was, in short, a vicious smear campaign.

Rumors swirled that Buchanan's ads were being financed by another candidate. That would explain both Buchanan's campaign largesse and his targeting me instead of the other candidates. And in this line of reasoning, it was obvious that the source of Bucky's money and mean-spirited ads was none other than the frontrunner himself: Roy Woofter.

As my campaign staff and I puzzled over this development, we came up with a plausible theory:

Roy Woofer was a good friend of Joe Conforte, the owner of the Mustang Ranch, a brothel in northern Nevada, who had been the prime mover in getting brothels legally allowable in rural counties that wanted them. It was suggested that Conforte might have funneled the attack money to Bucky. Conforte's apparent motive was to help a man whom he hoped would win a powerful position in law enforcement in the state's largest county. That political favor could be valuable to Conforte in case he wanted to legitimize his trade in Las Vegas, a potential gold mine.

The funding of a weak candidate by one contender to attack a rival is a common ploy in politics; the thinking goes that the voters don't like the politician who takes a cheap shot at an opponent. So the top contender often helps one of the lesser candidates go on the offense. Bucky might have bought into this strategy because he was low in the polls and knew he couldn't win. But another likely factor influencing him was that he bore a grudge against me, given our clashes when I was JP. Again, the reason he was running at all could have been to hurt my candidacy. He may have seen the nasty campaign ads as his opportunity for some retribution.

I never did determine conclusively who supplied Bucky with the funds to launch the advertising assaults. But the experience was a big wake-up call to me. I realized with dismay that Bucky's ads would not be the last of their ilk were I to continue running for office. My baptism as a political candidate was a bath of ice water. In my earlier run for JP, I'd had to cope with a second Robert Miller on the ballot. Now, in the DA's race, I was coping with sleazy attacks on my family. It was personal, and I was sickened and infuriated. But I also knew I needed to maintain my composure and resist urges to punch the SOB attacking my mother.

Mom, naturally, was furious. She was a sweet, simple lady, a woman who attended Mass every day at the Guardian Angels Shrine on the Strip. She was incensed at being targeted in such a wanton and cruel way. But she knew as well as I that the only sound course was to respond to the ads publicly in the context of the campaign. My camp took the stance that we were outraged that an opponent would attack my mother and my deceased father.

As it turned out, a lot of voters agreed.

I won the primary with 42 percent of the vote. George Franklin ended up with 31 percent and Roy Woofter finished third with 19 percent. Bucky Buchanan* received less than 8 percent. The general election against Republican Alan Bray, a former FBI agent, was not as difficult or controversial, and I won by a 2-to-1 margin.

I walked away from the entire experience hurt but wiser, and emotionally prepared for future attacks along the same lines as Bucky's. I digested the bitter truth that for me, a person who'd grown up in a Las Vegas casino family in the 1950s and '60s, character assassinations founded on innuendo about my parents just came with the territory in running for public office.

Competitors and critics were going to look back at the old Las Vegas, whose casinos were operated by those who'd learned the trade in illegal gambling outside the state, and suggest that even though we were now

---

* In 2006, Bucky got to star in a reality show on the Court TV cable network. It was called *Las Vegas Law* and featured the now-bald jewelry-draped legal eagle in custom suits and $5,000 alligator shoes, driving a Bentley and representing drug dealers, prostitutes, and others agreeable to his cash-only billing system. He died in a single car crash in November 2009.

living in a new Las Vegas, Bob Miller's family's interest in casinos and his father, Ross Miller's, history and early connections should be a reason to disqualify me from serving the public in an elected office. I simply refused to believe that voters would buy into this line of thinking. I would absolutely not accept that I was unfit to be DA, or any other public position I might seek. I was not my father. I did not have his background or associations. He was a part of the early founding era of Las Vegas; I was a part of the transition to the modern metropolis. And what was more, I resented third parties trying to slant and disparage the man he had become in his years in Las Vegas.

It would turn out that throughout my political life, my adversaries would take every opportunity to use my father's career in gaming and his business associations against me. To this day I feel these were cheap shots, especially given the fact that my father had already passed away by the time these accusations were made. I never shied away from my father or who he was—and I never will.

Unlike my father, my mother had actually witnessed and even been attacked personally during her lifetime. For those who knew my mother it would seem reprehensible. She was quiet and spent all of her time doting on her family. Although I would never hear "the Irish Songbird" sing on many occasions, I saw her brighten a room with her contagious laugh. Unlike my father's stoic exterior she would always be smiling. Sadly, she died of leukemia at the age of fifty-seven in 1979, a mere four years after my father. As I had with Dad, I spent countless days at Sunrise Hospital waiting, hoping, and watching for a recovery that never happened.

From right: Eugene Miller, center: Ross Miller, on his left (white shirt) Herschel
Miller. Circa late 1930s or early 1940s. *(Courtesy of Bob Miller)*

Bob Miller in Chicago, age 7
or 8. *(Courtesy of Bob Miller)*

Ross and Coletta Miller
with Governor Grant and
Bette Sawyer, 1963. *(Courtesy
of Las Vegas News Bureau)*

Ross Miller in front of Riviera hotel, 1964.
(Courtesy of Las Vegas News Bureau)

Bob Miller (holding son,
Ross Miller) and Bob
Hope at the 3rd annual
Ross Miller Memorial
Golf Classic, 1978.
*(Courtesy of Dee Ennis—
DeePics Photography)*

To Bob Miller—
With appreciation and best wishes,

Bob Miller with President George H. W. Bush and Barbara Bush at National Governors Association meeting, 1989. *(Courtesy of The White House)*

From right: Governor Bob Miller and Arnold Palmer, 1990. *(Courtesy of Joann Dost)*

Justice of the Peace Bob Miller, 1975. *(Courtesy of Dee Ennis—DeePics Photography)*

District Attorney Bob Miller at White House, presenting victims of Crime Task Force Report to President Reagan, 1982. *(Courtesy of The White House)*

To Robert Miller
With best wishes,

Ronald Reagan

On the campaign trail: Governor Bob Miller, serving as pillow for Ross and Corrine Miller. *(Courtesy of Sandy Miller)*

Governor Miller and family at Governor's Office: Ross and Corrine standing, Sandy (seated) holding Megan, 1994. *(Courtesy of Nevada Department of Transportation)*

Forty-seven-year-old Governor Miller voted MVP in charity game, versus members of then L.A. Raiders football team, 1992. *(Courtesy of Nevada Department of Transportation)*

Governor Bob Miller and John Walsh on the set of "America's Most Wanted," 1992. *(Courtesy of Walsh Productions, LLC)*

In the White House, from left: Arkansas Governor Bill Clinton, Hawaii Governor John Waihee, Nevada Governor Bob Miller, and President George H. W. Bush. *(Courtesy of The White House)*

National Governors Meeting in Las Vegas, 1998. *(Courtesy of Corrine Miller-Liebe)*

President Bill Clinton attending National Governors Meeting in Las Vegas (Corrine Miller-Liebe with camera in back). *(Courtesy of National Governors Association)*

Governor Miller talking to Michael Jordan at Governors Conference, 1998 (President Clinton was frequent attendee, so buzz that day was Jordan's appearance). *(Courtesy of National Governors Association)*

Miller family holiday card (1998) from left: Corrine, Bob, Sandy, and Ross, Megan on top of suitcase. *(Courtesy of Larry Hanna Photography)*

Governor Miller with Russian Heritage Highway Co-Chair Mikhail Gorbachev, 2004. *(Courtesy of Cashman Photo Enterprises)*

Editorial cartoon in 1999, when Bob Miller considered running for the U.S. Senate. *(Courtesy of Jim Day, Las Vegas Review Journal)*

15

Being District Attorney— Carl Thomas and Vegas Stereotypes

The past, they say, is never really past. And after I became district attorney, my past—or should I say Ross Miller's past—became the present.

Carl Thomas was one of my father's business partners and a close family friend for many years. He was also, prosecutors would later allege, one of the architects of a massive skimming operation from Las Vegas casinos on behalf of the Chicago syndicate. Thomas and others, including high-ranking members of the mob in the Midwest, would be indicted for skimming more than $2 million from Strip establishments. Some of those involved—Kansas City mobsters Nick Civella and Carl DeLuna—would be represented by Oscar Goodman, the mob's mouthpiece who decades later would be elected to three terms as Las Vegas mayor. For some people, the past stays the past.

I wasn't so lucky. I was at a national District Attorneys Association meeting in Hilton Head, South Carolina, in 1979, when I received a call from one of my staff that the media were trying to reach me. It seemed that the indictments were the fruits of surveillance of many of those accused and Carl Thomas was on one of the wiretaps talking about the new district attorney of Las Vegas in November 1978. This was the man who was alleged to be the mob's man in Las Vegas, orchestrating the skim operation, talking about me.

I was stunned, to say the least. Carl Thomas was the last casino executive I would have guessed to be implicated in a skimming scheme. In fact, he was the only one of the defendants who had been licensed by Nevada gaming regulators. My bigger concern was what any of this had to do with me.

It turned out that the basis for Thomas's indictment was an FBI wiretap tape of Thomas in conversation with Nick and Carl Civella. These wise guys were among the targets of the FBI's extensive five-year surveillance investigation of reputed crime figures suspected of involvement with the Stardust and Fremont, Tropicana, and other Las Vegas casinos. On one tape, Thomas's voice can be heard saying, "I just had breakfast with the new district attorney, and he's a real stand-up kid."

If this were all that was said, I would have faced some serious insinuations, fortunately during the follow-up conversation Thomas was asked by the others if they had supported me and he replied definitely not. You did not want him.

Although this was an exoneration of sorts for me, future political opponents would take Thomas's mention of me out of context and use it against me time after time.

Although I'd known Carl and his family for many years, I didn't spend any time with him after this story broke. I'd appreciated that, after my father died, Carl had proved himself a very supportive friend of our family by helping my mother through the tough times, calling her regularly to see how she was doing, seeing if she needed anything as if she were family.

From my perspective, Carl Thomas was a very caring man. His involvement in the skimming scheme came as a shock not only to me but many others in Nevada, as state gaming authorities previously had said he was just the type of individual you would want in the casino business.

Carl Thomas was a local boy made good. He'd been a young card dealer at the Stardust when my father first met him. They were both Shriners, and Carl had helped Ross Miller hone his skills in public speaking, an art with which he'd had little experience. Carl was industrious, bright, and well read. He'd even earned a master's degree from the University of Nevada, Las Vegas in his spare time. My father ended up bringing Carl over to the Riviera to learn casino management.

Thomas's involvement in cheating, linking him with the likes of hardened gangsters such as the Civella brothers from Kansas City, and known mob associates Anthony "Tony the Ant" Spilotro, Frank "Lefty" Rosenthal, and others who'd been rumored to have their fingers illegally in some casinos, was an inexplicable dichotomy and I found it very sad. Thomas had seemed to us Las Vegans as an exception to so many casino operators of that era. To us, he was a hometown guy who'd bootstrapped his way up the ranks and was educated, polished, and unblemished by shady dealings with out-of-town interests.

Former Nevada Governor Bob List, among many other prominent officials including member of the gaming control board, professed shock at the news about Carl Thomas.

Thomas eventually plea-bargained, testified against those he had met in organized-crime circles, lost his gaming licenses, and was sentenced to fifteen years (later reduced to two because of his cooperation) for conspiring to skim $280,000 from the Tropicana.* I expected that his conviction was going to give ammunition to my political opponents in my next runs for public office, simply due to my parents' previous business partnership with him and his allusion to me in the FBI wiretapped conversation. Of course, my expectation would be met.

The Carl Thomas indictment was one of two controversies during my tenure as district attorney that would have staying power. The other involved a legendary Vegas figure, Benny Binion, who ran the Horseshoe Casino in Glitter Gulch.

Binion was a colorful gambler who'd come from Texas in 1946 with a

---

* A few years later, out of prison, Carl Thomas died in a tragic one-car accident in Oregon. Some people speculated that foul play was involved. I frankly doubt it. The kind of culprits who kill someone to make a statement that the death was retribution for the victim's actions generally like to make the killing obvious, such as by using a car bomb. Besides, those who knew Carl know he tended to drive too fast.

reputation as the kind of man you didn't cross with impunity. He became a legend as a Las Vegas casino pioneer with innovations at his Horseshoe, including carpets (when many casinos had sawdust on the floor), high limits, free drinks for all players, and limo service for preferred patrons. He also founded the World Series of Poker. Benny had lost his Nevada gaming license because of tax-evasion convictions related to his former activities in Texas, but his sons, Jack and Ted, as president and manager, ran the Horseshoe. And they continued their dad's unwritten policy that the club's security staff would forcibly handle any criminal problems, such as pickpockets or slot cheats, right there on the premises, instead of calling the police.

In May 1979, a thirty-eight-year-old player named Rance Blevins evidently grew unruly after losing his money and resisted leaving the Horseshoe after being asked to by security guards. When Blevins finally departed, he reportedly kicked and shattered a plate-glass window. Witnesses told police that a club security guard in uniform and another man in plainclothes chased Blevins. He fell to his knees on the street, and according to the witnesses, the man in plain clothes took the security guard's gun and shot Blevins in the head. They initially identified Ted Binion as the triggerman.

I assigned one of my seasoned deputies, Dan Bowman, to prosecute the murder case. Then the witnesses tossed a curveball, changing their testimony to implicate a Horseshoe pit boss, Walter Rozanski, instead of Ted Binion. Rozanski, represented by Oscar Goodman, pleaded guilty to manslaughter and was sentenced to probation. Years later, Bowman told the *Las Vegas Review-Journal* that police and our staff in the DA's office suspected that Ted Binion was the gunman, but that we couldn't secure a conviction given the witnesses' changed testimony. The bottom line was: We had no proof that Ted Binion* was the gunman.

---

* Ted Binion was killed in September 1998. His death has been a subject of controversy; girlfriend Sandra Murphy and her lover, Rick Tabish, were initially charged and convicted in Binion's death, but were later granted a new trial and acquitted on the murder charges. Binion had buried millions of dollars both near his house and outside of Las Vegas in a sub-desert

Las Vegas was changing as I became district attorney and I wanted to be part of that change. And the progress was not without sad ironies. Ralph Lamb, the cowboy sheriff who ran the town the way an Old West lawman did, would lose the same year I was elected.

He'd come from an era when Clark County was smaller and he knew all the important players, and his rough, old-fashioned notions of law enforcement still seemed to work. In 1978, Ralph's bid for reelection faced real opposition for the first time, from his former vice squad commander, John McCarthy. I believe that deep down Ralph is a shy man who didn't much take to crowds or strangers. For whatever reason, during the campaign he took to spending a lot of his afternoons working at his favorite activity: roping cattle on his ranch. This, of course, cut into his campaigning time. Coupled with this, as I've said earlier, the incumbent DA, George Holt, surprised the political establishment by tossing his hat into the sheriff's race. Holt's stated reason was that he'd had a dream one night instructing him to "rid the valley of Ralph Lamb."

Though Holt lost to McCarthy in the primary, his attacks on Lamb had an impact in weakening Lamb's candidacy. In the general election, McCarthy prevailed in a landslide, ushering in a new era of law enforcement in Las Vegas.

I decided there would be a new way of doing business in the district attorney's office, too. I had been affected by victims' stories on the campaign trail and I wanted to make the office more responsive. I also wanted to make the office more reflective of the community. There were very few women working there when I was elected. But my administration ended up hiring more female deputies than the Clark County DA's office had ever seen.

The problems that frustrated me most were our relationship with victims. The lack of personal contact engendered suspicion and frustration in victims. Many of the local victims-rights' groups were critical of the DA's office. Members of the Rape Crisis Center and of Parents of Murdered

---

vault. Some of it has never been found.

Children had picketed outside the Clark County courthouse. They complained to the media. They wrote letters to the editor of the local newspapers. And I suspect they represented only the tip of the iceberg of public discontent with criminal prosecution in Clark County.

I hit upon a plan: to create a citizens' panel that would give the public a voice within our office to help revise our policies and improve communication with victims. It seemed the most practical, common-sense solution. The director of my victim witness unit, Tom Tait, set upon the task and found that these associations were delighted to have direct input into our policies.

What's more, I decided to require the approval of the crime victim, or barring that, my personal approval, for a plea bargain to be reached. Not surprisingly, this change met with a good deal of resistance from the more seasoned deputy DAs. Their position was that they were the ones trained in the law, not victims, and therefore I was stepping on their toes by requiring them to clear their decisions with victims. What's more, they already felt overburdened by the crush of criminal cases. Now, with the new approval policy, they faced expending more time and energy in persuading victims of the merits of a plea bargain before resolving their cases. Victims, the deputy DAs said, were not only ignorant of the law, but too emotional to make the right decision when presented with the rationale for plea-bargaining.

I didn't buy their arguments. "Yes, victims are more emotional," I said, "but that's because they had a gun held in their face or were raped or someone in their family was killed by a drunk driver or murdered. Still, most of them are reasonable people. And while they don't have a legal education, you do, and you should be able to use your education to convince them this is the right result. And if it's not the right result, then you shouldn't be convincing them. If it is the right result, and you can't convince them, then you can convince me."

These innovations would later lead to my being nominated in 1982, by President Ronald Reagan, to serve on the Presidential Task Force on

Victims of Crime. There were nine members, and I was one of only two Democrats on that task force.

Bob Miller, whose father had associated with men who created victims of crimes, was now a nationally recognized advocate for victims of crime. I think my father would have appreciated the irony.

I also think my father, who along with other residents of his time put up with all sorts of anti–Las Vegas stereotypes, would have appreciated that I was responsible for excising a ridiculous bylaw that prevented the National District Attorneys Association from ever meeting in Nevada. I had no illusions about the origins of my home state, but this seemed a stretch. When I asked board members for an explanation, I was told that when a prior meeting had been held in Nevada, a DA from New York State had double-dipped on his travel expenses. I didn't learn the specifics, but evidently he'd charged the trip to his office's budget and also been reimbursed by a private source back home. After this came to light, the DA was charged and convicted of embezzlement.

The NDAA's board had somehow concluded that the DA in question wouldn't have gone astray if not for the fact that the association's meeting had been held in Nevada. This was the same old prejudice against the Silver State that held Nevada up as a pariah, as an evil realm of sorts, because of its earlier gaming history. In my dad's era, this anti-Nevada attitude would have been taken in stride by most Nevadans. Well, times had changed. The gaming industry had moved on from mobbed up to mainstream. And not only was I offended by this preposterous bylaw, I was unwilling to ignore it. I decided to seek the ultimate redress. I made up my mind that not only would I get this rule removed, I would get an NDAA conference scheduled in Las Vegas.

I eventually got the bylaw changed, with the help of two of my deputies, Ray Jeffers, who knew a lot of people in the organization and explained that he'd lived in Las Vegas most of his life. He said it wasn't the Sin City these fellows imagined it to be, but was a family town that actually had more churches and Boy Scouts per capita than almost anywhere else, and Rex Bell, my assistant, whose parents were the cowboy actor of the same name* and the queen of the silent screen, Clara Bow.

I'm pleased to say that after the anti-Nevada bylaw was removed, both Reno and Las Vegas eventually hosted NDAA conventions. Somewhere, Ross Miller was smiling. His son had helped Vegas go legit.

---

* Rex himself had spent his early childhood on the giant Walking Box Ranch, near Searchlight south of Las Vegas, which his actor parents owned and where they often entertained Hollywood friends such as Clark Gable, Carole Lombard, Norma Shearer, and Errol Flynn. Rex succeeded me as the elected district attorney and was reelected, retiring after eight years.

16

Crushing Tony the Ant

My father's associations would continue to be a political roadblock for me as my career continued its upward trajectory. But so, too, would the remnants of the mob in Las Vegas.

In 1979, a wiretapping operation caught Las Vegas mob enforcer Tony "the Ant" Spilotro talking with Ross Miller's old friend, Allen Dorfman, the head of the Teamsters' Central States Pension Fund, seeking my help as DA in getting Spilotro's name removed from the Black Book—that's the mechanism gaming authorities used to ban people from casinos. Allen Dorfman was a frequent visitor to Las Vegas. He had helped arrange many of the early hotel financings through his connections with the Central States Pension Fund. These hotels included not only the Riviera but Jay Sarno's Caesars Palace and Circus Circus. When I was with my father, I'd seen Dorfman on occasion, but seldom if ever after Ross Miller's death.

Dorfman did, however, phone me up at one point when I was DA and posed a vague question about how state judges were selected to preside over various cases. He asked how the process worked and if it was possible to get a case transferred. I told him the assignment of judges was random and transfers were not possible. That was the substance of our conversation. The subject of Anthony Spilotro never came up, and I thought little more about the call. I later learned that Dorfman's inquiries were related to Spilotro, who had just been charged with a Black Book violation, namely entering a hotel-casino, and had a court date pending.

If Dorfman had, indeed, been trying to feel me out, to see if I could be of assistance to his friend, I would have been among the last people on Earth to go to bat for Tony the Ant. To the contrary, my DA's office was working with the feds to have him and his Hole in the Wall Gang locked up. And that was quite a battle. When it came to Spilotro, we had to go against stiff legal representation in the form of Oscar Goodman. Another challenge for us, of course, was Spilotro's suspected practice of the traditional Mafia tactic of silencing potential witnesses. Some of those were immortalized in the film *Casino* by Joe Pesci, who presented a vivid depiction of the vicious criminal.

I wanted to put Spilotro behind bars and so did the new sheriff, John McCarthy, a former vice squad commander, who fit the mold of the disgruntled employee who'd seized the reins of power and was on a mission to show how things should be done. He surrounded himself with like-minded commanders, zealots who also saw the world in black and white and set about getting the bad guys. Foremost among their targets was Tony "the Ant" Spilotro.

That was certainly admirable, given that Spilotro, a ruthless mob enforcer, was a public menace. There was good intelligence that a Las Vegas Metropolitan policeman, Joe Blasko, was actually a Spilotro associate. He was accused of tipping off the criminals with inside information on upcoming raids. This caused the FBI to cut off the sheriff's office from a lot of information. Blasko years later was found guilty of burglary and racketeering as a member of Spilotro's Hole in the Wall Gang.

While I agreed with McCarthy and his associates about the need to nab Spilotro, I had concerns about their methods for accomplishing the goal. A deep-seated mistrust developed between Metro's top management and the DA's office. They resented that we would not rubber-stamp all their tactics. The strained relationship was graphically illustrated by a wiretapping operation of Frank Bluestein, who was an associate of Anthony Spilotro's, and several others suspected of racketeering and other crimes. Metro authorities applied for the wiretap with an affidavit, and our office staff reviewed the affidavit to ensure the request met statutory requirements. A district court judge authorized the wiretapping, and the affidavit was sealed, unavailable for viewing without the court's approval.

The wiretap operation proved extensive. After it concluded, my chief criminal deputy DA, Don Wadsworth, prepared a notice to go out to each person whose conversations had been intercepted. This was in accordance with the law; each of these people was served by registered mail or in person, informing the person of the court order and that his conversations had been intercepted, and that he had a legal right to listen to those conversations if desired.

Shortly afterward, a story appeared in one of the Las Vegas newspapers reporting on the wiretapping operation. And shortly after that, Don Wadsworth told me that a sergeant he knew in Metro had called a meeting with him. The sergeant and two others from Metro showed up in Don's office, and one of them plopped a tape recorder on the table and began quizzing Don about his alleged contact with the newspaper reporter. Don didn't even know the reporter, much less had spoken with him or passed along news tips.

I was furious. It was obvious that Metro had initiated an investigation of our office, to determine whether we'd leaked privileged information to the press. I called Sheriff McCarthy and explained that the DA's office was beginning our own investigation of Metro's possible leak of information about the wiretapping. Eventually, the state attorney general's office conducted an independent probe and absolved Metro and us. Although it remains unclear where the reporter had obtain the information, it is likely it could have come from any of the individuals who'd been wiretapped, then served with a copy of the court order.

My relationship with McCarthy's office was so tense that there were times he didn't even take my phone calls. Meanwhile, as he crusaded against public enemies and perceived enemies, less glamorous crime was afflicting the city. Left relatively unchecked, prostitutes plied their trade all over the Strip, aggressively soliciting tourists on sidewalks, even stopping cars to offer themselves. The McCarthy administration seemed to think it had bigger fish to fry. I was less concerned about headlines and more concerned about the city's image of countenancing rampant prostitution.

It would take tremendous resources to put Tony the Ant out of business. The effort was considered vital: He, more than anyone, embodied the mob's resilient power in Las Vegas even as its grip was being broken.

Spilotro was the enforcer ensuring that the right people cooperated and the skim went where it was meant. He lived a few miles from our house; one of the few times I laid eyes on him was during my first term as DA, when I'd gone into the Food Factory, a hamburger joint frequented by Vegas locals. I looked over and saw him and some of his associates at another table. I recognized him from photographs. Spilotro was a short, stocky guy with a beaverlike coif of dark-brown hair who didn't look particularly menacing, although his reputation would give anyone chills.*

A small but sturdy man who stood just five-foot-six, Spilotro had first earned underworld notoriety in Chicago in the early 1960s by reputedly squeezing a loan deadbeat's head in a vise until one of the man's eyes popped out. Spilotro furthered his infamy by, as the story went, rubbing out a suspected FBI informant by hanging the man on a meat hook, torturing him, and leaving him there to die slowly over the next few days.

Spilotro had supposedly gotten his nickname after longtime FBI agent William Roemer Jr. referred to the Mafia capo as "that little pissant." The moniker also may have stuck because of Spilotro's short stature. Either way, he was a very lethal species of insect. When Tony the Ant was sent to Vegas in 1971, to oversee the skim, he brought along a crew of Chicago underlings who were scary in their own right, yet terrified of their chief. In the years following their arrival, Vegas's murder rate leaped 70 percent.

---

* The fact that I literally had been in the same room as Anthony Spilotro—that is, we had been in the same restaurant at the same time—was enough fodder to produce a Las Vegas Metro intelligence report on the incident. Obviously, this was another of John McCarthy's political tactics. Ironically, on the very same day I'd spotted Spilotro at the Food Factory, I'd told my own investigators, and had them tell Metro, that I'd seen Spilotro in that restaurant. His whereabouts, I thought, was useful information.

In Vegas, Spilotro worked with his childhood friend, Lefty Rosenthal, to embezzle casino profits. Lefty handled the brains end; Tony the Ant supplied the brawn. But Spilotro wasn't content with just keeping the skimmers in line and getting his cut; he greedily branched out with his group of goons to engage in loan-sharking, shakedowns of illegal bookies and drug dealers, extortion, home-invasion robberies, arson for hire, and, as their signature crime, heisting jewelry from stores. The gems and other stolen merchandise were brazenly sold or fenced in a store, a block from the Strip, called the Gold Rush Ltd. This was co-owned by Spilotro, his brother Michael, and former Chicago bookmaker Herbert "Fat Herbie" Blitzstein.

What was particularly galling to those of us in local law enforcement was that organized crime in Las Vegas traditionally had been confined to profiting from the casinos; the supposed agreement among underworld bosses was that the rest of the city was off-limits, since the wise guys didn't want to draw attention to themselves and risk exposure of their lucrative gambling-club scams. But Tony the Ant crawled on his own path. He was committing street crimes.

His crew's method of boosting jewelry was cutting holes in walls to bypass store alarm systems. That's how Spilotro's bunch ended up being dubbed the "Hole in the Wall Gang" by us in law enforcement, borrowing the name given the coalition of outlaws such as Jesse and Frank James, and later, Butch Cassidy, who'd used the impregnable Hole-in-the-Wall Pass in Wyoming as a hideout in the 1800s and early 1900s.

The modern-day Hole in the Wall Gang seemed just as committed to the outlaw life as their Wild West namesakes. Besides Spilotro's brother Michael and Fat Herbie, his cohorts included longtime sidekick Frank Cullotta, Samuel and Joseph Cusumano, Ernesto Davino, Lawrence "Crazy Larry" Neumann, and a few others from Chicago. Also they were aided by Joe Blasko, a Las Vegas Metro Police detective. Blasko was reputed to have worked as a mole keeping gang members apprised of law-enforcement efforts to nail them, and even provided electronic equipment for counter-surveillance.

All bad things must come to an end, thankfully. Eventually the Hole in the Wall Gang bungled a job. Six members were caught burglarizing Bertha's Household Products on July 4, 1981, attempting to get their fingers on $500,000 in jewels. Then the thieves began turning on each other. Cullotta, frightened that Spilotro was going to kill him to prevent him from spilling the beans as a state witness, surprisingly turned FBI informant the following year and was placed in the federal witness protection program. Cullotta ratted on Spilotro's alleged involvement in numerous crimes. Spilotro was indicted in Las Vegas on murder and racketeering charges. During this period he also was tried in Chicago for two 1962 murders there, but beat the rap in front of an Illinois judge. (The judge, incidentally, later was convicted of taking bribes in several unrelated cases.)

Spilotro was crafty. When running his Vegas street-crime operations, he communicated using eye and hand motions and shrugs, or with cryptic words. He knew the feds were following him. But Tony the Ant's odds of continuing to be a public peril were growing ever longer. There were our local efforts to take him down, via Metro Police and the DA's office, plus, on the federal level, the FBI, Internal Revenue Service, and Drug Enforcement Administration. When a federal grand jury in Kansas City, Missouri, produced indictments in October 1983 against fifteen alleged participants in Vegas casino skimming (including at the Tropicana, in addition to the Stardust), the defendants included mob bosses in Chicago, Kansas City, and Milwaukee, Spilotro, the enforcer in Vegas, and my father's old friend, Carl Thomas.*

Somehow, Spilotro kept winning his gambles. Despite continual battles with the law during his fifteen years in Vegas, Spilotro was never convicted of a crime during this period. His racketeering charges related to the Hole in the Wall Gang bust ended in a mistrial in April 1986.

But there was one form of justice he couldn't escape.

---

* This indictment was separate from the 1981 case, which revolved around the Tropicana Hotel. This case centered on the Stardust Hotel.

The Mafiosi chiefs were not only angered by Tony the Ant's inclusion in the Black Book, they apparently were furious that he'd jeopardized the skim through his greedy extracurricular misadventures with the Hole in the Wall Gang. They blamed Spilotro for the diminishment of the skim to a trickle, following the federal indictments. Finally, it was said the mob bosses were enraged that he'd violated a Mafia code by sleeping with the wife of an associate. Spilotro, it seems, had been fooling around with Geri Rosenthal, Lefty's spouse.

According to credible accounts, Tony the Ant and his brother Michael were summoned in June 1986 to a meeting with higher-ups in Illinois. One story says they were to meet at a hunting lodge; another version says it was at a basement in a suburban Chicago home, where Michael was going to be inducted into the Outfit. Either way, the results were the same: The Spilotro brothers were given a "dirt bath." They were savagely beaten, perhaps with baseball bats, and their bodies dumped in an Indiana cornfield, where they were discovered by a farmer and identified by dental records. They may have been buried alive or strangled to death beforehand.

Thus ended the career of a man credited with twenty-five murders. Nevada historians say Spilotro's passing marked the demise of much of the mob's remaining influence in Vegas.

17

Becoming Dick Bryan's Lieutenant

As I was weighing my bid for reelection as DA in 1982, I was approached by the state's attorney general, Richard Bryan, with a different idea.

Bryan, eight years older than I, was one of the bright, younger Nevada Democrats. He had grown up in Las Vegas, where his father, Oscar, had been a justice of the peace, and he had lots of political support in southern Nevada. His political stock also had risen as AG; in the federal courts he'd successfully defended Nevada's Gaming Commission and the Gaming Control Board, the regulatory structure for our gaming industry.

Bryan was planning on running for governor against incumbent Robert List, a Republican who had bested Bryan in the election for AG eight years earlier. At our meeting, Bryan encouraged me to run for AG, telling me I'd be the strongest candidate. It made sense: I was the elected prosecutor of the largest county in the state. I also knew Bryan, himself, had an excellent chance of beating List.* The sitting governor was not very popular, and

---

* Indeed, Dick Bryan defeated Robert List by 11 percentage points. At a recent public event several past Nevada governors, including myself, joined the present governor in an informal conversation of the job. One question was, "What else do you wish you could have done as governor?" List's witty reply was "serve a second term."

127

what's more, registered Democrats in Nevada far outnumbered Republicans at that time. This imbalance could be traced in part to the fact that few Republican candidates ran for statewide office in Nevada in that era, which meant that a voter would have to register Democrat to be able to vote in the majority of statewide primary elections. In addition, politically conservative Nevadans often registered as Democrats, because Nevada Democrats traditionally have been far less liberal than mainstream Democrats.

But I decided to pass on Bryan's suggestion. While serving as AG could be a stepping-stone to running for governor, as it was for Dick, I didn't harbor that ambition. But evidently some people in the state Democratic Party had me on their list of future gubernatorial candidates. Bryan's pitch to me had included a reminder of Clark County political history: "No DA has ever been reelected. You will never be governor if you follow that path."

Governor, I thought. Who said I wanted to be governor? I never began with such goals. I just looked for what could be my next challenge and what would have pleased my dad. I just wanted to get reelected DA. My abiding aspiration was to do the best job I could as Clark County DA. Toward that end, I had unfinished business to tend to. I knew that the major changes I'd made in the office's structure and policies during my first term needed to be institutionalized, instead of being left at risk of being rolled back under a successor. What's more, I had a chance of being elected president of the National District Attorneys Association, which would give me a platform for promoting criminal-justice issues on the national level. My reelection was without opposition. I would thereafter call this the secret that had evaded my predecessors. At the same time former undersheriff John Moran defeated John McCarthy to become the new sheriff overseeing the Las Vegas Metropolitan Police Department. I openly supported Moran's candidacy.

Looking back, I made the right decision in foregoing a run for attorney general in favor of seeking a second term as Clark County DA. One reason was that, during those second four years, I was able to become more involved with the National District Attorneys Association and pursue a position in leadership.

When Newman Flanagan, the district attorney for Sussex County, Massachusetts, was president of the NDAA in 1982, he encouraged me to run for president-elect, despite the fact that I was facing reelection in Clark County to an office that no one had been reelected to for a four-year term. Newman then spread the word to the NDAA members to support "Miller." One member mistakenly approached Ed Miller, the DA from San Diego County, to offer his support. Ed responded by saying, "Thanks. I will run." I had been through the two-Miller scenario before, so withdrew and ran the following year instead. I enjoyed a lot of support, and was chosen president-elect, allowing me to serve as president from 1984–85.

All in all, I forged a broad network of valuable connections in the NDAA. One man I'll never forget was a guest speaker at one of our conferences during my first term as DA. His name was John Walsh. He was introduced as the father of a six-year-old boy, Adam, who had been kidnapped outside a Florida department store in 1981 and at that time was missing but was later found to have been murdered. Ultimately, only Adam's head was recovered. The prime suspect was never charged; police lost key evidence. The heartbreaking experience had mobilized John Walsh into becoming a staunch activist for victims' rights, and an indefatigable crusader against violent offenders.

His presentation at the NDAA conference was powerful, to say the least. Walsh was very critical of the criminal-justice system. He related that as he'd sat in the police station in Hollywood, Florida, in the immediate aftermath of his son's disappearance, he'd noticed that bulletins from other police departments in the region were going unnoticed. The Hollywood police told Walsh that they were putting all their efforts into locating his son. But Walsh quickly reasoned that law-enforcement agencies in Florida and neighboring states would also be unaware of Adam's abduction, if their personnel were similarly ignoring bulletins sent by other agencies. So he visited as many of these agencies as he could to inform them of his son's case.

Walsh also told us that it had taken much longer for notice of Adam's kidnapping to appear in the FBI's National Crime Information Center's database, whose information is shared with state agencies linked to the database, than it had for information about a stolen car. His speech moved me to tears.

I met Walsh afterward and we began working together on victims' rights issues. He testified before President Reagan's Presidential Task Force on Victims of Crime, on which I served, in 1982. Ultimately, John really made a difference: he had a tremendous impact on the creation of important victims' rights legislation in many states and nationally. Walsh's and his wife, Revé's, valiant efforts led to the creation of the Missing Children Act of 1982. This law authorized immediate entry of missing-children reports into the National Crime Information Center's database. Walsh would later become the host of the popular television program, *America's Most Wanted*.

I had persuaded the NDAA to support Walsh's lobbying efforts on this legislation, although some law-enforcement groups would not back it, fearing political reprisal from the FBI. At the same time President Reagan signed the Missing Children Act, he signed the Victim and Witness Protection Act, which mandated, in part, that a "victim impact statement" be filed to help a judge when determining a criminal's sentence, which can include restitution to a victim who suffered bodily harm or property loss.

In Nevada, I testified before legislative committees on victims' rights bills, and was a chief sponsor of the Crime Victims Compensation Program, which allows for funding for people who can establish they are victims of crime and have incurred financial needs because of the crime. Sources for the funds include bail forfeitures, administrative fees for writing bail bonds, and a small percentage of prison-industry wages earned in excess of minimum wage.

In retrospect, I must say that my greatest accomplishment in my years as Clark County DA was improving the treatment of crime victims, especially with creation of the Citizens' Committee on Victim Rights, and the change in the office's policy regarding plea-bargaining. My participation with the NDAA allowed me to be involved in crucial campaigns for federal laws protecting crime victims.

I couldn't have anticipated it then, but my friendship with John would come into play several years later, during my campaign for the office of lieutenant governor.

Near the end of my second term as district attorney, Gov. Dick Bryan approached me again—this time about running for lieutenant governor.

The circumstances had changed for me from four years earlier, when he'd asked for a meeting and proposed I run for the attorney general post he was leaving, as he campaigned for the governor's office. Unlike then, when I'd craved another term as DA, I now felt I'd accomplished my goals as a county prosecutor. A statewide campaign appealed to me.

Bryan explained he was seeking reelection and wanted a lieutenant governor whom he could work with and trust. He saw me as a viable candidate. The public saw me as tough on crime and a defender of victims' rights: core issues in my political image, which sprang from my law-enforcement background. That sort of reputation plays very well in Nevada. A shortcoming for me, though, was that the lieutenant governor's post really has more to do with promoting the state's economic agenda than any other issue. The job had been expanded during the previous term, through the lobbying of lieutenant governor Bob Cashell.* Cashell, who'd been elected as a Democrat but switched parties to Republican, was an energetic Texas transplant who'd become a self-made casino owner in northern Nevada. As lieutenant governor, he'd chaired the state's commissions on economic development and on tourism.

Even with the added responsibilities, the lieutenant governor's duties were light. The task of presiding over the state Senate was largely ceremonial, and would only be necessary every other year, given that Nevada's legislature is biennial. Indeed, the lieutenant governor's position was considered to be part-time, and whoever filled it was expected to have an outside job, as well. This was to my liking. If I managed to get elected as lieutenant governor, I also would have a chance to catch on with a law firm

---

* At the present time Bob Cashell is in his second term as mayor of Reno, Nevada. A Republican, he has supported my son, a Democrat, in both of my son's elections.

and practice in the private sector for the first time, to see whether that was appealing to me. I realized I didn't plan on spending my entire career in public office.

But there was a special nuance to the lieutenant governor's race in 1986. Even though Bryan didn't mention this in our meeting, there was widespread speculation in political circles that he intended to run for the U.S. Senate two years hence. That created this scenario: Bryan wins re-election as governor, then, midterm, runs successfully for the Senate. The lieutenant governor becomes acting governor for the remaining two years of the four-year gubernatorial term.

The scenario seemed likely to play out to a tee. First, Dick Bryan was a heavy favorite to win reelection to the governor's mansion. The Republicans did not seem to have a strong opponent to field against him. The candidate, who finally did step forth, Patty Cafferata, was not perceived as a formidable challenger to the popular Bryan. She was the daughter of Nevada U.S. Rep. Barbara Vucanovich and in 1982 had become the first woman elected as Nevada treasurer. Cafferata probably could have won reelection as treasurer, but gamely agreed to be her party's long-shot candidate for governor.

The second part of the scenario involved the 1988 race for the Nevada U.S. Senate. Bryan would have to knock off the incumbent, Republican Chic Hecht. And if ever an incumbent seemed eminently beatable, it was Hecht: an ultraconservative who was embarrassingly ineffective on Capitol Hill, Hecht was consistently rated the least effective member of the U.S. Senate. Such was his record, he occasionally found himself half of the losing tally in a 98-to-2 vote; the other nay vote would come from North Carolina's Sen. Jesse Helms, whose leanings sometimes seemed rooted in another era: the Antebellum South.

Against this backdrop, I considered whether to run for lieutenant governor. If Dick Bryan, as governor, ran for Chic Hecht's Senate seat and prevailed, then I, as lieutenant governor, would ascend to the position of acting governor for the remaining two years of the four-year gubernatorial term. It was a heady thought, indeed, that if everything fell in place, I could end up governor: the most important elected position in the state. It would be the opportunity of a lifetime to make a difference in citizens' lives, pushing the issues most important to Sandy and me, such as boosting funding sources for public schools and higher education, and strengthening victims' rights and tough sentencing for criminals.

Yet, questions persisted about whether Dick Bryan would really run for Senate. Many high-powered Republicans believed that he would have difficulty vacating the governor's mansion if the next-in-command of the state were a member of the opposing party. If the Republicans could manage to get one of their own into the lieutenant governor's office, it could very well keep Bryan staying put in the governor's mansion instead of taking on Hecht in 1988.

As I contemplated a run for lieutenant governor, I knew it would be very tough running a statewide campaign for the first time. But this campaign, I fully realized, would be an especially fierce and draining battle, given the extrahigh stakes of the peculiar political landscape that featured the governor's office and the U.S. Senate as chips in the pot.

After talking it over with Sandy, who said she would support whatever I thought best, I decided to jump into the race.

Sig Rogich had managed both my campaigns for DA. But by this time, Sig had been active in campaign work for President Reagan, who specified that none of his consultants could work for Democrats. So Sig referred me to an independent consultant, Kent Oram, a plain-talking man who had his own small but aggressive consulting agency in Las Vegas. I sat in Oram's office for our first meeting. He was a stocky, gruff, rough-and-tumble guy. We chatted a bit, and he scribbled notes on a pad, but I wasn't quite sure what to make of him. I told him the date Sandy and I had settled on for making the formal announcement of my run for the lieutenant governorship, and asked, "What do you think?"

"I have no clue," he replied.

I shot him a funny look, internally questioning whether this guy was worthy of his big-shot campaign guru reputation.

"Why don't you know?" I asked.

Oram bent over his desk. He rummaged through a stack of folders, and pulled out one he'd begun as his Bob Miller file. He started firing questions:

"How do your credentials put you in good shape to run for lieutenant governor?"

"What would you tell the general public why you're running?"

"What is your general campaign platform?"

My mumbled responses were far from articulate. The fact was I had not done my homework, which for me was unusual. I looked at the position from the perspective of transition … possibly to governor or possibly to the private sector because its part-time nature would allow me to practice law at the same time. Oram made me realize that I needed to concentrate on how I could use the position to help other people. That had always been the attraction of public office for me.

As I discussed the election and the position with Oram, we concluded that as lieutenant governor, I could affect criminal justice and victims' rights statewide. That's how I became Bob Miller, the law-and-order candidate for lieutenant governor.

My opponent, Oram and I knew, would do everything in his power to shoot that image full of holes.

The Republican candidate for the lieutenant governor's race was Las Vegas lawyer Joe Brown, a partner in one of the state's largest firms, Jones, Jones, Close and Brown (which later became Jones Vargas). Brown was a University of Virginia graduate who had moved to Las Vegas after his graduation, and I knew him personally. At the outset of the race he told me he would not run a negative campaign. "We were friends before this race started," Joe said. "We'll be friends during and after. I'll never say anything bad about you."

I looked at him. I pointed out the truth. "Joe, we've been friends and we may be friends at some point after the election. But we will not be friends during the election, and you will say something bad about me."

Based on my experience campaigning for DA, I anticipated a rough outing. I expected to be hit with attacks against my parents, as before. I knew my record as DA would be picked apart and negatively exaggerated.

What I never anticipated was Joe Brown would get a personal plug from the White House.

Brown was well connected in his party's circles, all the way to the top. He had the support of Nevada U.S. Sen. Paul Laxalt, who was best friends with Ronald Reagan. President Reagan, at Laxalt's urging, had appointed Brown to the State Justice Institute (which supports the improvement of state courts) and to the Foreign Claims Settlement Commission (which adjudicates property-loss claims of U.S. nationals against foreign governments). And it so happened that the president would be in Nevada on his party's business during our campaign.

The year 1986 was full of important U.S. Senate races. Ronald Reagan was committed to stumping around the country on behalf of GOP senatorial candidates, trying to maintain the conservative momentum in American politics. Nevada was one of the targeted states, because longtime Republican Sen. Laxalt was not seeking reelection. U.S. Rep. Jim Santini was vying for that Senate seat against Democratic U.S. Rep. Harry Reid. Santini originally was elected to Congress as a Democrat, but now was a Republican. Reagan was making a stop in the Silver State to raise campaign funds for Santini. Laxalt was a very close friend of Reagan's, and inveigled the president to carve out time for taping a TV commercial supporting Joe Brown for lieutenant governor.

And that's how the president of the United States ended up appearing in an ad opposing Bob Miller's candidacy for the office of lieutenant governor of the state of Nevada. This proved the axiom that there should be no surprises in politics. Still, how could I not have been surprised? What's more, I was unsure how I would counter whatever surge for my opponent that Reagan's ad generated.

Kent Oram, fortunately, came up with an idea.

Oram recalled our first meeting together to plot campaign strategy, at which I'd mentioned how I'd befriended John Walsh during a National District Attorneys Association meeting.

"Can you get hold of this John Walsh guy?" Oram asked. "I'd like him to do a TV spot for us."

I told Oram I could, but that Walsh sort of stayed in seclusion. Oram was adamant. A Walsh plug for my campaign would be key, he said. I called John and he agreed to do an ad. However, when he looked at the script, he threw it to the side. "I know what I want to say. Just roll the camera," he said.

I couldn't have anticipated the poignant power of Walsh's delivery. He cut the spot in one take. Speaking from the heart, he related how he'd fought for better protection of children and prosecution of child killers, and finished by giving me credit for supporting him from the start. He noted that he was a Republican while I was a Democrat, yet I'd followed through on my support of Walsh's campaign. I did what I said I'd do and helped Walsh change the laws. And that's why I deserved people's vote. Unexpectedly, his eyes welled up as he said this.

Bob Patrick, the cameraman, was not an emotional guy; but just like the rest of us when we saw Walsh's spot, Patrick got teary-eyed during the shooting. Immediately after wrapping the take, he phoned Kent Oram and said, "You're not going to believe this spot. I don't think I could edit the last part where Walsh begins to tear up."

About a month before Election Day, a TV movie about John Walsh's life was coincidentally scheduled to air in that period. We bought the broadcast time and our John Walsh ad ran during a commercial break in the movie. The ad immediately made a big impact with voters. It was such an effective plug that the opposition realized it gave me a huge boost in the run-up to the election.

A heated counterattack was in order. Joe Brown angrily claimed I was trying to mislead the public into believing I was a Republican candidate, because I had run ads pointing out that I had served on President Reagan's nine-member National Task Force on Victims of Crime. Brown's camp kept up the fierce personal attacks against me.

We kept on running our John Walsh ad.

The contest for lieutenant governor had taken on a fevered pitch. And the impact was felt right in the Miller household. Any candidate in a rough race has to steel himself or herself against personal attacks. But if the candidate has young children it can get tricky explaining to them why bad things are being said about Daddy or Mommy on the television or radio.

At age eight, Corrine thought her daddy was perfect. When she'd see TV commercials or hear radio ads from my opponent attacking me by name, she wouldn't exactly understand the gist of the attacks, but the tone was enough to make her mad. I'd patiently explain to her what the ad was saying and the justification for it, though I'm not sure how much that mollified her. In Corrine's mind, Joe Brown was an awful guy to be saying such mean things about her daddy. Well, I knew she'd be hearing an earful of even worse things as the race entered its final phase.

The weeks leading up to Election Day shrank to three. Oram was a fanatic about polling, and was proud that we'd built up a lead of more than twenty points. Joe Brown was holding press conferences almost daily, it seemed, stumping all over the state, in Reno, Carson City, Minden, Elko, Ely, and Tonopah. He assailed my administration of the DA's office. He got truly nasty in attacking my office's handling of a case in which two gamblers were beaten by security guards at one of the casinos owned by the Binion family.

Brown's campaigners insinuated that I was a sleazy DA who was too cozy with certain casino owners, like the Binions, and would compromise any police investigations of these casinos by tipping off my friends there. In fact, the Binions had known about the pending charges long before my DA's office sought the personnel records. And it was a Clark County District Court judge, not I, who had decided my office couldn't prosecute the case. But in the fast-paced tempo of a political campaign, a short-attention-span public can't be expected to digest all the facts. And a political campaign can't chop up such facts into bite-sized pieces fit for quick public consumption.

Brown's twist on the Binion case put a crimp in my campaign. Polling showed my lead had shrunk to twelve points. We decided it was time to counterpunch—hard.

Kent put together two particularly strong radio spots that branded Joe Brown as a liar. The script of one spot ran: "On October 23rd, Republican candidate Joe Brown told United Press International that Metro police are concerned about leaks in the DA's office. He said police fear Miller will tip targets of future search warrants. This statement by Joe Brown is a total lie. The truth is, every major police group in Nevada has endorsed Bob Miller. Three weeks ago, Bob Miller was chosen Law Enforcement Man of the Year by the Nevada Conference of Police and Sheriffs. Further proof that Brown has lied about how our police feel about Bob Miller comes from Sheriff John Moran. We quote Sheriff Moran: 'Joe Brown's statements are political garbage. Police have total trust in Miller and his staff. The truth is Bob Miller is a 100 percent honest person and one of the finest people I know.' We believe Sheriff John Moran's words sum it up well. As to Joe Brown, your vote for Bob Miller is the best way in the world to teach Joe Brown that Nevadans don't like liars."

I was frankly galled by the tone and content of that ad, and told Oram so during a meeting of the campaign staff's inner circle at his office. "I'm just getting all kinds of negative comments about our ads," I told him. I was especially worried how they'd play up in northern Nevada, where people weren't used to the big-city mudslinging that happens in Vegas races.

"He's hurting us, we're countering him," Oram said tersely.

My opponent's camp kept up attacks.

My campaign staff kept running our liar ad, and the John Walsh ad.

With days to go before Election Day, two of the major daily newspapers in the state, the *Las Vegas Review-Journal* and the *Reno Gazette-Journal,* endorsed Joe Brown for lieutenant governor. The editorial boards decided that Brown had been involved in the business community, and that this background related more to the lieutenant governor's duties than my career as a county prosecutor and justice of the peace.

I took those endorsements in stride. Brown's business experience primarily was as a law firm partner, and from serving as an officer with the

Nevada Development Authority, a nonprofit agency that works to diversify and boost southern Nevada's economy by attracting new businesses and helping current ones network.

But neither those newspaper endorsements nor President Reagan's TV commercial managed to get Joe Brown elected lieutenant governor. I won by 25,000 votes. As for Dick Bryan, he handily earned another term as governor, capturing each of the state's seventeen counties as he took 73 percent of the general election vote.

In the afterglow of my victory, I felt sincere gratitude to John Walsh, whose ad, I am convinced, made the difference for me. To my satisfaction, I was eventually able to repay the favor.

18

Sticking It Back to Chic

After eight years in the high-pressure post of Clark County district attorney, serving half time as lieutenant governor and half time as a private lawyer was a transition, indeed. I joined the law firm of Beckley, DeLanoy, Singleton and Jemison, which had offices in Las Vegas and Reno. The firm's practice areas included business and commercial litigation. The partners were good to me, giving me plenty of time to carry out my duties as lieutenant governor.

The four-month legislative session began that January. Presiding over the State Senate, ceremonial though the post was, gave me a front-row seat to lawmaking. It was frustrating not being able to participate other than calling the daily session to order, but very educational in seeing the process of bill-making and bill-passing up close. There's an old saying: "The two things you don't want to see being made are sausage and laws." Nevertheless, I got to see some veteran lawmakers in action, including Reno Republican Bill Raggio*, who was a fifteen-year veteran of the Sen-

---

* Senator Raggio would resign in 2011 after serving longer than any member of the State Senate. He would pass away during a trip to Australia in 2012, and be remembered by many, including me, as one of Nevada's finest ever elected officials.

ate at that point, and that year was the new Senate majority leader and the chairman of the powerful Senate Committee on Finance. There is a real craft to the messy business of finishing bills and mustering votes, of twisting arms and cutting deals. But the whole process made me think of Mark Twain's quip in a dispatch to the *Territorial Enterprise* newspaper in Virginia City while covering the close of a session of the Territorial Legislature: "They meet once every two years for sixty days. Having observed the process, my recommendation would be that they meet once every sixty years for two days."

Outside of attending legislative sessions, during my first year as lieutenant governor I found it interesting to chair the Nevada Commission on Economic Development, and the Nevada Commission on Tourism. Each panel had six members who were leaders in their fields. It gave me a new perspective on private enterprise. It also afforded me the opportunity to travel abroad on behalf of Nevada.

One aspect that made my work as lieutenant governor more interesting than for others who've occupied that office is that political insiders knew I could very well end up governor in a couple years. So when lawmakers or lobbyists, civic or industry leaders with long-term plans met with the governor, they would visit me afterward to discuss issues. That helped prep me for the role should I ever get it.

The seeming insignificance of the post of lieutenant governor took a dramatic shift, as expected, after Dick Bryan declared in early 1988 that he was running for the U.S. Senate. Now, as next in line to be governor (should Bryan win), I was treated as a public figure of consequence in state politics. That was very helpful to me in preparing for serving as governor. But my position also had an immediate downside: It set me up as a potential target for Bryan's opponent, Sen. Chic Hecht, as part of his campaign strategy to hold on to his seat.

Dick Bryan was an excellent campaigner with a broad network of political support in the state. He jumped ahead by a wide margin in the polls. But Chic Hecht, as incapable as he had proved to be as a lawmaker on Capitol Hill, had made a career of flouting the odds and confounding conventional wisdom. While he was a heavy underdog at the start of the race, he began staging a comeback as the months wore on. He certainly had been born under a lucky star. It was as if fickle fate grinned on him.

Two factors helped Hecht slice into Bryan's overwhelming lead. One, Michael Dukakis, the Democratic presidential nominee in 1988, disclosed that he accepted Congress's naming of Yucca Mountain in southern Nevada as the nation's initial repository for high-level nuclear waste. Yucca Mountain was (and remains) a hot-button issue in the Silver State, and the fallout from Dukakis's statement turned some Nevada voters toward Republican candidates in general. Second, President Reagan, a lame duck who still enjoyed vast appeal among his party's faithful, made campaign appearances in Nevada on behalf of Hecht.

Voters who embraced the "Stick with Chic" slogan sensed a possibility of overcoming those who sported the STICK IT, CHIC buttons and bumper stickers. As the weeks wound closer to November and Election Day, the Hecht staffers reveled in their man's newfound momentum, and cranked up the negativity dial. They poured huge amounts of money into two ads. One focused on Bryan's use of the state plane, which was a small jet owned by the Nevada Department of Transportation and represented an upgrade from a propeller plane. Hecht's ad depicted it as "the governor's personal jet," implying it was an extravagant use of taxpayers' money.

The second ad's message was: Bob Miller is unsuitable to be governor of the state of Nevada.

Once again, my family's past connections in the casino business were being bandied about to besmirch me. The gist of Hecht's ad was that the business relationship between my late father and his business partner, Carl Thomas, made me an unacceptable person to assume leadership of the state. Thomas, as I've mentioned, had been charged with skimming from several Vegas casinos, though not the one (Slots-A-Fun) Dad had co-owned with him. (What's more, Thomas's transgressions had occurred after my father's death.) This ad was airing frequently on television. It claimed that my background probably would disqualify me for a state gaming license. It painted my late parents and me with the same ugly brush.

The initial attack revolved around the letter written during Thomas's sentencing hearing. The decision whether or not to write a letter had been one of the most difficult in my life. I knew politically it would not play well but, on the other hand, I knew the man and felt a need not to defend him but to give the judge a complete impression from which to base a decision. And I could not ignore the kindness he had shown my mother. So I decided that politics was secondary to the need to recognize that he had been my parents' friend and had some positive qualities, despite his extremely poor decision-making.

I'd begun the letter by indicating to the judge that I was making no recommendations as to the sentencing nor offering any excuses for Carl Thomas's behavior whatsoever. Associating with mobsters and conspiring to skim from the Tropicana were certainly criminal activity. But when a judge considers sentencing a guilty party, he or she makes a determination based on the individual's character as well as the crime. I felt compelled to point out that part of Carl's nature was his kindness and generosity, which he'd exhibited by helping my mother through her grief and confusion following my father's death. Carl had proved himself to be a caring individual in that sense, I wrote, and the judge could decide whether that had any bearing on his sentencing.

It would have been easier for me, with my political aspirations to consider, to have never written the letter, to have taken a duck. But Carl had been a loyal friend and business associate of my parents for many years. Carl Thomas deserved the opportunity to have the sentencing judge know about his positive attributes. And, I wouldn't have been able to live with myself if I had completely turned my back on a close friend of my family.

So now I was paying a political price for my connection to Carl Thomas. Hecht's ad disgusted me, especially since it tossed mud at my parents. My father had been dead for thirteen years, and my mother for nine. Their memories didn't deserve this spurious sullying. But I gritted my teeth.

Hecht was closing in the polls; I wondered if Dick Bryan's camp was going to respond to the negative Carl Thomas and governor's jet ads.

Bryan, however, seemed content that his lead was substantial enough so that he didn't have to respond to the attacks. And then he caught a break. A Republican state senator came forward to publicly respond to the ad about the jet, noting that he himself had voted in support of upgrading the plane because the state as a whole needed it, and the jet was not, in fact, owned by the governor's office. So Dick Bryan was now out of the firing line completely. But I was still very much a target, suffering the political bullets all by my lonesome. Hecht had even gone so far as to say there was "a cloud of suspicion" hanging over me.

That was the turning point. Enough was enough. I was sick and tired of my family being smeared with the stain of mob association.

It was time for me to rebut the Carl Thomas ad.

I got on the phone with key officials in law enforcement who knew me from my terms as Clark County district attorney and would vouch for me. Then I called Dick Bryan and said, "I want you to know that I'm having press conferences tomorrow in Las Vegas and Reno to rebut those Carl Thomas ads."

I had assembled quite a roster of bipartisan officials, including the elected sheriffs and district attorneys from Washoe (Reno) and Clark (Las Vegas) counties, as well as Las Vegas attorney Stanley Hunterton. If anyone was an inside expert on the federal government's ultraaggressive prosecution of organized-crime figures, it was Stan Hunterton. He'd served as a special attorney with the U.S. Department of Justice's Organized Crime and Racketeering Section, first on the Detroit Strike Force for four years, then on the Las Vegas Strike Force from 1978 to 1984. After that he'd spent a year as the deputy chief counsel on the President's Commission on Organized Crime. Stan had recently entered private law practice in Las Vegas. Since he no longer worked for the government, he was free to publicly offer his opinion on whether Bob Miller had ties to mobsters. Stan was offended by the Hecht camp stirring up innuendo about me. He was happy to join the press conferences to speak his mind.

The first conference was in Vegas, after which we would hop on a small jet plane borrowed from a campaign donor and fly to Reno for the second conference. Stan Hunterton's words were very persuasive. He told the media that at the time of the Carl Thomas indictments, when I was Clark County DA, he had been concerned about my connections to Thomas through my parents. But those concerns had evaporated when no evidence linking me to organized crime figures ever came up during the extensive physical and electronic surveillance. As Stan emphasized, the FBI, IRS, and Justice Department offices in Chicago, Kansas City, and Las Vegas were all looking at the Chicago and Kansas City organized-crime connections with Las Vegas, in investigations that went on for years.

As Hunterton recalls: "We were all running wiretaps. Sometimes we were tapping the same phone from different places. If there had been any connection of Bob Miller to these people, somebody would have found it! This was a very thorough investigation, it went on for years in three different places, with indictments returned in three different cities, people called before three different grand juries. Bob was never even enough of a figure to be called before a grand jury and asked any questions. And he obviously was never indicted, never considered a subject or a target."

Billy Vassiliadis, Dick Bryan's campaign manager, subsequently had a full-page ad composed and printed in the daily newspapers in Las Vegas and Reno, containing the pro-Miller quotes by the law-enforcement leaders. The theme of the ad was: "Who are you going to believe: Chic Hecht or Nevada's leading law-enforcement chiefs?"

At that point, both of Hecht's ads had been rebutted, even by members of his own party. This ensured the dissipation of his gains in the polls. In the end, Dick stuck it to Chic in the election, taking 51 percent of the vote to Hecht's 47.

The campaign had an interesting postmortem discovery for me. Through the grapevine, I learned just how much of a blow my press conferences had been to Hecht's reelection hopes. I was told that his advisers informed Hecht that my conferences had led to his defeat. This no doubt sprouted a prickly grudge in him toward me, one whose thorns I would end up feeling nearly a dozen years later.

For now, Dick Bryan would be joining Harry Reid as one of Nevada's solons on Capitol Hill in Washington. And Bob Miller, son of a gambling man, was headed to the governor's mansion in Carson City.

Part III

Governing in the Shadow of an Exploding State

19

Acting as Governor, a Role I Never Imagined I Would Fill

Two things happened in 1989 that no one ever would have thought possible: The son of a man indicted for skimming and tied to the Chicago Outfit moved into the governor's mansion and, ten months later, a joint opened on the Las Vegas Strip that had a volcano and dolphins—and it had to make an impossible $1 million a day to survive. I'm not sure which was the longer shot, but both events would later be seen as watersheds in Nevada history. I became acting governor of Nevada at the dawn of a new era in gaming as the little state of my youth surmounted the one million mark in population and the industry, as it had before, reinvented itself with a megaresort era that would prove to be no Mirage. This was not my father's Slots-A-Fun; this was the time for the full flowering of Steve Wynn's genius, one that would inspire and catalyze others up and down a five-mile stretch of real estate that was a dusty, sparse boulevard when I arrived three decades earlier. And now, the young boy who scoffed at one impresario (Jay Sarno) now had been given the task of being the ringmaster for the entire gaming industry, the man charged, among other things, with shepherding Las Vegas into a new era and the country's fastest-growing state into a new, mature phase.

In the coming years, I would deal with issues against the backdrop of

151

the country's fastest-growing state, undergoing a metamorphosis that Ross Miller could not have dreamt of when he came to Nevada almost a half century earlier. This was not the Nevada Ross Miller knew anymore, and his son had to keep up with the mercurial economic and political environment, fend off a different kind of charge about my closeness to the casinos than what I had confronted before about my dad's associations (these were mine and mine alone), and seek to become the longest-serving governor in Nevada annals.

Was I up to it? On January 3, 1989, as I assumed the reins of state government, I had no idea.

On the morning of my first day as acting governor, I was sitting in the Governor's Office in the Capitol Building when the secretary of state, Frankie Sue Del Papa, walked in to see me. Frankie Sue was a friend of mine, a moderate Democrat who'd grown up in Las Vegas, was a high school classmate of Sandy's, and had become the first woman elected secretary of state in Nevada.

"Tag, you're it," she said, handing me some documents to sign, indicating I was now acting governor.

I acknowledged the knot in my stomach. As lieutenant governor, you constantly try coming up with tasks to accomplish and ways to become involved in government. But that mentality ended the very instant I was officially governor. The entire workings of state government now focused on me. I thought to myself, OK, you've got this job now. What are you gonna do?

I would always be cited in history books as a Nevada governor. I had a sense of history. I realized I was an anomaly, an acting governor, with a half term to fulfill. There hadn't even been a swearing-in ceremony. There was no need, since I'd been sworn in, along with the other constitutional officers, as lieutenant governor in 1987. Oddly enough, I still was lieutenant governor, only acting as governor because of Dick Bryan's ascent to the Senate. No one was sure what the protocol was for making the transition. That was among the first issues I needed to address. I couldn't appoint a lieutenant governor as a replacement, because no statutory provision existed to permit that. Nevada law simply provided that the lieutenant governor became acting governor if the sitting governor vacated the office. And this was the first time in recent memory—in fact, since the year I was born—when Nevada had faced this situation.[*]

Since I held both positions, I decided to dissolve the staff of the lieutenant governor's office and refuse my salary for that post. This would save the state money. Frankly, it was an easy decision to make. In contrast, the two-month transitional period between Election Night in November and my official first day as governor had been fraught with difficult choices.

First, I'd had to assemble my cabinet and administrative staff. I wanted people qualified for the posts who shared my political values and with whom I could communicate well. This was not unlike my father surrounding himself with trusted friends at a casino. I'd pulled in some of the people who'd served me as lieutenant governor. I named Scott Craigie my chief of staff, my right-hand man. He would administer my staff and serve as liaison to my cabinet and the legislature. Scott, a former marine sergeant in Vietnam, had chaired the state's Public Service Commission after working as a consumer advocate for senior citizens, including hosting a Las Vegas TV show. Scott had neither worked for me previously nor been involved in my campaign. But I knew of his reputation for honesty and hard work, and his passion for improving the lot of senior citizens and young people. Craigie's appointment would set the tone I wanted for my incipient administration. My cabinet would be gender and ethnically diverse—I wanted it to be the face of a changing Nevada. Most would be outsiders.

As I'd geared up to officially take office, one unexpected crisis reared its head. Since 1989 was a year with a biennial legislative session, set to convene the first week of February, I had to get to work right away examining the budget that Dick Bryan and his staff had developed. Bryan had

---

[*] In 1945, Edward Carville resigned as Nevada governor to finish the remaining two years in the U.S. Senate term of James Scrugham, who'd died. It seemed like an unlucky Senate seat; Scrugham previously had resigned his elected post in the House of Representatives in 1942 to finish the unexpired term in the Senate of Key Pittman, who, yes, had expired in office (just days after his election). Lt. Gov. Vail Pittman, Key's brother, stepped in as acting governor upon Carville's resignation, and fulfilled the remainder of the term.

put one of his cabinet members in charge of preparing the transitional budget. But my chief of staff, Craigie, and legal counsel, Brian Harris, were stunned to learn, in meetings with the staff of the state budget office, that only a skeleton of a budget had been prepared by Bryan's people. In other words, we had to start from next to nothing. I am sure this was done to allow us flexibility, and it did—along with giving the new kids on the capital block our share of stress.

Craigie reviewed previous budgets and discovered they were so complex that it was obvious that only someone intimately familiar with Nevada's governmental workings and budgeting could ever hope to put together a workable executive budget proposal. My cabinet went into panic mode. We reviewed possible scenarios. The one we finally went with was to call the man and woman who had served as Dick Bryan's budget director and assistant budget director and see if we could enlist their help in preparing a budget.

Bill Bible, who had been Bryan's budget director, already was pursuing another career route, chairing the state's Gaming Control Board. Bible, much like me, was a bridge to the past, too. His father had been a U.S. senator in the 1950s, '60s, and '70s. I entered direct negotiations with Judy Matteucci, who had been Bible's assistant, to hire her as my budget director. I appealed to her sense of duty to the state. I told Judy that I wanted to maintain consistency with the previous budgets, and that the state needed her expertise. I added that if she wanted to, and if I won the governorship for the following term, she could remain as budget director beyond the two years I'd be serving as acting governor. Fortunately, she signed on.

The backdrop to my acting as governor would have been daunting to someone intimately familiar with state government, much less a relative newcomer. Nevada was booming, especially in the southern part of the state. The Las Vegas Valley was the fastest-growing metropolitan area in the country, and would remain so for years to come. In Clark County, an average of two acres of desert was being developed every hour. The ethos was: Whatever it is, bring it on, we want it, get it here as fast as you can. Growth limits? That was for the older, more established cities in the north—Reno, Sparks, and Carson City—and for the World War II–era town of Boulder City.

Such staggering growth brought dire social needs. It seemed that traffic congestion could not be ameliorated in Vegas. Freeways couldn't be extended fast enough. Vegas was now a city, very much resembling a Southern California metropolis, not the small town in which I alighted when Ross Miller picked us up those many years ago.

I knew that of all the state's needs, the one that would be most immediately affected by the exploding growth was public education. As a parent, with a schoolteacher as a wife, and now as governor, I wanted my first priority to be improving the state's public education system. Ross and Coletta Miller had not had many choices when they sent me to school after we moved to Las Vegas. But now the issue wasn't so much the lack of alternatives, but the lack of resources to keep up with the growth.

Nevada traditionally has ranked near the bottom among the fifty states in terms of funding for public education. That never sat well with me nor, not surprisingly, my wife, Sandy. As first lady, she had plenty of input on the subject of increasing funding for the schools.* Of course, Sandy was much more knowledgeable about the technical and practical matters of education than was I. She explained to me that the most critical years of a student's formal education are in the first few grades, when the foundation is established for the basic skills of reading, writing, and arithmetic, as well as the ability to pay attention to the teacher.

When classes are overcrowded in the primary grades, it severely challenges students' abilities to learn, particularly when the child is not getting a helping hand at home. There is only so much personalized attention

---

* Sandy's support for education during my tenure as governor was acknowledged when an elementary school, the Sandy Searles Miller Academy of International Studies, in Las Vegas, was named after her. I'd already had the Bob Miller Middle School named for me in Henderson; Sandy's school naming was the only time two spouses each have had that honor in Nevada. Sandy's namesake school achieved a special honor in 2008 when the Magnet Schools of America organization named it the best of the five thousand such schools in the U.S. Bob Miller Middle School was listed as the top middle school in Nevada in 2010, and is the only school ever in Nevada to have two teachers of the year on staff. Sandy and I have great pride and a little rivalry in being the namesakes of such great schools.

a teacher can give with thirty or more students in a class. Nevada was experiencing an unprecedented population growth, the highest in the nation. Schools in the boom areas, such as Clark County, were bulging at the walls. Early-childhood education was one of Sandy's professional specialties, and she saw very clearly, having worked as a public-school teacher, that investing in people at the front end saves tremendous resources later on. A child who is nurtured early on, and develops learning and social skills, is much more likely to become a productive member of society and much less likely to become a burden on the system.

It was obvious to me that improving our public schools with moves such as reducing class sizes would be a wise investment in Nevada's future. After all, it came down to "pay now, or pay later." Children who don't succeed in school end up as adults who don't succeed in society. They add to the soaring costs of the criminal-justice system, which I had seen first-hand many times, and become drags on governmental services. Given Nevada's crowded schools, I felt the urgency and responsibility to act quickly.

After much deliberation with my cabinet, I decided to include a budgetary line item specifically to reduce the teacher-student ratio in grades one and two to an average of no more than nineteen students per teacher. That would mean more than one teacher in a classroom, in some cases, and it would be expensive.

So here I was, acting as governor and my first act would be to raise taxes for my class-size reduction proposal. Here my naïveté helped me. I hit on the concept of diversifying the revenue base by raising the tax rate on the mining industry.* Nevada is the world's third-largest producer of gold, and is rich in other minerals such as silver and copper, gypsum and lithium, gravel and sand. The mining companies pay property, sales, and use taxes, plus a net-proceeds tax. But their rates in Nevada were then lower than what they pay in some other jurisdictions.

---

* Nevada's general fund is fed by seven main tax sources: sales, gaming, casino entertainment, business licenses, cigarettes, insurance premiums, and mining.

It wasn't long before I had red flags waved in my face. Matteucci, my new budget director, was adamantly opposed to my radical proposal of reducing class sizes and funding the hiring of more teachers by increasing taxes on the mining industry. She'd run budgets through the legislature, and she said she didn't think my proposal had much chance of surviving. Matteucci and several others advising me raised another, political consideration: If I, an acting governor, introduced new taxes, I'd never get elected if I ran for governor next year.

A schism developed in my cabinet over the class-size reduction proposal. Scott Craigie had taught in schools before and remained passionate in pushing for the proposal. He enlisted the support of two of my advisers during this transitional period, consultant and ad man Billy Vassiliadis, and John Cummings, the insightful executive director of the Nevada State Education Association. On the last day of budget preparation, when the final version was put together (with some proposals to be eliminated), the various proponents argued hard for their preferences. Class-size reduction was a big sticking issue. It ultimately was my decision to make the call, and I would have to live with the consequences.

In making up my mind, I asked myself: What is the sense of being governor if you can't make big decisions that will lead to positive changes? The whole point of being governor is to use the position's power, not merely to stay in power. I also believed that this was needed and that Nevadans would understand if the purpose was explained to them. This was a new Nevada, one that Ross Miller could not have imagined in those bygone days, one with real problems and real dilemmas. Tough decisions, unlike any made before in this brave new world, were needed.

Class-size reduction stayed in the budget.

As I settled in as governor, I knew full well that I was virtually unknown to many Nevadans. Who is familiar with the lieutenant governor? And as for those who took an active interest in who was filling the chief executive seat in their state, they couldn't be blamed for considering Bob

Miller to be nothing more than a caretaker governor, a beneficiary of circumstance.

A major opportunity to establish myself as Gov. Bob Miller in the eyes of Nevadans would be coming up only two weeks after I took office: the televised State of the State speech. I wanted to make the most of this appearance.

It took Scott Craigie and me many long hours over that two-week span to finish the State of the State address. When we were done, I not only was satisfied with it, I was excited. I saw it as a stirring speech, hitting many strong emotional buttons. The script waxed so sentimental in one spot—an anecdote illustrating the dire need for the state to provide better care for our vulnerable senior citizens—that my eyes welled up with tears. The script ended on a strident note as I made my case for the mining industry to contribute more to the tax base of our state, whose natural resources were making mining companies rich. I'd added my own special line, a real zinger, to punch up that section.

I was eager to deliver the State of the State address, but nervous, too. I knew I was no glib orator. Every day I rehearsed my thirty-five-minute speech, so often that Sandy and some of my aides could recite entire sections of it. I fairly well had it memorized, which was important to me. When the time came for me to stand at the podium in the state assembly chambers, I was not going to read off a teleprompter (the state didn't own one at the time), but refer to the written text if needed. It would be my first televised address, and it would set the tone for my administration and reveal our charted course. It would make me some allies and, I knew, some enemies. I would be serving notice that I was no stand-in governor, but one with ideas and plans to tackle the critical issues facing Nevada.

Finally, the day of the State of the State address arrived. The major newspapers in Las Vegas and Reno announced it on their front pages. I read the articles with interest.

That morning's *Las Vegas Review-Journal* carried a story headlined, "Children's Issues to Be Key Focus Among Miller's Priorities as Governor." The story noted that the previous governor had galvanized public support with a State of the State address that tackled an issue that touched a vein with the average Nevadan: high hospital costs. The story said that Bob Miller needed an issue to rally Nevadans, and that issue could be children. The veteran capital beat reporter, Ed Vogel, quoted me as saying, "The primary focus will be children" in my speech.

What I wasn't prepared for was the column by the *Review-Journal*'s Jon Ralston, which ran on the op-ed page.

Ralston had a way of digging up information, which was evident in the column's headline: "Mining Bashing, Drug Czar to Highlight Miller's Big Speech." Ralston led into his piece by pointing out that I was still relatively unknown to many Nevadans, saying, "Tonight, the acting governor will have to start acting like a governor on the state's political stage." Then Ralston transitioned to the meat of his column, revealing the main points that would be in my address. His column continued, "according to sources close to Miller, here are some of the highlights."

My jaw dropped. Ralston had scored quite a scoop. He did, in fact, reveal several of my major proposals, including creating the position of a state drug czar, having stricter enforcement of child support, and giving teachers a 5 percent pay raise. I had no idea who leaked him all this information. But what irked me the most was Ralston's revelation that "Miller plans to try to subvert the miners' PR slogan, 'Mining. It works for Nevada.'"

Talk about stealing my thunder by giving away my best line before I could even deliver it in the speech! I was furious, but I had to get past it. There was a speech to give—the most important one of my life.

That evening, in the assembly chambers, I faced the bright lights illuminating the podium and the lenses of the TV cameras. I realized I was being watched by hundreds of thousands of Nevadans across the state viewing this live broadcast. But these are the moments that a politician lives for. I felt a surge of electricity, like a performer in front of a packed house after the curtain rises. My speaking voice, which I'd been told tended toward the monotone, was charged with emotion. And then, several minutes into my address, I hit the passage about improving care for our senior citizens, which included the tearjerker of an anecdote that Scott had contributed.

"The immeasurable debt we owe our parents (certainly in my case, I owe everything to a dad who worked endless hours seven days a week and a mom who took me everywhere and joined every parents group imaginable) and grandparents is just as important as our obligation toward our children and young adults," I said. "It is impossible to measure the wealth of knowledge, experience, and caring our parents and grandparents provide us with.

"How can we adequately repay these people who took care of us when we were young, fought our wars, forged new territory, developed new industry, and are most responsible for the benefits we enjoy today? Sometimes . . . they need our help."

Toward the end of the speech, I reached the issue of the mines tax. I led into it by saying, "Teachers' compensation is too low, there are no funds for counselors in the early grades, and the battle against drug abuse demands much more emphasis. Where can we get the needed funding, without burdening homeowners and wage earners?"

That set the stage for my pitch to raise taxes on mines.

"Mining in Nevada has never been more lucrative. Nevada is this country's largest gold producer, and Nevada mining companies supply 65 percent of all the gold that the U.S. produces. We lead the nation in the production of silver and we're among the leaders in the production of lithium, mercury, and barite. The mining industry earned $1.4 billion in Nevada last year. One-point-four billion dollars! The industry every single day produces fourteen gold bars worth a quarter of a million dollars each. That's three and one-half million dollars of Nevada gold every day—three hundred and sixty-five days a year!

"Remember those facts the next time you see a television commercial or newspaper ad that says, 'Mining, it works for Nevada.' Well, it is not working hard enough."

The hall exploded in applause. But not every lawmaker was amused by that line. Venerable Speaker Joe Dini, the dean of Democrats in the legislature, turned his head and scoured the seats until he spied Scott Craigie. Dini, from rural Lyon County, was a solid supporter of the mining industry. The withering glare he fixed on Scott could have roasted the garlic growing in the fields around Dini's hometown of Yerington. He assumed incorrectly that Craigie had added that wicked sentence.

The lobbying by vested interests was fierce and relentless during the session. My mining-tax initiative failed (although voters would approve one in a special May election), largely due to the political influence of the mining industry and its angry workforce. However, other new taxes were accepted that session bearing the imprint of the Republican leaders in the senate and assembly, who could claim they'd held the line against the governor's steep tax proposals. That's the way the game is played.

Happily, my class-size reduction proposal had gained such broad support that it was implemented under the Republicans-endorsed tax plan. I was secretly glad to let it be "their" tax.*

I didn't know it then, of course, but class-size reduction would turn out to be one of my proudest accomplishments as governor. It positively affected the education of Nevada schoolchildren from its implementation to this very day. Unfortunately, instead of expanding smaller class sizes to other grades, my successors shrunk the program.

Besides the battle of funding class-size reduction, there was one other defining moment from my first legislative session as governor. And it was one that was akin to Ross Miller taking some misbehaving gamblers to the woodshed to teach them a lesson. My handling of the fallout from a bill calling for a tripling of the state's contribution to the lawmakers' pensions was only slightly less subtle, although any blood on the floor of the Legislative Building would be metaphorical.

It didn't take a genius to foresee that if lawmakers passed this bill, the public would react with indignation. Journalists had reported on the bill,

---

* In subsequent budgets, the mining industry would work with me to assist in needed funding.

and a constant refrain I heard from citizens, during my rounds at public events, could be summarized as: "What the hell's going on? You're not going to sign that bill, are you?"

I kept telling legislative leaders that the bill was a bad idea and I wouldn't support it. But I couldn't sway them. They were off in their own world, sequestered in the legislature. They were basically locked in a building for long hours five days a week, for months at a time, essentially surrounded only by one another and professional lobbyists. In their minds, they believed they were justified on the pension issue. They felt (and, perhaps, rightly so) that they were underpaid for the amount of work they put in. By the state constitution, they received a small daily salary of $130 for the first sixty days of a regular session, and for the first twenty days if a special session were called, but no pay for additional days except for a thrifty per diem allowance for food and board.

My point was that trying to bring their compensation in line with their work all at once, by such a steep increase, was not going to sit well with the public. And when the bill came across my desk toward the end of the session, I vetoed it. But the legislators, in the shortest time in state history—eighty-five minutes—voted to override my veto. One reporter told me later that Speaker Joe Dini, a fellow Democrat, said that this would put me in my place.

Sure enough, the reaction of constituents was loud and angry. There were letters to the editor, and even editorials, in the state's leading newspapers. One of the biggest critics was former Nevada governor Mike O'Callaghan, who now was executive editor of the *Las Vegas Sun*. He (as had many legislators) was receiving mail heatedly opposed to the pay hike. I can only imagine what my father would have said had he been alive. But he surely would have praised me for brandishing the veto pen and he would have had some choice words for what I should do to those legislators.

It was the sort of deafening umbrage that could carry over into elections. Chastened lawmakers—the same ones who had stuffed my veto back in my face in record time—asked me to use my power as governor to call a special session to repeal the new law. In Nevada, special sessions tend to be rare and short; this session was the shortest in Nevada history. The vote to repeal the pension boost lasted just over two hours in the senate; to the chagrin of the bill's backers, several ended up losing their next elections anyway. There was blood, even though I did my best to stop the bleeding for them.

I remember a reporter from the *Review-Journal* saying that my veto of the pension increase should remove the word "interim" from in front of my name, that the decision had in fact established me as an effective governor of Nevada.

I didn't have to wonder what Dad would have thought. I knew.

20

Becoming Governor Proves to
Be No Mirage

Historians may someday cite November 22, 1989 as the day the new Las Vegas dawned. Steve Wynn, who was to the new gambling era what Jay Sarno, that man who came to our family dinner so many years before, was to the old: a bold impresario pushing the development envelope on Las Vegas Boulevard South, opened the Mirage. The resort was spectacular—its tropical theme accented with a faux volcano—but its prospects, at an unheard of cost of $630 million, seemed like, well, a mirage.

The resort embodied the quintessence of the Nevada gambling spirit: a dreamlike venture of fantastic proportions rising in the desert, as if anticipating some invisible force of the universe to bestow upon it success. A popular catchphrase that year came from the movie *Field of Dreams*: "If you build it, they will come." Opinions in Nevada on the Mirage were strongly divided between skeptics and believers on whether guests would come, and if so, in numbers necessary to the resort's success.

I was in my first year as acting governor, and saw the opulent Mirage as offering a brilliant new opportunity to promote Nevada to the rest of the nation. (I wonder how the former head of the Riviera would have felt about that!) I was involved with the Western Governors Association, and lobbied successfully for the organization to hold its annual winter conference at the Mirage, which at that point was still under construction. This was a gamble. The conference was scheduled to begin four days after the hotel's grand opening that November.

Two weeks before the conference, my chief of staff Scott Craigie and I went to see Steve Wynn at his new property. We walked through the front entrance. We were stunned to find that work crews were pulling up all the carpet in the foyer and gaming area. We walked into the cafeteria area. Steve Wynn came and sat with us.

"They're taking the carpet up!" I exclaimed.

"I know," Steve said, "it's horrible! Did you look at it? It's the wrong color!"

"Steve," Scott said, "people are going to be here in, like, ten days."

"Aw, don't worry about it," he said. "It's in the mill and they're manu-facturing the new carpet right now."

"Manufacturing it? Where?" Scott asked.

"In Great Britain," Steve said.

It just didn't seem like anything was rattling him.

I couldn't help blurting out a thought that bothered a guy like me, whose family had been in the Vegas gaming business long before the era of a behemoth resort like the Mirage.

"Wow, the overhead must be amazing."

"No," Steve replied. "Only a million."

I was astonished. "A million a week?"

"No. A day," he said, matter-of-factly.

"No problem," Steve continued. "We will make a few hundred thou-sand on rooms, several hundred thousand on food and amenities, several hundred thousand on slots. And then the table games will all be profit."

The Mirage, of course, was finished and gleaming, carpets to chande-liers, for the grand opening. When the twenty-two members of the West-ern Governors Association arrived, each one's suite boasted a big bouquet of flowers, a smattering of gifts from various industries in our state, and a card listing all the big Vegas shows. Steve Wynn had provided a video message to all his employees, encouraging them to be proud of this oppor-tunity and to go the extra mile to help everyone attending.

Las Vegas and the state were undergoing a transformation, one that would usher in a building boom that eventually would make the Mirage look like a lower-end property compared to what was to come. That was inconceivable at the time. But as the man charged with overseeing the kind of growth, both on the Strip and in an exploding Las Vegas (the county's population was approaching three quarters of a million people), I had two jobs. I had to assure the continued vibrancy of the state's primary industry while ensuring that the community sprawling on both sides of the Strip had the resources to give the residents a good quality of life. I had a new reason to think about my education legacy, too, as a "surprise" named Megan arrived as I was gearing up for my 1990 campaign to remove the word "acting" from my title. Megan was only the second child born to a sitting first family in Nevada and would become a fixture in that campaign. She was frequently on my arm, earning the nickname "Velcro baby"—that phrase came from the press corps because I had a habit of holding Megan when I thought I might need to deflect some tough questions on the campaign trail. But the Las Vegas, the Nevada of her future, would be one that the son of Ross Miller would have to help lead through a time my dad could not have conceived.

As I prepared to run for governor in 1990, I had a balancing act. I had to take much of my campaign money from the state's primary industry while also trying to indicate that I was not beholden to the barons of Las Vegas Boulevard.

I was not sure what my prospects were for a full term as governor. But, fortunately for my chances, I received strong early support from key Democratic insiders. What I was told was that the political powerbrokers in the Nevada's Democratic Party—the people who could raise the several million dollars and provide the network of connections my campaign would need for winning the primary and general elections for the highest office in the state—saw four assets I possessed that would make me attractive to voters.

First, I was the incumbent, having served two years as acting governor. Unlike my opponents, I wasn't starting from scratch in running for governor. Frank Schreck, the Las Vegas gaming attorney whose fierce loyalty to the Democratic Party had led him into an unofficial role of major fund-raiser for candidates for everything from the Clark County Commission up to statewide offices, signed on as my chief fund-raiser, along with casino executive Mike Sloan, a longtime political stalwart.

My second key asset was my résumé. It featured certain plusses that endeared me to those whose purse strings would have to be loosened by Frank Schreck were I to raise the kind of money necessary for a long, hard campaign. Foremost, my background in law enforcement would play well into the political process. Two terms as Clark County DA, and having worked as a judge and, before that, legal adviser in the Clark County Sheriff's Office and its successor, the Las Vegas Metropolitan Police Department, gave me solid credentials as a crime fighter. And crime always is an issue near and dear to voters' hearts. I had earned this despite the continuing efforts of political opponents to suggest that my father's associations made me untrustworthy. Added to that, my four years in Carson City, with two as lieutenant governor and two as acting governor, told voters I knew the job of working as chief executive in the state capital. The fastest-growing state in the union faced pressing budget issues that would tax any governor. But having gone through one legislative session already, I could tell donors and voters that I'd been there and done that. I wouldn't have to learn on the job. And I wouldn't turn out to be a wild card.

Third, in any candidacy, a candidate's personal image counts for a great deal. In general, the electorate votes as much on emotion as on reason. Well, I'd done what I could to smooth my image, as I've said, sanding off the rough edges while still being what I was, for better or worse, a "regular guy." I was the son of a gambling man, not a good old boy, but a guy Joe Six-Pack could relate to. "Just Call Me Bob" read the headline in the *Las Vegas Review-Journal* when I took over as acting governor; I was not smooth, but I was a man of the people. That was even better, I thought. Dad would have agreed.

The trait of being down-to-earth strikes a chord with Nevadans, perhaps best exemplified by former governor Mike O'Callaghan, who was a role model for me. He was "Governor Mike," a man of the people; I wanted to be the same kind of chief executive. I naturally avoided flowery language or polysyllabic words. And I was no haranguer or whiner. I came off as calm and casual (that is, since I'd learned to restrain myself from speeding up and letting my voice grow shrill when I spoke on issues I was passionate about). I'd worked hard to overcome one of the question marks political supporters had about me, by greatly improving my public-speaking skills. I hoped this would stand me in good stead during the crucial televised debates during the heat of a campaign.

A fourth asset I had in my favor was, unlike Dick Bryan before me, I wasn't shy about soliciting money from donors.

Why was I uninhibited in pitching donors? Probably one simple reason: my competitive nature. And in my own way I was still trying to accomplish things that I knew would have pleased my dad.

To win a grueling election, you have to have the money to run. I wanted to win. While I didn't enjoy asking for money, I wasn't afraid to ask for the means to enable me to win. My opponents were on the same mission I was.

As it turned out, the 1990 gubernatorial race didn't present me much opposition in the primary.

I'd expected my Republican opponent in the general election to be Brian McKay, the two-term state attorney general who was popular and even bore a physical resemblance to John F. Kennedy. McKay happened to have been a neighbor of mine in Las Vegas. Eight years before, as my first term as Clark County DA was winding down, he'd walked down the street to my door and asked if I was planning on running for attorney general. I told him I wasn't; McKay, a deputy AG, did run, and won.

But now, in 1990, he'd opted out of seeking his party's gubernatorial nomination. He left and went to practice law, taking a position with the state's most prominent law firm, Lionel, Sawyer and Collins. There was speculation in political circles as to why Brian bowed out instead of running for governor. Las Vegas political columnist Jon Ralston claimed in his book published in 2000, *The Anointed One: An Inside Look at Nevada Politics*, that leaders in the state's gaming industry decided to back me for governor in 1990 and put the word out not to contribute to McKay's campaign. Brian McKay disputes this assertion. He personally told me that he'd simply made a decision not to be in public office anymore. He'd had his fill of politics, and wanted to go into the private sector, which he did, and which offered far more remunerative rewards than a public salary. But there is no question that the gaming industry titans had made it clear to McKay that he would not get money, so when former governor Grant Sawyer offered him a job, only he knows what role that played in his decision to forego the race. And it is hard to argue with Ralston's assertion, simplistic and sensationalistic though it may be, made in the blurb for the book: "The mob may have lost its grip, but the corporate titans who run the Las Vegas Strip maintain a stranglehold over the political system that the capos of La Cosa Nostra would envy."

With Brian McKay out of the 1990 race, the man who stepped up as the GOP candidate was Jim Gallaway, a relative newcomer to Nevada.

Gallaway was a former marine who'd gone to law school, and later became wealthy after founding and running a string of telecommunications and computer startup businesses. He'd recently moved to the Silver State from California. He felt drawn to run for governor, and spent a lot of his own money to win the primary. After that, he expected to have the support of the Republican Party.

He no doubt was disappointed to learn that I had received endorsements from several former Republican state party chairmen. Such is the benefit of being a longtime Nevadan with many years in public office, compared to a recent transplant whose background was in the private sector. Nevada, despites its growth spurt, was still a small state. Like Ross Miller, Bob Miller was a guy known as a straight shooter and reliable. Gallaway was unknown.

My opponent also made some big missteps. One was during the only debate we had during the campaign. He came out for decriminalizing marijuana, which was not a widely popular issue in the Silver State.

(Ironically, the state now allows medical marijuana and I am not sure that an initiative to legalize pot wouldn't be close.)

The leaders of my own party were behind me, of course, and I felt it was quite a coup to have locked up bipartisan backing. The media took a different angle. One newspaper ran a story headlined, "Miller Ruins Two-Party System." It criticized my ability to gain support from both major parties. I remember thinking at the time, Isn't anything good news?

The general-election campaign for governor in 1990 was not as ugly as my runs for district attorney and lieutenant governor had been. Every major Nevada casino owner and the powerful Culinary Workers Union, representing hotel and restaurant employees, had given me their support. I stumped all over the state, and my wife, children, and I especially enjoyed the visits to the more relaxed rural locales.

I defeated Gallaway by more than 2-to-1*. Later, in his book, Ralston would suggest I was "anointed" by the powers that be, that the anointment forced McKay out of the race and ensured I would coast. Anyone who has ever run for office would chafe at such descriptions—even if your opponent is overmatched, it is still hard work that strains families and exhausts you. But call it what you want, I was no longer filling Dick Bryan's shoes: I was the governor of a state entering a transformational decade and I had a lot of work to do.

---

* On Election Night, the Velcro baby would "phht" every time she heard the name Galloway. Nearby her teenage brother and sister were rolling on the floor, laughing at the trick they had taught her.

21

A Vegas Visionary

As I took office in January 1991 as an elected governor, it seemed like the headiest of times in the Silver State. Even the most astute economist would have been hard-pressed to assert that something closer to the hardest of times was in store, and would arrive very quickly.

The world's economy had vacillated between slowdown and revival throughout the late 1980s. On "Black Monday" in October 1987, the U.S. stock market crashed, with the Dow dropping by nearly 25 percent. Yet it seemed that every time experts claimed there was a full-blown recession in the United States, consumer confidence and spending belied that prognosis.

Las Vegas happened to be in the initial stages of a spectacular construction boom, one that seemed as improbable, perhaps, as the city's emergence as a thriving metropolis in the desert.

For Steve Wynn, the Mirage was just the beginning. He had plans for a 2,900-room, $430 million megaresort to be called Treasure Island. A moat would surround it, featuring a pirate show four times a night that ended with an invitation to spectators to walk down the plank into the hotel-casino. And beyond this dream, Wynn eventually would build something even more extravagant: a masterpiece that he would call the Bellagio, and open in 1998 at a cost of $1.6 billion.

Some say a rising tide lifts all boats. Steve Wynn was the tide that hoisted the other hotel-casinos. They had to sail along or sink.

Circus Circus built the 4,000-room Excalibur, based on the King Arthur tales, which opened in June 1990. Many more magnificently themed "mega casinos" were in the works. Kirk Kerkorian bought the small Marina Hotel. He planned to knock it down and put up a new, 5,044-room MGM Grand, complete with theme park. Caesars Palace set to boosting its profile by building its Forum Shops, a major high-end shopping complex with an hourly show featuring animatronic statues. That would open in 1992.

Unfortunately, while Nevada's fortunes seemed to be riding high on a lucky streak, things weren't all so rosy for the near future with the nation's economy.

As 1991 progressed, high unemployment and negative production growth were about to cause a massive suction effect on leisure spending. And tourism-fueled Nevada—our fortunes typically reflecting the nation's economy—would be as vulnerable as anywhere to the drastic downturn.

In a matter of weeks in late spring 1991, I started sensing that I had a massive budgetary crisis on my hands. Hindsight, as the saying goes, is 20/20. When my staff and I had prepared my executive budget proposal for the 1991–92 fiscal cycle, I was buoyed by a bright forecast for state general-fund revenues, based in large part on the casino boom on the Strip.

The two-year budget for state government I'd sent to the legislature contained a 30 percent increase in spending—based on projected increases in existing revenue sources, primarily gaming and sales taxes—over the previous biennial budget. The legislature passed the budget, making a few changes to my plans, but I was confident we had done what was necessary to keep up with the state's growth and providing for educating our children. The session had been relatively uneventful. But we passed a mining tax this time with industry support and a business tax increase to fund the budget and keep the state moving forward. Or so I thought.

Even before the start of our new fiscal year, to begin in July, the chickens began coming home to roost. And they were less than plump. Our sales- and gaming-tax revenue figures were showing up far under estimated levels. The plunge in the tourism trade nationwide boded ill for the immediate future, and perhaps longer.

The recession had arrived, and we were mired in its depths.

Operating in the red was not a legal option. The Nevada constitution requires that the state budget be balanced. That meant drastic cutbacks were urgently in order for state spending, which ultimately meant scaling back our payrolls and projects.

Slashing the budget would be a very time-consuming and painful process. No one would be happy. Not state employees, whose contracts wouldn't be renewed or who would be working in understaffed offices. Not taxpayers, who wouldn't be receiving the level of services they'd expected (and who, during an economic downturn, needed more social aid). And not lawmakers, who would be hearing the outcry from unhappy constituents.

I pondered what to do. One option was calling a special session of the Legislature, to revise the budget. That seemed impractical, to say the least! It would mean twenty-one senators and forty-two assemblypersons, each with an agenda, battling over an interminable list of budgetary items. It portended the longest and nastiest special session on record—not to mention, the costliest. Most lawmakers recognized this. Some played up to their constituents by publicly calling for a special session, yet privately sent word to me via a third party with the opposite message. A lawyer, legislative aide, or lobbyist would phone me to say, "By the way, so-and-so doesn't really want a special session."

I understood. What lawmaker wants the aggravation of being tugged a dozen different ways by the lobbying of vested interests? And the fact was, I'd already decided I was going to revise the budget myself. It needed to be done now, not months from now. I was the chief executive; the buck stopped with me. It would be lonely being the one who had to do it. I knew whatever cuts I made, people would be very upset. Everyone would want the hatchet to fall on someone else.

Indeed, state lawmakers bristled that programs they had funded in the latest session could end up being trimmed severely. That year, the Democrats had finally earned a majority in the state Senate. I sent Scott Craigie, my chief of staff, to meet with the Democratic legislative leaders. He explained that I would never go along with the spending that lawmakers insisted stay in place. Cuts were going to happen. The chairman of the Senate Finance Committee, Nicholas Horn, called our staff and said that the Democrats enjoyed a majority in the Senate for the first time in a long time, and they were going to spend what they wanted to on the programs they supported, and that was that.

Right off the bat, the negotiation with legislators had moved into hardball territory. In the days of Ross Miller, some casino enforcers carried baseball bats; in the Bob Miller administration, I carried a big stick, and I wasn't afraid to use it—just as in my sport of choice, I was never afraid to take a jump shot.

We moved swiftly. Craigie and I came up with a tactic that would send the right message. We enlisted the old maxim: People who live in glass houses shouldn't throw stones.

Politics, to a degree, involves gamesmanship, like a competitive sport. You want to play it clean and fair, but you play it to win. You do what you need to do, within propriety, to achieve your objectives. The ball was in the governor's court, so I whacked a return volley with a lot of spin on it.

We sent a letter to the Legislative Counsel Bureau, whose staff serves the legislature, requesting a list of all the bureau's employees and the salaries they were paid in each of the past three years. I expected the salaries would be about twice that of what my cabinet members were paid. The response from the bureau was a list of all the staff positions and what the bureau's budget for salaries was at present and for the next fiscal cycle.

Scott and I discussed our next move. "Let's just get this real clear," we decided. "We did not ask for what was budgeted for them. We did not ask what's being budgeted for them next cycle. We want to know what's on their W-2s. And if we don't get a list of the amount of money that is paid to each of these people, that was on their W-2s, we're going to the press, and we will go to court."

Scott delivered a letter, signed by me, to the bureau. Six hours later we received the requested information.

The legislators knew what position they were in now. The state government was in serious financial straits, and these lawmakers were still paying hefty salaries to their own staff, and refusing to go along with the governor's game plan to move state spending out of the red. If the media got hold of this story, it would do little to improve the legislators' public image.

They were prepared to play ball with me now. I had learned from my father not to start a fight but never to back down from one, either.

The first order of business for me in cutting the budget was shrinking the payroll for the approximately 13,000 state workers. The issue of compensation for state employees had loomed large during the legislative session. Lawmakers had passed a bill authorizing collective bargaining with the State of Nevada Employees Association. But I'd vetoed the bill; if negotiations with the AFL-CIO–affiliated employees union were to break down, I reasoned, arbitration could cost the state dearly.

In my first legislative session I'd raised public employees' salaries by 5 percent in each of the two years. State employees were still expecting the pay increase, included in the budget, for this year and next, and their union's director, Bob Gagnier, was unwilling to back down. During his tenure, Gagnier had fought with and criticized each Nevada governor in office. I'm sure that is how Gagnier built his own support among the union membership, by constantly saying they were not being paid enough.

I held a meeting with Gagnier in my office. He proved to be arrogant and obstinate. I told him I could avoid cutting state jobs if there was an agreement by his union to just delay the recent pay raise, which was about 4 percent. He refused. He knew I would lay off based on seniority—"last hired, first fired," as the saying goes—so his most senior members would not be affected. I did, and still do, feel his resistance to delaying the pay raise to preserve the number of employees was shortsighted and selfish. I got the sense all he cared about was preserving his own job by protecting the personal needs of the people who would keep him in his job.

I had declared a hiring freeze in May. I also convened a meeting of my full cabinet, the directors of every department and agency, and asked that they hold back on their offices' travel and major purchases. Of course, they all were disappointed by this prospect, but knew it had to be done. The belt tightening had begun. And a few months later I announced that the state governmental hiring freeze would last through at least the current two-year budget cycle.

In October, I told the directors of each state entity to prepare for 20 percent budget cuts. The following spring, I lopped an additional $52 million from the budget, sparing only the prisons system and other public-safety coffers. With savings from the nearly 1,700 state jobs left vacant, I'd managed to trim more than $170 million from state spending.

Every state in the nation was struggling to cope with budget shortfalls, with many of them facing record deficits and their leaders seeking new sources of tax revenue. California, Nevada's giant neighbor to the west, was hit especially hard, falling short billions of dollars in estimated income. For a time, the Golden State's government issued scrip, à la the Depression, to employees, and also in place of state tax refunds. The ratings of California's general-obligation bonds were continually downgraded.

We were more fortunate in Nevada. Our swift cutbacks, painful as they were, maintained our AA bond rating, reflecting that we had acted swiftly and appropriately. I was comfortable with my decisions, even with the protests that ensued.

The bitterest demonstration came from mental-health activists. To me, this was ironic; I'd increased funding for mental-health services more than any of my predecessors, and I'd minimized the slashing of those services more than any other agency outside of public safety. Nevertheless, after the revised budget was announced, the activists staged protest rallies and even placed coffins on the front lawn of the governor's mansion, which is an open residential area with no fences or restrictions, to bemoan what the demonstrators claimed was the demise of state mental-health services.

I went outside the mansion to address the thirty or so demonstrators. This made state trooper Angelo Webster, in charge of the governor's security, nervous. He stood in the area as I told the protesters I was truly sorry the state was suffering through a budget crisis, and I understood their concerns, but we couldn't spend what we didn't have. I'd increased the budget for mental-health services more than any previous governor, and tried to cut it less than other areas in the budget, I said. "But the reality is right now, we have to do it across the board."

The protesters listened politely, but they were unhappy. I did my best to take their demonstration in stride. But the truth is, the coffins upset me. If a public official ever tells you his skin is so thick that he isn't affected by criticism of his actions, then I don't know if he should be in public office in the first place. I care about people and about helping them, and did not enjoy cutting services that citizens sorely needed. By the same token, the bottom line was that the state couldn't spend money it didn't have.

I ate so many Tums during and after chopping the budget, I probably increased their stock value.

22

Controlling a Riot

When the Millers came to Las Vegas in 1955, the city already had gained the unfortunate appellation of "Mississippi of the West." The city—and state—was plagued by institutional racism that would continue for decades, a place where black headliners such as Sammy Davis Jr. and Harry Belafonte would play the Strip, then be escorted out a back door and forced to stay in what is still known as the Westside, the African-American area near downtown Las Vegas. My father lived in that milieu at the Riviera and his son would have to deal with it in a very different way decades later.

It came not too long after my first year as nonacting governor. In too many ways, despite the state's rapid growth, Las Vegas remained almost a de facto segregated city in 1992, with the African-American population overly concentrated on the Westside. That would matter on Wednesday, April 29, when a Southern California jury acquitted three Los Angeles police officers (reaching no decision on a fourth) of most of the charges related to using excessive force in the beating of an unarmed motorist named Rodney King.

As news of the shocking verdict and video clips of the ensuing unrest were broadcast by network TV news, mob mayhem spread on smaller scales

181

in additional cities, including New York and Atlanta, Dallas and Omaha, San Francisco and Seattle. Undoubtedly, those prone to rioting were riled up by the constant TV images of anarchy gripping sections of L.A., captured by helicopter-borne news crews.

The Rodney King verdict had surprised me, as well, and I was concerned that it might lead to serious violence in Nevada. The atmosphere in the country was highly charged. The day after the verdicts, hundreds of people took to the streets of the Westside, some in a peaceful demonstration to express their outrage at the verdicts, but others bent on violence by firing weapons or tossing rocks and bottles at police and firefighters, businesses, and passing motorists.

I felt great sadness at this development, as if a preordained tragedy finally had been realized. In my youth, the Westside was the area that literally was on the wrong side of the railroad tracks. It was a largely impoverished section of town populated by disadvantaged African-Americans. During my senior year of high school, two of my teammates on my city-league basketball team lived on the Westside, and I'd give them rides home after games.* In the Westside, among the decent-looking homes, were rows of trailers and shacks.

Any time you isolate an element of the community and its residents feel mistreated and harbor deep-seated resentment, there is always the potential for an outbreak of violence. Now, in 1992, it had erupted in response to the Rodney King verdict, which had fired up an abiding rage of perceived racial injustice.

The wildness fed on itself like wildfire. In a twenty-four-hour period, Las Vegas Metro police responded to more than 9,750 calls, and the city's fire department to some 300. Two deaths were reported: one victim shot by a gang member; another burned to death in a ravaged store. Buildings and cars were torched; homes and businesses were destroyed. Nucleus Plaza, an L-shaped strip mall with a large parking lot filling a city block in the

---

* The mother of one of my friends, Glynn Walker, would come to own the Moulin Rouge, which is where black entertainers would perform each night after leaving their Las Vegas Strip engagements.

Westside, had been turned into a jumble of concrete block and rebar, and there was heavy damage of property on surrounding streets. This terrible destruction had taken place within a fifteen-minute walk of downtown.

The common wisdom in the 1950s and '60s was that the mob bosses in casinos kept a tight rein on mayhem that could tarnish the city's tourism image. Trouble was not tolerated on the streets, and muscle was employed to ensure tranquility. Well, even the old-time gaming chiefs with security guards and foot soldiers at their disposal couldn't have stopped this frightening unrest.

Fear gripped the population across the Las Vegas Valley. Mobs had rumbled through business districts in other cities. Would chaos and destruction spread toward downtown Las Vegas, the world-famous Glitter Gulch? That was a grim scenario, indeed. Beyond the most critical perils— the threat to life and property—news headlines about rioters rampaging downtown, or on the Strip, could cause incalculable harm to Vegas's image as a safe place for tourists and the region's economic lifeline that was already being choked by the recession.

The night of the verdict, a large group of angry Westside residents began walking en masse toward the downtown area a mile away. Metro Police showed up to monitor the situation, although they took care not to openly confront the marchers or erect barricades to impede their progress. They avoided actions that could have ratcheted up the tension and triggered a riot. Meanwhile, rumors were flying, as they do in times of distress, and one story said carloads of rioters were on their way from California to Las Vegas to wreak carnage on the Strip.

As all this was going down, I happened to be out of state. The terrible timing of the unexpected crisis erupting while I was away added to my anxiety as I began contemplating how to get back to Nevada as quickly as possible.

Watching the images flashing on the TV newscasts in our hotel room, Sandy and I were alarmed, like millions of our fellow Americans.

One's first concern in such a situation is the welfare of one's family. While Ross and Corrine were up in Carson City, Megan was staying at Sandy's parents' house in North Las Vegas. From the initial reports I'd gotten from my staff back home, North Las Vegas seemed to be close to harm's way.

I called my father-in-law and said he should take Megan to our house on the other end of the Las Vegas Valley, but Jim Searles was adamant about staying put at his own house, vowing to defend it if he had to.

Up in northern Nevada, Adjutant Gen. Tony Clark, the commander of the Nevada National Guard, knew he might be ordered to dispatch his troops to quell any rampage by rioters in Las Vegas. Gen. Clark called Scott Craigie, my chief of staff, and Brian Harris, my staff legal counsel, who happened to be in a meeting together in Carson City. Gen. Clark told them to come down immediately to the Guard's headquarters in Carson City.

The command center was in a bunkerlike setting, and recently had been outfitted with a new communications system that included a wall-sized television screen. When Scott and Brian arrived, they saw airing on the immense screen the footage that was being captured by police officers roving the streets of Las Vegas with video cameras. Video images alternated from different angles showing police vehicle lights flashing in the night, and glimpses of crowds milling around. It was like a War Room. Some twenty people in uniform were gathered, each attached to a military or police organization from somewhere in the state. A similar gathering was taking place down south in a command center in the Las Vegas Metro Police complex. Law-enforcement and National Guard efforts were being carefully coordinated.

Gen. Clark was in continuous phone contact with leaders in Vegas. He explained to Scott and Brian that a crisis situation was brewing, with the potential for a riot in downtown Vegas. Local media already were on the scene and more were arriving from California and elsewhere. Scott asked Gen. Clark which Guard units were available to deploy, if needed. Clark mentioned the 72nd Military Police Company, headquartered at the Henderson Armory. As an MP company, the 72nd was ideally suited for handling a civil disturbance, Clark said. Its soldiers had performed combat-prisoner-of-war operations when deployed the previous year during the Gulf War.

Scott reached me by phone and passed on what little he knew at that point. We quickly set up a conference call with leaders in the Vegas command center.

As the conference call began, I immediately laid down the law: Any and all media inquiries would be handled as if I were in the state and in command of the situation; no leak of information would be tolerated. Meanwhile, I said, I would do my best to fly to Las Vegas and get to the command center as soon as possible.

The briefing by the Guard and police leaders commenced. My main concerns were intertwined: to not let the crowds on the Westside streets energize into an orgy of chaos that got out of control, and to not provoke the crowds into getting out of control. The twin visions I dreaded were (1) angry civilians rampaging, attacking tourists, and wreaking destruction in the downtown hotels, and (2) uniformed soldiers turning their weapons on civilians, creating a bloodbath. The situation was incredibly delicate.

I approved the command-center leaders' recommendation to have uniformed police officers deploy in the area but remain at a comfortable distance from the crowds on the street so that there would be no engagement. No officers would assemble into formation and rush the mob. We wanted to see if the numbers on the street would begin to decline and the danger die down on its own.

Barricades were erected on downtown streets, but they were only lightly manned. No rifles were displayed. Fortunately, no riot erupted that night.

I had boarded a plane and flown back to Las Vegas.

Sgt. Harvey Weatherford, the state trooper who was my primary driver when I was in Las Vegas, drove me to City Hall, where the command center had been set up at Metro Police headquarters. Scott Craigie, Brian

Harris, and my press secretary, Mike Campbell, flew to Vegas on a Nevada Air Guard transport plane. There we joined Bob Walsh,* my chief deputy in southern Nevada, who had been on the ground in direct contact with all the involved authorities.

The next twenty-four hours would be critical. The crisis would probably be coming to a head. Whatever elements in the Westside community that could spark a confrontation—a massing of people that would move toward downtown in a menacing manner, with violence surely at the climax—had to be neutralized somehow.

I was in agreement with Clark County sheriff John Moran and Las Vegas mayor Jan Jones on the immediate need to send in guardsmen alongside Metro officers to restore order and to impose a curfew on the Westside. Then a new consideration materialized.

Billy Vassiliadis, my friend and political adviser, was well connected to a great many different community and business interests in southern Nevada, including the African-American leadership in the Legislature. As the crisis situation developed in the Westside, local African-American leaders had called Vassiliadis, asking for a meeting. Billy told me he was going to a meeting that would include not only Las Vegas city councilman Frank Hawkins and National Association for the Advancement of Colored People chapter president Jesse Scott, but leaders in the Westside community who were quite unhappy.

About 150 members attended the meeting in a Westside bar. Billy heard out their complaints and concerns. These men begged to differ with us about the wisdom of sending in the troops, saying it would only spark greater hostility. Billy relayed all this to me.

Time was ticking away. I knew that if the violence wasn't contained during the remaining daylight hours, but was given a chance to build and spread, any operation to control and subdue it would become harder, and undoubtedly bloodier. The guardsmen and Metro cops would end up

---

* Walsh is presently the chief deputy in southern Nevada for my son, Ross, who is the secretary of state of Nevada.

having to go into unfamiliar terrain in the middle of the night, like an armed invasion. Dangers real or imagined could trigger firefights and serious carnage. On the other hand, if I immediately ordered the troops in, their appearance in riot gear could very well pour more fuel on the fire, exacerbating the situation by making people in the Westside feel they were being sealed off.

The stakes were steep. I was starting to feel butterflies like a general must when a dangerous battle is about to begin. I decided to pursue a middle path. I would hold off, for the moment, on ordering the troops in. And I agreed to meet with African-American community leaders.

I called Billy and told him to put together a small delegation from the Westside community to come to Metro headquarters that afternoon for an emergency meeting on averting a possible showdown between demonstrators and police and guardsmen.

The Metro Police and National Guard leaders gathered in the giant conference room at Metro to meet with the Westside delegation. The men formed a huge circle. Now I had a brain trust assembled that would help me develop the soundest plan. This was the best possible situation.

"Everyone must remain calm," I began. "Each group here needs to designate spokesmen. And I want to hear perspectives from around the room."

I started with the Westside leaders, who included not only Frank Hawkins and Jesse Scott but state senator Joe Neal and state assemblyman Wendell Williams. One of the other men in the Westside group was a reputed gang leader, but I was willing to hear him out, too. I wanted to restore order, and was willing to listen to anyone who could help bring that about.

The Westside leaders expressed the grievances of residents, in particular feelings of racial discrimination that had boiled to the surface after the Rodney King verdict. They felt targeted and oppressed by the police. Their young people didn't have equal opportunities to get hired at the hotel-casinos. What's more, the leaders said, there was fierce resentment in the community that Sheriff Moran had ordered a nighttime curfew for the Westside only, and not for the entire county, in response to the riot risk.

A spokesman for the law-enforcement leaders then gave a status report on their deployments to that moment. The Guard troops already were mustered, gear ready, at Cashman Field Center, the minor-league baseball park downtown, which was just a five-minute drive from the Westside, in case they were sent in to physically take control of the Westside streets.

I was pleased that the tone of each group's summaries was even-keeled and to the point, even though anxiety and antagonism roiled below the surface.

One of the African-American community leaders raised an urgent point: If even one shot were fired, it would trigger disaster and would turn into a bloodbath. The leader had a suggestion: What if the troops were sent in, but without ammunition?

I called for a break so that the groups could convene among themselves. The members did so, heatedly at times. Expletives could be heard, but at least they were swearing among one another, I thought, and one group wasn't attacking the other.

If there was one fact that was bringing the different sides together, it was this: Everyone in the room knew that at any moment a report could come that an unruly mob was forming on the streets. For us, no news was good news. But it was now approaching 4 P.M. With sunset only a few hours away, time was not on our side. It would have been pitch dark on the Westside, because the day before protesters had knocked down telephone and power poles and the power lines were out. For Westside residents, this only contributed to the feeling of being under siege and the collective sense that the crisis was heading inexorably toward some violent escalation.

I knew a plan needed to be finalized and set in motion. The deadline could be thought of in the literal sense of the word. Could we defuse the situation and its potential for a riot? Or would the madness of a mob prevail and the result become mayhem and death in the darkness of night?

When the meeting resumed, I was relieved that both sides seemed eager to reach a middle ground, a moderate position, a compromise.

I said the curfew needed to be set citywide, not just on the Westside. The Guard spokesman said if troops were deployed in a nonconfrontational way, where they would have a presence on the street but not in a show of force that could provoke anger and attacks, it could pacify the situation while still leaving the option of armed containment, if necessary.

Then the African-American leaders made a proposal that was as bold as it was intriguing. They said they'd recruit responsible leaders in the Westside community, including church ministers, elected officials, and business owners, to hit the streets, calm residents, send angry youths home, and restore order. They would stay out all night, walking every street as citizen monitors. They would light up the streets with any available illumination, even lanterns and flashlights, since the power lines had been cut off in the previous rioting. They would disperse restive groups and counsel any unruly characters against bringing ruin to the Westside, by telling them to get back in their homes, that, "We're not going to have this happen tonight." They would create an all-night community and take responsibility for the actions of their residents.

I brought the meeting to a close and summoned five men to join me in a separate room: Frank Hawkins, Jesse Scott, Billy Vassiliadis, Scott Craigie, and John Cummings, who was executive director of the Nevada State Education Association, a man with close connections to legislators and ties to the community. I sat on a table and they sat on chairs, and we reviewed the worst-case scenarios.

These scenarios were far from pretty. What if the African-American leaders and their fellow Westside community stalwarts failed to keep agitators from gaining sway on the streets? What if guardsmen came under fire? It would be night, and they wouldn't know the terrain. Or what if they mistakenly believed they were under attack and responded with force? Innocent people, fellow Nevadans, could end up caught in the crossfire. In a battle zone, in urban combat, with bullets flying, anything can happen. And the reverberations of such tragedies, and the bitter memories they instill, can last for generations.

Any bloodshed would be on our hands—more specific, on my hands, since I was the one who had to make the call here. An easy decision, on paper, would have been to respond with force, to send in the troops as a buffer against mayhem spreading to the commercial core. But in the real world, it is no easy decision at all.

"You know," I said, "the best choice we can make for the community is not the best choice you can make for elected officials. But that's why we're here: we're here to make what are the right decisions."

I looked at Hawkins and Scott. "I'm counting on you and your leadership more than anyone else," I said. "You're the only ones who can really deliver this through this night."

The men gave their word they would do their utmost.

I emphasized that they needed to explain to the residents they encountered that the Guard and Metro personnel were on alert and would respond forcefully if needed.

The plan I approved was incredibly risky. Imagine General Clark being told he could deploy a limited number of guardsmen into the Westside, taking up points off the main street, and without ammunition. The plan we settled on was designed to avoid the potential of a Kent State–type disaster, with inexperienced guardsman firing on college students without sufficient cause or threat of danger. Only Guard officers and non-commissioned officers would carry ammo. If the lower-ranking guardsmen did end up needing bullets, their superiors could immediately provide backup with firepower and supply the ammunition. As far as residents knew, all the guardsmen were carrying rifles locked and loaded. In reality, we had limited the ability to react to those guardsmen with the most experience.

If ever I needed to bank on the trust that law enforcement had in me because of my background as a district attorney, and my tough-on-crime stance, this was the time. I'm not sure if a governor without those credentials could have persuaded Metro Police and the National Guard to give the African-American leaders' proposal the time it needed to prove itself, to relay that message down the chain of command to the people who would be on the streets. And if not for my strong standing with the Democratic leaders in the Westside, I'm not sure if they would have stuck their necks out, trusting that I would follow through by ensuring (to the best of my abilities) a restrained approach by the police and the Guard.

TV news crews were on hand that evening as about fifteen National Guard trucks and Jeeps from the 72nd Military Police Company arrived in a convoy at Cashman Field Center, on Las Vegas Boulevard North, just outside downtown. The 125 soldiers dismounted, garbed in olive-drab battle-dress uniforms and black combat boots, body armor, and Kevlar helmets, and clutching M-16 assault rifles. Their belts carried canteens, gas masks, and packs for extra ammunition. The Guardsmen quickly assembled in formation, then marched into the auditorium next to the baseball field.

As the men sat on the floor in their squads, the TV cameras captured squad leaders handing out rifle ammunition and soldiers loading their clips. What the cameras did not catch were the four platoon sergeants collecting the clips afterward and carrying them to the rear, where a sergeant guarded them under strict orders about their security. The ammo was to be issued to the soldiers only on my direct order, which would have gone to Gen. Clark and then down the chain of command.

It's when a crisis erupts that an elected leader's political capital can truly be weighed and his political connections counted. And foremost among my connections was Billy Vassiliadis, with his connections. The Nevada Power Co. happened to be one of the clients that Billy's advertising agency, R&R Partners, represented. Billy contacted Nevada Power's president, Chuck Lenzie. That night, around ten o'clock, as soon as it appeared that the adult leaders in the community were maintaining the peace and calm on the Westside streets, Nevada Power workers brought in big trucks with the blazing lights that are used for nighttime work. Crews set to work repairing the downed lines. Then the guardsman walked in. They did so carefully, in a nonaggressive manner, politely greeting residents they encountered.

At about 2:30 A.M., the streetlights began coming on in the Westside. Electricity had been restored, and for the people in their homes, it must have seemed that sanity had returned as well. At that wee hour, when anger, fear, and despair can grip hearts and minds especially powerfully, relief had come. Refrigerators hummed on. Hot-water heaters started. These were powerful hints that the peril had passed and normalcy resumed.

At the command center, we felt like winners. Anything could have gone wrong—one stray gunshot, or even a firecracker—could have set off a disastrous chain reaction. Now, we could relax a little, even allow ourselves to feel the fatigue that adrenaline had masked for thirty-six hours.

The best way for me to emphasize that Las Vegas still was one community, working together to solve our problems, was to mix with the African-American community. In past years I'd attended services at the Second Baptist Church in North Las Vegas. I knew the bishop. I decided to attend service at the church that Sunday. I told my security chief, Angelo Webster, that I would go in alone. Only years later did I learn that he sent in two plainclothes African-American troopers despite my order. I was probably the only person in the church who did not realize it, but my presence did serve its intended purpose.

In the weeks that followed, Mayor Jan Jones formed the Multi-Jurisdictional Community Empowerment Commission, comprised of movers and shakers in the city, to prepare a report with recommendations for addressing root causes of the urban unrest in the Westside.

I followed through on my promise to the community leaders at our ad-hoc meeting during the troubles. I went to hotels in Vegas and asked that they start employing ethnic-diversity standards in their summer-work programs for students. Bob Maxey, an executive with MGM, approached me with an offer to donate $1 million to a program to benefit minority youths in Vegas. The money came from MGM chairman Kirk Kerkorian's philanthropic foundation. Kerkorian wanted to make the donation anonymously. Ultimately, we created the Nevada Partners Program to accomplish the task and coordinated with a work-training program that Mayor Jones had been working on.

In the end, the forces that threatened to rend the city instead pulled Las Vegas a little closer together.

23

A Question of Eligibility

One of the benefits of becoming governor in 1989 was that I was able to participate in the National Governors Association (NGA), where I met a colleague by the name of Bill Clinton. We became friends almost immediately—and it was friendship that would later pay significant dividends for Nevada. We shared political ideals and had similar senses of humor. That's where the comparisons ended. I didn't project magnetism and suavity. I couldn't walk into a room and light it up with my dazzling smile, dapper dress, and deft wit. And I didn't play any musical instrument.

When Clinton decided to run for president in 1992, I felt good about offering my help. At the National Governors meetings he always seemed to know more about the issue at hand than any of the rest of us. He was knowledgeable on an incredibly wide variety of issues and seemed to know at least a little about any subject that came up. Most impressive to me was his ability to convert complex concepts into simple, easily understood descriptions. His politics were moderate and pragmatic, and so were mine. I became the second governor, and one of only a small number of elected officials in the country, to endorse him, and I volunteered to run his campaign in Nevada.

Nevada was a longshot for the Clinton campaign—the state had voted for the Republican nominee since 1964. But I introduced him around the state to donors with the help of Mike Sloan and Frank Schreck and left no stone unturned to help him. Initially I was the only elected official in Nevada supporting him. On Election Night, I was thrilled that he had won Nevada as part of his victory and called him to tell him so. One day later, the mastermind of Clinton's campaign, James Carville, said to the national media in recapping the elections: "I can tell you that we won every state that we targeted, and we lost every state we did not target. There was only one exception, and that was Nevada. We did not target Nevadans, but we won."

I can't take sole credit for that—Ross Perot siphoned enough votes to help Clinton take the state. But our bond was only cemented that night and later, my access to Clinton would elicit promises from him to help stop the federal government's plan to entomb waste at Yucca Mountain, only one hundred miles from Las Vegas, and to apply federal to tax the gaming industry. The son of a gambling man getting the president of the United States to help the state Ross Miller called his adopted home and the industry that made his career. My father would have been amazed—and proud.

As 1993 approached, with the biennial Legislature set to convene in February, I considered that class-size reduction in grades one through three in our public schools was adequately funded, but I wanted to make more strides in the quality of education. I knew that growth led to the need for more teachers, and I wanted to retain them by paying them higher salaries, and to give them better technology. All this would require more tax dollars. And I couldn't very well ask lawmakers to approve raising taxes unless I could persuade them, and their constituents, that I was doing my best to eliminate unnecessary spending from government.

I knew it was high time to take a very close and critical look at each of our agencies and commissions, departments, and divisions. The organizational chart was a horrific hodgepodge of 47 state agencies and 173 free-floating boards and commissions. There was overlap in services; there were little departmental fiefdoms competing for prestige and power. All that added up to governmental waste of resources and money.

What was needed now was a citizen's panel to provide constructive and effective guidance on streamlining our government. They would have to be unpaid appointees motivated by civic concern, and whose backgrounds qualified them as managerial experts. That's how I formed the nonpartisan Commission on Government Reorganization, comprised of seven successful business leaders from northern and southern Nevada. Chairing it was a Republican, Kenny Guinn. His résumé was impeccable: He'd risen through the public-education ranks to become superintendent of the Clark County School District for nine years, then switched to the private sector and served as vice president and chairman of the board of Nevada Savings & Loan (which became PriMerit Bank), and then president and chairman of Southwest Gas Corp. Throughout those years, he'd consistently declined overtures from his political party to run for statewide office—that is, until I was done and he was elected to succeed me and then reelected for a second term.*

The panel's task seemed daunting. As I said, there were more than two hundred state agencies, boards, and commissions.

That legislative session, I signed laws that reduced the hodgepodge of entities down to eighteen. I would be proud of that achievement. But it would be another initiative that session, reforming the troubled workers' compensation system over the objections of my labor allies, that would threaten my political future. But first, I had to find out if I could even run. The Nevada constitution has a two-term limit for governors. But I had served only half of Dick Bryan's term, so I thought I was eligible. But was I?

The question, not surprisingly, was raised by the state employees union, still smarting from our battle royale over compensation. They had a case. A 1970 amendment to the Nevada constitution said that the governor is the sole elected executive official subject to a limit of two four-year terms in office. The amendment further stated that an individual succeeding to an unexpired term of two years or more is only eligible to serve one

---

* Kenny, who had also served as an interim president of UNLV at a salary of one dollar, would tragically die in 2010 when he fell off his roof. His funeral was attended by huge crowds and covered live all over Nevada on television. I described him as a man who, while elected as a Republican, served as a Nevadan.

four-year term after fulfilling the unfinished term of his predecessor. This provision parallels the 22nd Amendment of the U.S. Constitution.

After I'd become acting governor in January 1989 to serve out Dick Bryan's term, I'd served two calendar years plus a few days. I checked with several legal sources to see whether that disqualified me from running for a second elected term in 1994. The first opinion I got was from the Lionel Sawyer Collins law firm, suggesting I was not eligible. The key point was that my term as acting governor had exceeded the number of actual calendar days allowed to qualify as only two years, or a half term in office. The same conclusion was reached by the state's Legislative Counsel Bureau (possibly at the request of Republican legislators): that I had served more than two years of another governor's term, and therefore could not be elected to the position of governor more than once. I'd taken over as governor for Dick Bryan on January 3, 1989, with that term officially expiring on January 7, 1991. Therefore, I had served four days past two years.

I decided to seek a second opinion from another law firm, of which my longtime friend Frank Schreck was a partner. Brian Harris, the legal counsel in my cabinet, started researching the issue, too. As a result, Brian begged to differ with the opinions of Lionel Sawyer Collins's lawyers and the Legislative Counsel Bureau attorneys. Brian believed that the language put into Article 5, Section 3, of the Nevada constitution in 1970 regarding term limits was, in his words, "basically a statutory construction issue." Brian held that the language in Article 5, Section 3, was "an intended reference to the midpoint of the constitutionally mandated 'four-year' term set forth in Article 5, Section 2."

Brian's argument was incredibly simple. He said a "four-year" term was not a calendar-day term but a term which, pursuant to Nevada state law 223.030, runs from inauguration day (the first Monday in January) to inauguration day (the first Monday in January four years later), regardless of the actual number of calendar days in between.

Frank Schreck's firm, specifically Todd Bice, reached the same conclusion, which Brian expressed in a letter: "The most logical way of marking the 'years' of a Governor's term, then, is from first Monday in January to first Monday in January for four years. In this regard, Dick Bryan would have completed two years of his term on Monday, January 2, 1989. Bob became Acting Governor a day later on January 3, 1989, the day Dick Bryan resigned and began his term as U.S. Senator. Counting from first Monday in January to first Monday in January, Bob did not serve more than two years of Dick Bryan's term."

It should not be ignored that the favorable opinions came from my counsel and my close friend and fund-raiser. Fortunately for me, the attorney general, a Democrat and another friend of mine, Frankie Sue Del Papa, sided with their argument. As assistant attorney general Brooke Nielsen wrote in the AG office's opinion, on December 31, 1992: "The word 'years' as used in Nevada Constitution Article 5, Section 3, means 'official years' not 'calendar years.' Governor Bob Miller, therefore, has not served 'more than two years' of another person's term as governor and is eligible to seek reelection to the office of governor at the 1994 general election."

I proceeded to file to run for governor with the secretary of state. But the eligibility issue was not dead. Gagnier, the head of the state employees union, with whom I'd tangled over my proposed budget cuts during the 1991 fiscal crisis, promptly filed a legal challenge.

The uncertainty over my eligibility was one of the reasons that, unlike my first gubernatorial campaign in 1990, I suddenly faced a strong opponent for the Democratic primary: Las Vegas mayor Jan Jones.*

Jones had burst into Las Vegas politics in 1991 as a surprise first-time candidate running for mayor. She enjoyed a high familiarity rating with Vegas voters due to the whimsical television commercials she'd appeared in for the car dealerships owned by her then father-in-law, Fletcher Jones. Jan was an attractive woman with champagne-tinged blond hair and a bubbly personality. In the commercials she'd appeared in various

---

* Some media had referred to it as the race of the century.

getups, including a Red Riding Hood costume, and in flashy casino attire as she stroked the tail end of a shiny new car. As a tagline, she needled her miserly father-in-law, chirping, "Nobody's cheaper than Fletcher Jones."

She'd even appeared in clever commercials with female impersonator Kenny Kerr, who was a popular attraction in showrooms on the Las Vegas Strip. She had become an attractive and recognizable figure to television viewers throughout southern Nevada.

In 1991, Jan proved to be much more than a flashy blond newcomer to office who favored short skirts and big earrings. She had brains and business savvy. Her grandfather, Roger Laverty, had founded the Southern California grocery chain that came to be known as ThriftiMart. Jan was a Stanford graduate with two decades' experience in the business world in marketing and personnel positions, and had sat on boards ranging from Security Pacific Bank to the National Conference of Christians and Jews. She and her then husband, Ted, were mainstays of Vegas high society. She was well connected, energetic, and confident.

The heady success of her initial run for office, however, may have left her prey to overconfidence. Political consultant Dan Hart, who'd engineered Jan's campaign for mayor, now promised her a bigger prize: the governorship of Nevada. Hart touted her chances against me, as did some leaders of organized labor* and others who wanted to see Bob Miller defeated. These people included Joe Brown, my Republican opponent when I'd run for lieutenant governor. I imagine their voices were flattering and persuasive to Jan's ears. I'd found myself in a similar position before, as a young election winner being peddled blue-sky visions by political Svengalis.

Jan Jones had yet to complete her first term as mayor, and now she was

---

* In the previous legislative session Nevada faced a crisis—in our Workmans' Compensation system we had an unfunded liability of $2.3 billion. I had decided to abolish an oversight board and take personal control. Some in labor resented this plan. The state-run system was eventually privatized and its successor is run by Doug Dirks, whom I had given oversight of my reforms, and Ann Nelson, my former staff attorney.

being prodded into a far rougher arena: running for the top executive office in the state. She was being told that she had to seize the window of opportunity to run for governor while it was open. That window was open, the smiling faces told her, because of the uncertainty as to whether Bob Miller was eligible to run, and because I was a weak incumbent after taking on labor during the legislative session. To bolster their spiel, they pointed at early polls showing her beating me by ten or eleven points.

In the end, Jan ignored the advice of mutual friends of ours, including Billy Vassiliadis and Steve Wynn, and filed to run for governor.

I could understand why someone such as Jan Jones would consider me a beatable incumbent. After all, I'd inherited the job to start with, and then won election two years later against an insubstantial opponent, Jim Gallaway. Jan considered me vulnerable on several points. She saw me as soft on issues of particular importance to women, minorities, and labor. I had appointed many women to high-level positions. I had a good record with minorities and unions, up until the workers' compensation reform issue. But Jones and her advisers know that memories are short in politics, so they played carpe diem.

Jones positioned herself as a strong progressive liberal. She announced she was pro-choice. She spoke out against an initiative drive to amend the state constitution to prohibit spousal status for gay couples and deny certain other legal protections. She cast herself as pro-union, declaring her support for "project labor agreements," which are negotiated between construction owners and trade unions at the start of construction projects, to avoid labor disputes during a project.

On paper, Jan Jones arguably looked stronger than I did as a candidate. Besides her charisma, in 1994, female candidates enjoyed tremendous appeal among a large section of the electorate. Women were making big strides into major positions on the political stage. Jan also could count on a head start in statewide campaigning. I couldn't announce my bid for office until most of my work related to the 1993 legislature was completed.

Jan, though, declared her candidacy in fall 1993, giving her a half-year lead on me. She already enjoyed positive ratings in Las Vegas. Now she was traveling the state, getting herself known to voters in the Reno metropolitan area and in the rural "cow" counties, defining herself as a candidate for governor.

But perhaps I was in better political shape than I seemed to Jan. It was true that I am, personally, pro-life. I'd publicly stated that I favor the preservation of life. But I'd emphasized that I would respect the Nevada voters' decision to enact pro-choice laws. They had made abortion legal in the Silver State. And while Jan had strong ties to the gay/lesbian community, she failed to recognize that I, too, was an outspoken critic of any laws or actions that were discriminatory. Politics is a game of addition, not subtraction, and I was proud to have earned the support of gay-rights advocates. I had signed Nevada Senate Bill 466 in June 1993, repealing the state sodomy law, because I believe that what two consenting adults do in private is none of the state's business. The following year I would take a lead role in actively opposing the initiative drive in 1994 by a group called the Nevada Citizens Alliance. I unmasked this as a discriminatory group of bigots attempting to punish homosexuals based upon that reason alone. This was a civil-rights issue, and I had no qualms about supporting equal treatment under the law for gay people.

Nevertheless, Jan Jones pushed ahead aggressively in her bid for governor. As fate had it, my campaign would proceed as well. The Nevada Supreme Court ruled 5–1 that I was eligible to run.

24

The Campaign for Governor— A Worthy Opponent

It was no secret that Nevada labor leaders had encouraged Jan Jones to run against me. Winning the AFL-CIO's endorsement was a major goal of candidates in the Democratic primary, given the large number of union members working in the hotel-casinos.

I knew getting the endorsement wouldn't be easy for me. The State of Nevada Employees Association was affiliated with the AFL-CIO. I visited individually with leaders of other unions associated with the AFL-CIO. I emphasized the actions I'd taken as district attorney and governor that had supported their causes. One was trying to break the impasse between the Elardi family, who owned the Frontier Hotel & Casino on the Strip, and the Culinary Workers Union, which struck the hotel in September 1991. More than five hundred maids, waitresses, bartenders, and cooks had walked off the job, claiming unfair treatment by management.

The Elardis held fast to their stance that they couldn't afford to pay union wages, and the pickets had continued daily year after year. Federal arbitrators couldn't break the stalemate. I knew that it was critical to the state's economy that a balance be maintained between the powerful gaming companies and the unions. Nevada was growing very fast in population, and there needed to be a partnership between labor and gaming. The ability to hire and retain employees was critical to sustaining overall prosperity. I had managed, at least, to get the Elardis to sit down with union negotiators. Tom Elardi and his attorney, as well as key union officials, had attended the meeting, but it was evident that the Elardis would not budge. His mother, in reality, called the shots, and the family was determined not to compromise.

Fortunately for me, union officials, especially from the Culinary Union, understood that I'd earnestly tried to get the lengthy strike resolved.* They also remembered that, as Clark County DA, during a citywide strike by union members, I'd decided not to prosecute hundreds of nonviolent trespassing charges issued to picketers, although I did authorize prosecution of picketers who'd actually committed batteries or other crimes during the strike. For these reasons—and, perhaps, some of my advisers' closeness to the unions—the union officials decided to support me.

The *Las Vegas Sun* reported on how elated my camp was to earn the endorsement, and how bitter Jones's camp was. Jan's campaign manager, Dan Hart, went on the record accusing me and labor leaders of backroom wheel-dealing and "strong-arm" tactics to secure me the two-thirds majority of votes to win the union's endorsement. Walt Elliott, president of the bartenders' union's Nevada chapter, responded that Jones's staff was full of sour grapes.

Jones had to realize she was now in a real dogfight. She found herself as a political neophyte up against an experienced campaign team that knew how to play the inside game (the AFL-CIO endorsement) and the outside game—media, message, etc. The way she saw it, my campaign handlers were making shrewd move after move to better position me on what were perceived as my weak points with voters. I'd hired a woman, Patty Becker†,

---

* In 1999, billionaire Phil Ruffin bought the Frontier and promptly settled the strike. In 2007, he would sell the Frontier and the following year he purchased and now owns the Treasure Island (TI).
† In reality, gender was never for me a reason for hiring anyone. Of the four chiefs of staff over my ten years, two would be women. My last year in office my chief of staff was Catherine Cortez Masto, who is presently serving in her second term as Nevada's attorney general. I would also receive the Breaking the Glass Ceiling Award from the national Association of Women Executives in State Government.

as my chief of staff. I publicly defended gay rights. Meanwhile, I had an invaluable ace in the hole: the support of the gaming industry. That was understandable. I was the incumbent, and therefore a known quantity. Jan, however, as a political outsider, was a wild card. Were she to become governor, it was unclear what moves she'd make that might help or hinder gaming in the state. She could appoint people adversarial to the industry as members of the Gaming Commission or Gaming Control Board. Why take the risk?

As the weeks wore on, the campaign heated up. Jan and I traded attacks and counterattacks. She daringly insisted I was too soft on crime. She charged that I was too cozy with the casino industry. And after Jan's campaign people found that the big donors were supporting me rather than her, they may have felt somewhat desperate. That may partly explain why Jan ended up committing to an audacious, and even shocking, gambit that was practically the equivalent of going all in very early in a high-stakes poker game.

Frank Schreck, my campaign fund-raiser, was attending a gaming commission meeting in Carson City when he received a phone call from Billy Vassiliadis, my campaign strategist. Billy's voice was alarmed. "Oh, Frank, God, we're in trouble!"

"Why are we in trouble?" Frank asked.

"Jan Jones has announced that she's going to be on the federal courthouse steps, and is going to slam you for raising all of Miller's money from gaming people, and then appearing in front of the gaming commission, which he appoints." Gaming meant something different than it did in my dad's today. This attack wasn't about the mob; it was about political influence. But it could be damaging nevertheless.

Frank is nothing if not a quick thinker on his feet. "You got to be kidding me!" he said. "Billy, that's the best news I've ever heard! Christ, Billy, what is she going to say? She's going to say that somehow the people who are appointed to these positions are bought because I raise money for the governor? Listen to what I'm going to say when I get back. And have some press people waiting. I'll be back by four o'clock."

Sure enough, Jan gave a news conference from the steps of the federal courthouse in Las Vegas, slamming me and criticizing my use of Frank as my chief campaign fund-raiser. Because Frank was a partner in a high-powered Las Vegas law firm representing big gaming clients, Jan questioned whether a lawyer who regularly appeared on behalf of clients in front of the Gaming Control Board, whose members were appointed by the governor, should be the key person raising money for my reelection. The implication was that the votes of Gaming Control Board members could be, or had been, compromised.

Well, TV and print reporters were waiting for my campaign's response. I was immediately available for their interviews. My retort to Jan's allegations, as quoted in the *Las Vegas Sun*: "It's apparent she's willing to run a negative gutter campaign. The important thing here is the fact that the mayor is willing to besmirch the reputation of anybody for her own political gain. She was not specific and says she has no evidence."

Frank Schreck got his two cents in with the media, as well. He pointed out that he'd raised money for Jan's run for mayor from the same people from whom he was building Bob Miller's campaign chest. He continued that Jan had approached him to raise money for her governor's campaign. Frank pointed out that four of the five gaming commissioners had not been appointed by me, but were in their seats from previous appointments. Then Frank fired off his own attack:

"Jan Jones goes out and collects money from gaming licensees in Las Vegas, and she sits as mayor of Las Vegas on the licensing board, granting them licenses and ruling on their zoning."

Jan later responded that the state, not the city, grants gaming licenses. But Schreck, the lawyer, pointed to the state statute saying that no gaming license can be issued until the local municipality grants it.

In the end, Jan's shots at my campaign on the courthouse steps backfired. Her early lead in campaigning, and her hard work defining herself to voters as an aggressive, progressive woman with a spotless record, was subverted by her move toward a negative campaign. Frank Schreck and Billy Vassiliadis were elated.

Ironically, Jan and I did (and do) like each other. On a personal level, we got along fine. That January in 1994, we'd found ourselves on a chartered airplane flying from Las Vegas to Arkansas for the funeral of President Clinton's mother, Virginia Cassidy Kelley. I was going as a friend of the president while Jan had befriended Virginia when the spunky Southern woman was in Vegas to give a campaign speech on behalf of her son during the presidential campaign of 1992. Jan and Virginia had ended up spending the day together. The night Bill Clinton was elected, Jan had been there at campaign headquarters in Little Rock.

On the plane, we were joined by Brian and Myra Greenspun and their daughter Amy. Amy had just commented on how friendly Jan and I were despite being political opponents when we were adjusting the cushioned seat, and I remarked, "Yeah, this is what it's going to be like through the whole campaign: push, shove, push, shove."

And it was. Running for governor, Jan discovered, as I had in my previous race, is a faster, nastier game of hardball than running for mayor, and the cleats are sharper. The opposing camps are ever vigilant to catch each other's candidate off base. It is challenging for either candidate campaigning against a member of the opposite gender. If a man is running against a woman and he comes on too strong, he seems like a bully. If the woman comes on too strong, she's unfairly considered to be a different word beginning with "b." But neither side wants to appear timid. Jan and I were always trying to strike the right tone.

Jan and I would be going face-to-face in a series of televised debates. And that worried my camp greatly. Although Billy V. was running my campaign, we brought in Kent Oram to help out. Kent, as I've said, is an expert at grooming and preparing candidates for public speaking. We all knew that Jan Jones was awesome on camera, just a natural actress. Billy V. and other key aides hoped I could manage to earn a tie or just lose a little to her in our TV debates. They were hopeful I would come across to viewers as at least as appealing, or nearly as appealing, as she. But Kent had a loftier goal: to make Jan look like just a pretender to the office, and to make me look like the Governor, the man in charge and in the know.

Jan had done tremendous homework. She'd prepared a hundred-page booklet detailing her positions on issues, and distributed them to the media. But Kent Oram understood sound bites. "She has all the positions, but you're the governor," he told me. "You're under fire and make the tough decisions. If she attacks you on specific issues, throw out facts as fast as you can, then get back on your own turf, running the state."

Kent also counseled me against shying away from engaging in verbal sparring with Jan, just because she's a woman. Jan was a formidable foe, Kent said. "You can't be afraid to fight. Be yourself. If she starts punching you with statistics or facts that just aren't right, you say, 'Jan, you're not right. Here is what the facts are.'"

Jan and I each went into the televised gubernatorial debates very hyped-up and anxious. As the night of the first of the three debates approached, it seemed that every political pundit in the press, and most of the players in Nevada politics, pretty much predicted she would mop me up. After all, Jan was extremely entertaining and funny, and a gifted speaker, and tough as nails. I was seen as someone rather stiff who did not connect particularly well with audiences either on television or in a big room.

Billy V. prepared me for the debate by having me practice in a mock setting against Gene Porter, who was the Assembly majority leader. From my dealings with the legislature, Gene knew very well the chinks and foibles in my political armor. In our rehearsal, he came on like an over-zealous sparring partner looking to make me taste the canvas. He pounded away at my positions and my background. Billy wanted to give me the worst of it so that the actual debate wouldn't feel as bad. Well, Gene gave me a verbal bruising.

Afterward, my advisers told me I'd done fine, but Sandy begged to differ. "You've got work to do, partner," she said.

The debate was held at the beginning of summer at a studio at the public TV station. "Just be the governor," Billy V. had told me. "You're the man who helped the state through tough budget times, and we're now enjoying good economic times, and you've created the class-size reduction program in Nevada. You have great bona fides. So just be the governor."

My advisers had helped me develop a series of responses to any question that fell within one of the big-message categories of the campaign. One of those categories was law and order. Jan went after me almost from the start on that subject. She noted that my budget director, during my drive to slash state spending, had proposed an early-release program for low-level and white-collar prisoners. She also leveled a charge, which she also used in one of her TV ads, that inmates in our state prisons had cable TV. The implication was that I was mollycoddling the inmates.

I began my rebuttal by listing my law-enforcement credentials: that I had served as a peace officer, deputy district attorney, justice of the peace, and two terms as Clark County DA, and that my candidacy for governor was supported by all the major law-enforcement agencies in the state. This established a great level of credibility by the time I got to directly answering Jones's attacks. Whatever I said at that point didn't matter all that much, in fact, because it would be perceived by viewers as a well-considered point made by a true-blue crime-and-punishment proponent. But I pointed out that there was no way I ever would allow the release of dangerous criminals back to society. "Some of these people I actually put in jail," I said. As for the cable TV access in prisons, it was provided to comply with a federal mandate.

Jan also attacked me as the candidate of the gaming industry, a man whose parents had been part of that industry. I cut that discussion right off by saying I would not engage in defending my family and that I was offended by anyone bringing my family into this political debate. And when Jan hit me on how much campaign funding I'd received from the gaming industry, I pointed out that the gaming industry is the number-one employer in the state of Nevada, and the greatest revenue generator, and the casinos' contributions to my campaign were not disproportionate to their participation in the state.

When my car pulled into campaign headquarters afterward, I bounced out of the backseat and high-fived Billy V. so hard it nearly took his arm off. I knew I'd done great. It was one of those "I showed all of you" moments.

Billy V. told me I'd come out of the debate looking like the governor, while Jan Jones had appeared more like someone who just wanted my job. I'll never forget my feeling of elation after that debate. The sad truth is that I usually was my own worst critic, ruminating over things I should have said during a campaign appearance, and even brooding to the point of misery over how I'd left out a key point, or stumbled in my delivery, or had worn a jacket that was ill-fitting and puffy. There was always something troubling me.

But at least on that night, I felt good about the outcome. I thought to myself that I wished my parents, whose humble beginnings and hard work had put me in this position, could have been here tonight. I think they would have been proud of me. There wasn't much time to savor this feeling, though. I'd been through enough campaigns to know that anything can happen. The only certainty is that there are no certainties.

Election Day was still a long way off. Surprises would be in store.

My second televised debate with Jan Jones was held at the University of Nevada, Reno, sponsored by public-TV affiliate KNPB Channel 5. Jan was behind in the polls. If that weren't enough to spur her to go on the offensive, she was furious about a story that had appeared on the front page of the *Las Vegas Review-Journal* that very morning.

It seems that as mayor, Jan had vowed not to cast any of her votes on the city council on matters involving the interests of any of the contributors to her campaign. Of the hundreds of votes during her term to date, a few inevitably had concerned the dealings of her contributors. They were not major issues, things like maybe a zoning change from commercial to residential, and she had not been strident in mustering the votes of other council members to gain a majority. Nevertheless, the press took note, perhaps with a little help from my campaign. The headline over the *Review-Journal*'s story that morning read: "Jones' Votes Aid Contributors."

Once the TV camera lights went on in the stifling Reno studio, Jan came out aggressively, charging that our race had veered away from thoughts and ideas into dirty politics and character assassination. Soon we were engaged in a heated debate, and I mean that literally. Somehow, the air-conditioning system went out in the university's cinder-block building. It was summer in Reno, and the stifling warmth inside the studio, made worse by the blazing production lights on the set, threatened to take its toll on Jan and me, like boxers wilting under oppressive ring temperatures.

As taxing as the conditions were for me, they were far more unbearable for Jan. Veteran on-air personality that she was, she wore a fair amount of makeup. During the final twenty minutes of the debate, her face appeared as if it had melted. This predicament would have bothered anyone, and Jan seemed shaken. In contrast, nonflashy Bob Miller, with his average looks and minimal makeup, just kept on going in the same even-keeled mode, although sweltering in his suit.

At the conclusion, Jan seemed almost to collapse into the arms of some of her nearby staff. Some less charitable observers described it as the "the great meltdown." They had no clue; Jan and I had endured a veritable pressure cooker in the studio. She had been ready to faint.

My margin of victory in the primary that September was sizable: 63 percent to Jan's 28. With the campaign behind us, Jan and I became good friends. She called me to say she was sorry our race had gotten negative and that she knew I was a decent person and had Nevada's best interests at heart. I felt the same about her. As Las Vegas mayor, she supported the programs I pushed through the legislature the following two sessions. And I recognized how much more difficult it is to be gracious when you are on the short end.

The GOP contender in the general election was Jim Gibbons, a three-term state assemblyman from Reno.

On paper, Gibbons was a formidable candidate in Nevada. He was forty-nine, a Sparks native, and highly educated, having earned a bachelor's degree in geology and a master's in mining geology from the University of Nevada, Reno, and a law degree from Southwestern University

School of Law, in Los Angeles. He sported a varied résumé: hydrologist, mining geologist, mining and water-rights attorney, and three-term Nevada assemblyman. Gibbons also was a decorated military veteran. He'd flown combat missions in Vietnam while serving in the air force, and again in the Persian Gulf War as a member of the Nevada Air National Guard.

Gibbons was a staunch conservative, with a regular-guy image that played well with many Nevadans. His pickup truck bore a bumper sticker declaring FIGHT CRIME—SHOOT BACK. In 1993, he and his wife, Dawn, had authored the Gibbons Tax Restraint Initiative and collected 85,000 signatures from Nevadans to place a question on the 1994 ballot aimed at amending the state constitution to require a two-thirds vote in the legislature before a state tax could be increased.

Gibbons captured the Republican primary over Secretary of State Cheryl Lau in handy fashion, getting 51 percent of the vote to Lau's 32. Lau was an Asian-American who had some recognition in national Republican circles. Her campaign was overseen by Sig Rogich, who had run my first campaigns. Her husband, Garth Dull, ironically, was my secretary of transportation. I never held it against him that his wife had run for my seat, but I am certain he must have felt he was in an awkward position.

Jim Gibbons, and his wife, surely were ambitious. The first time Sandy and I met them had been a few weeks into my tenure as acting governor. Jim had just been elected to the assembly for the first time, and he and Dawn were among the guests attending the traditional reception for lawmakers at the governor's mansion on the opening day of the legislature. Sandy and I greeted guests as they came through the front door. Dawn exclaimed, "I want to live here someday."

Sandy, at that early juncture of our life in the mansion, thought to herself that she wouldn't mind not living in the mansion. After all, she was overworked with adapting to the role of first lady while also being mother to two teenagers and settling her family into a huge house. She still didn't even know where half her wardrobe was located.

Dawn Gibbons's comment may have sounded impertinent. But to Sandy and me, it surely was understandable. It's human nature to let one's imagination run in such a setting.

As fate would have it, Dawn Gibbons would have to wait another twelve years, until 2006, before moving into the governor's mansion as the first lady of Nevada. In the general election, helped by a late disclosure about a problem with Gibbons's campaign finance reporting, I prevailed with 53 percent of the vote to her husband's 41.*

---

* Gibbons would be elected to succeed Kenny Guinn. His single term was full of controversy, including the eventual divorce from Dawn. He became the only governor in Nevada history defeated in his bid for reelection during his own primary by Nevada's present governor, Brian Sandoval.

25

Taking on the Gaming Industry

Five years before the millennium, Nevada was a much different state than it was a half century earlier when Ross Miller's son came into the world. The dusty town the Millers had arrived in those many years ago was now over a million people. The Strip, once populated by mostly one-story, nondescript edifices, was now a neon-bursting international tourist draw, with tens of millions of visitors arriving at one of the busiest airports in the country. The state was booming, its largest city was thriving, and a son of a gambling man, who could never have imagined it all, was on track to being the longest-serving governor in history.

As a second-term governor, I had two legislative sessions left in which to leave my mark on state laws. One issue that had been near and dear to my heart since my days in the Clark County District Attorney's office was truth in sentencing. As the saying went, "If you do the crime, you do the time." But instead of serving out the sentence, convicts in Nevada were being released in half of a term, or less. Some were earning one day lopped off a sentence for every day served without incident behind bars.

I planned to introduce a special bill on truth in sentencing that I would lobby for in the 1995 Legislature. I also moved to create an Advisory Commission on Sentencing to review our state's criminal-sentencing struc-

215

ture for adults and juveniles. In my State of the State address in January 1995, I said I would direct this commission "to establish absolute, nonnegotiable prison terms. When a judge sentences a felon to five to ten years, it means five years and not a day less. And, if there is no rehabilitation, he'll do the ten years. Everyone will then know just what the sentence meant."

The 1995 session also gave me an opportunity to show that I was my own man in a state dominated by the casino industry, which had made my father's career and backed mine with money. I had always believed that part of a governor's role was to protect the vibrancy of the industry, but not allow the casinos to overreach. In 1995, they went too far.

The Las Vegas Hilton tried to persuade state lawmakers to introduce a bill capping jury awards to hotel guests for negligence due to inadequate security. The affair grew out of the infamous Tailhook convention of 1991, which had been held at the Hilton.

The Tailhook Association is a private organization whose members are active, reserve, or retired navy or marine aviators, plus defense contractors and others associated with naval aviation. Their thirty-fifth annual symposium was held over the first weekend in September at the Las Vegas Hilton. An estimated five thousand people attended, including four thousand navy or marine corps aviation officers. Tailhook had a tradition of drunken rowdiness by its attendees, but the gathering on this particular year may have included more unrestrained and outright degenerate behavior than others. Many of the pilots had returned from combat duty in the Gulf War and were looking to blow off steam. At the same time, the military was being downsized due to the end of the Cold War, and career pilots were stressed out about the possibility of losing their jobs. With that, many male officers who saw the aviation fraternity as the exclusive domain of their gender felt hostility toward the movement to allow women to fly combat missions. Mix in heavy drinking, and you had the makings for a free-fire zone with women as the targets of opportunity for despicable treatment.

Not much would have been made of what amounted to assaults on more than eighty female officers at the convention had not one of these women, a thirty-year-old decorated helicopter pilot, Lt. Paula Coughlin, blown the whistle and filed a complaint to her superior officers. The officers initially ignored her story about being groped, fondled, and severely frightened by a group of male officers in a third-floor corridor. Other victims of misconduct at Tailhook '91 refused to testify at first.

But Coughlin followed up by securing legal counsel to sue the Tailhook Association, the Las Vegas Hilton, and its holding company, Hilton Hotels Corp., alleging there was inadequate hotel security on the night she was attacked. She sought punitive damages. The national media began publicizing her crusade, and the navy had a major scandal on its hands. The Hilton had a potentially costly lawsuit to contend with.

In the wake of the attack, Coughlin suffered psychological problems, including post-traumatic stress disorder, which hampered her work performance. She knew her military career could be jeopardized if she filed an official complaint about the attack. But even though her superiors initially ignored her grievance, she pressed ahead. Other women eventually came forward with testimony following Coughlin's whistle-blowing, saying they also were attacked in the third-floor gauntlet of chanting, leering male officers. Some of these women reported that male officers threw them to the floor, pulled off their underwear, and molested them; many said that when they resisted, the assaults grew fiercer and they were called names such as "whore" and "bitch."

Coughlin's lawyers settled with the Tailhook Association for $400,000. The trial for the lawsuit against the Hilton and its parent company was held in U.S. District Court in Las Vegas. In October 1994, a jury awarded Coughlin $6.7 million, which the judge reduced by $1.5 million.

Hilton's lawyers appealed the case. And the hotel's executives decided to see what relief they could secure from Nevada's lawmakers, who would be convening for the 1995 legislative session.

Thanks to Hilton's lobbying, the Nevada Senate, by a 15–2 vote, passed Senate Bill 474, which would have prevented hotels from being liable for damages for injuries to guests resulting from a lack of security. SB 474 became known as the "Tailhook Bill," because it contained a clause that would retroactively apply to suits in which a final judgment had not been reached. That included Paula Coughlin's suit, which was under appeal, because the date of retroactivity included in the bill was just before the Tailhook '91 convention.

SB 474 was on its way over to the assembly. But the bill's backers would soon learn they had more to contend with than getting a majority vote in that half of the legislature.

One of the victims of Tailhook '91 had been in my office to speak with me. I already was ashamed and outraged by what had happened at that convention. For one, it gave a black eye to Nevada's chief industry, especially since the Hilton was a prominent property among Las Vegas hotels. One of my core beliefs is that gaming and tourism is key to our state's prosperity. But the reprehensible behavior suffered by the victims of the Tailhook convention, and the violation of their personal rights, stirred the prosecutor's ire in me.

On top of that, the casino industry's attempt at getting an ex-post-facto law passed in the legislature relating to a judgment in a civil trial was wantonly wrongheaded.

When news reached me that SB 474 had cleared the Senate, I couldn't contain my wrath and indignation. There was no way I was going to permit this heinous piece of legislation from seeing the light of day. I was going to quash it, quickly.

My first call was to Billy Vassiliadis. This was a preemptive strike. Billy was a key lobbyist for the gaming industry, and had the Las Vegas Convention & Visitors Authority and the Nevada Resort Association as clients. As was Billy's custom, he didn't personally get involved in the lobbying at the legislature until the session was nearing its end. Then he'd come up from Las Vegas to Carson City and see that lobbying efforts were wrapped up.

Well, he was about to be involved in unwrapping a lobbying effort.

I reached Billy as he was driving toward Carson in a rented car after landing at the airport in Reno.

I told him, "This is ridiculous. You better get that damned bill out of there. You go talk to your clients. This thing is going to become a national story."

I explained that the bill put Nevada in a position to be viewed as a state completely controlled by gaming interests, who could get whatever they wanted on the law books, where guests weren't protected in their hotels, and where it was OK to harass women.

Before Billy had a chance to get to the Capitol Building in Carson, I'd already called the chief gaming lobbyists into my office for a closed-door meeting. I explained to them, in no uncertain terms, that I would veto any such bill that came within a mile of my desk. No one left the meeting wondering where I stood, or what my intentions were.

In the end, lawmakers in the assembly removed the retroactivity clause from the bill. The issue has never come up again.

Throughout my ten years as governor I had gotten increasingly involved in the National Governors Association just as I had previously with the National District Attorney Association. In the summer of 1995, I was elected vice chairman of the association for a one-year term until the following summer, when I became chairman of the NGA for the next twelve months. During this time the Congress and White House were mired in partisan battles over welfare and Medicaid reforms. The Governors Association had always acted by consensus based on the experience that compromise and practicality were essential to our jobs in our respective states. We chose six of us, three from each party, to find acceptable compromises that would work with the Clinton White House* and the Congress. Ultimately we reached a consensus, which helped move federal legislation forward.† I can't say that NGA is nonpartisan, but overall solutions to national issues seem to reach bipartisan solutions more often than in the nation's capital.

---

* The White House liaison was chief of staff Leon Panetta. Leon, like me, was a Santa Clara alumnus.

† Much of the work was done by our staffs. In my case that was then chief of staff Jim Mulhall and deputy chief Nicole Lamboley, who is now my son's chief of staff.

It was also during my final term that I received a call from my friend John Walsh. This time it was he asking for my help instead of the other way around. He had been hosting the highly successful Fox network show *America's Most Wanted* for over seven years but in the fall of 1995 Fox decided to pull the show off the air. I was glad to help a friend but I also believed that *AMW* was a valuable program in aiding law enforcement. I contacted the National District Attorneys Association and at my request Nevada attorney general Frankie Sue Del Papa did the same with the AG's, both resulting in letters from the associations urging Fox to keep the show. I also spoke individually to all the governors, thirty-seven of whom signed a letter of support. Some six weeks later, John held a press conference to which I and a couple of others were invited, during which he announced that the show would return to the air. It was a good feeling not only to help him but in so doing to preserve a TV program that was performing a noble public service. He singled me out as the person most responsible. I doubt that was accurate but I felt very pleased to have played a role.

26

Your Excellency?

In late 1997, staff members in President Clinton's administration began floating my name as a potential appointment as U.S. ambassador to Mexico. During my years as governor I had developed many friends in Mexico* and had taken several trips there. As a Western governor, I had been to Mexico City to meet with President Salinas and later President Zedillo. And I had been the only governor to accompany the president during his official visit to meet with President Zedillo.† I had been very active, as well, in working with President Clinton to develop support among the nation's governors for his decision to provide financial assistance to Mexico during a time of financial crisis.

I certainly was excited at the possibility of returning to Mexico as the

---

* My son, Ross, would spend his first college year attending Monterrey Tech University while living with the parents of Adrianna Bremer, the wife of my good friend Carlos Bremer. In addition to studies, Ross played on their national champion basketball team, traveling throughout the country to play other universities.

† The official welcome ceremony was on a polo field in central Mexico City. The conclusion was to be a parade of assembled military in period costumes. As the commanding general came forward, he asked permission for the assembled forces to parade in review in honor of "President William" and after a long pause he concluded with "president of the United States." I believe in an effort to remember the president's middle name of "Jefferson" he forgot "Clinton." It was the momentary lapse I believe everyone has on occasion but at the worst possible time for him.

U.S. ambassador. So, too, was the lieutenant governor. That is, Lonnie Hammargren,* an eccentric neurosurgeon who held the number two post, saw a chance for moving into the governor's mansion as acting governor, finishing out the remainder of my term. He went so far as to tell a newspaper reporter that "Lonnie's luck" would work its magic, meaning that the U.S. Senate would confirm the president's nomination of me, and Lonnie would become acting governor.

But either Hammargren's fortunes were off, or some other force was at work, because the idea of my being named ambassador to Mexico eventually seemed to stall.

I couldn't figure out the reason why until I began hearing rumors that North Carolina Sen. Jesse Helms, chairman of the Senate Foreign Relations Committee, had something to do with it. In the meantime, I had support from many individuals, including some influential Republicans, among them governors and former Nevada U.S. senator Paul Laxalt, the latter who went so far as to call Helms's office to see if the resistance was emanating from him. Laxalt was assured that the source of the resistance was not Helms.

A few months later, I was back in New York when I got a call from President Clinton's chief of staff, Erskine Bowles. "I'm sorry," he said. "We've got a problem with Helms."

Without ever hearing the specifics, I withdrew my name from consideration and went about my business.

Several months later, Bill Clinton was in Las Vegas. On our way together to an event he spontaneously asked me if I wanted to be the next ambassador to Argentina. I told him I was flattered, but I wasn't sure if it was the right fit for my family and me. I said I'd think about it. Then I added, "Why wouldn't Jesse Helms have the same problem with me in Argentina that he had in Mexico?"

---

* In Nevada, governors and lieutenant governors are elected separately. In my first full term the lieutenant governor was Sue Wagner, a moderate Republican who had served as a state senator previously. We worked well together and when she decided not to seek reelection I selected her to serve on the State's Gaming Commission, which oversees our primary industry. Hammargren had been elected to serve during my final four years. In the primary he had defeated, among others, my close friend Bruce Layne.

The president smiled. "Because Jesse Helms only promised Chic Hecht that he would screw you out of Mexico," he said.

So that explained it!

Helms was an ideological soul mate with Hecht, Nevada's one-term U.S. senator, from their time serving as the two most conservative solons on Capitol Hill. Apparently, their bond of friendship, formed as partners riding the political fringe, continued after Chic left Capitol Hill.

It was still fresh in Chic's mind how I'd responded to the attacks with press conferences in Las Vegas and Reno at which prominent law-enforcement leaders had forcefully spoken in my defense as a man of character whose record as a district attorney had been unimpeachable. Those press conferences had helped torpedo Hecht's campaign comeback, leading to his ultimate defeat.

Now, nine years later, Chic had called on old pal Jesse for a personal favor: to keep Bob Miller from getting an ambassadorship. But, on the bright side, I was still on track to be in the history books as Nevada's longest-serving governor, although I had little warning of a health crisis that would threaten that possibility.

In October 1996, during a routine physical examination, my personal physician and longtime friend, Dr. Elias Ghanem of Las Vegas, checked my prostate. That was standard procedure, since I was fifty-one.

Ghanem possessed uncommon diagnostic skills, which was one of the reasons he had so many high-profile patients, such as President Clinton's mother and Elvis Presley. When the results of my prostate-specific antigen ("PSA") blood test came back, Elias didn't like them and ordered me to take an ultrasound. The images showed no problems but he still was concerned, so he ordered a biopsy. This was performed by a urologist in Las Vegas.

A few days later, I was in Las Vegas. Lt. Angelo Webster, the state trooper who headed the governor's security detail, was behind the wheel as we were driving. Good thing it wasn't me who was driving, as it turned out.

With a free space in my schedule, I got on my cell phone and called the urologist's office for the results.

"Well, did you talk to Elias?" he asked.

"No," I said.

"Well, it's positive," he said. "Come in tomorrow."

I stared at my mobile phone, thunderstruck.

I hadn't been experiencing any of the well-known and recognizable symptoms of discomfort associated with the disease. But, as I would come to learn, many men who develop prostate cancer never even know it. I also would learn that prostate cancer is the most common cancer in U.S. men, and that it kills more men in this country than any cancer except lung cancer.

I still felt relatively young and vigorous, but I was over fifty. Prostate cancer most often strikes men above that age mark. I was fortunate, though, in that my cancer was detected early. The immediate medical concern was that, like any cancer, the mutated cells could spread elsewhere, including to the lymph nodes or bones.

The urologist recommended surgery. He had an opening the following week. He outlined his treatment plan. I thought about it, and balked. For one, I didn't care for his bedside manner. Two, common sense told me I needed a second opinion.

I spoke with Elias, and he arranged for me to speak with specialists in California. He accompanied me on the trip. I found the consultations very valuable, and was relieved I'd sought them. The specialists told me that surgery wasn't advisable right after a biopsy had already cut into the prostate tissue. They explained that cancerous prostate cells are slow moving, so surgery could be scheduled when most convenient. What's more, they said, there were treatment options other than surgery to consider. None of this had been discussed with me by the urologist in Vegas.

Still, after undergoing additional tests and consulting with several doctors, I saw that surgery was the best option. It would remove the threat. And because I was in reasonably good shape, I stood to recuperate fairly quickly. I wouldn't be off the job long at all. That was important to me: I saw no need to have the unpredictable Lt. Gov. Hammargren take the helm, even for a few days.

I really liked one of the physicians I'd met, Dr. Stuart Holden. "Skip" was medical director of the Prostate Cancer Foundation, established by financier Michael Milken, a prostate-cancer survivor himself. Skip also was a urological oncologist practicing at Cedars-Sinai Medical Center in Los Angeles. Elias agreed that Skip would be an excellent choice. What's more, Elias said, "If we get you to California, we'll get you away from the press a bit, and you'll have a little more privacy. It's a tough recuperation, initially."

I firmed up my mind. Skip Holden would be removing the cancerous cells.

Once my plans were made, I called a press conference. It would have been impossible to keep my surgery secret, and I wouldn't have wanted to anyway. I was governor, so my physical condition was a public matter, not a private one. Nevadans needed to know that their governor was going under the knife, but that the procedure wasn't risky and would not impair my ability to serve as I recovered. What's more, my diagnosis was an opportunity to spread the word to other men my age to be sure to have their prostates checked annually.

At the press conference, I announced my situation and told reporters that, while I would have to take some time off, I wanted to reassure the public that I believed I could continue on in the office effectively. I tried to answer all the questions to the best of my ability. I spoke about the PSA test. I also mentioned the "DRE" exam. That led to a hilarious moment. One of the newspaper reporters innocently asked, "Could you explain in more detail what a digital rectal exam is?" I wish I had a photo of the faces of the other reporters in the room: they were dumbfounded. But I did offer to answer the question off-line after the press conference.

The news that I'd be having the surgery performed at Cedars-Sinai created an additional angle for news coverage: Why was Nevada's governor going out of state for medical treatment? One newspaper article included quotes criticizing my decision. And who was the source? None other than the Las Vegas urologist I'd declined to use. The article didn't mention that I'd rejected his treatment.

I bit my tongue when I heard of the criticism. It was typical of the kind of public response you get when you're in public office. Anyone with an agenda, or a need to gripe, often can find a way to take a public figure to task for some personal event or action.

When given a choice of getting the best medical treatment possible, or risking something less than that just to avoid getting eviscerated in the media, I think any sane person would choose the former option. On the positive side, I had an awful lot of people in Nevada praying for me. (Some of this may have had to do with Lonnie Hammargren being the lieutenant governor.)

The surgery to remove my prostate gland and the tumor within was successful, and my recuperation went well. I conducted a meeting of the state Board of Examiners over the phone the day after surgery. This was to demonstrate that I was capable and coherent, and there was no need for concern by anyone about my ability to run the state from my hospital bed or my recuperation bed back home.

I spent a few days in the hospital, but the rest of my recovery was at the governor's mansion. My staff members wondered how I'd be able to handle having to spend the required three weeks in recovery mode. After all, they'd sometimes joked about my resistance to treating ailments—about how I'd come back to the office, after playing basketball at lunchtime, with a bloodstain forming on a leg of my suit trousers because I'd skinned my knee on the court but neglected putting a bandage on the scrape.

A few months after the surgery, I tried to play in a charity basketball game and felt like I'd pulled a muscle. I found out that it was a bit more serious; my left hip was deteriorating and I was going to need hip surgery.

I considered that this may have been caused by a slight imbalance in the lengths of my legs, caused by my "football injury." This was the fracture all those years ago, in the eighth grade, when I'd tripped in my cleats while running across the street to the team bus. As I continued growing, my left leg ended up a tiny bit shorter than my right.

The hip surgery could (and did) wait until I was out of office. But my basketball days ended then and there. The doctor told me my condition probably came from jumping during all the basketball I had played.

I told him that his hypothesis was ridiculous: "I never left the ground."*

---

* The pinnacle of success of my basketball endeavors probably occurred at the unlikely age of forty-seven when I was named the MVP of a charity basketball game against members of the then L.A. Raiders professional football team. Photographs would seem to suggest that I actually did leave the ground at least that night.

27

The End of My Political Career, the Beginning of a New Life

With the 1997 legislative session behind me and my final years as governor approaching in 1998, I'd felt a subtle downshift in my duties. I was a lame-duck governor with little more than a year left on his term. There was plenty still to do in running state government, but the pressure didn't seem as intense. I focused on preparing for a transition to my successor. My chief of staff, Catherine Cortez Masto, prepared a book outlining as many details as would be helpful to the new administration. We also raised private funds to renovate the over one-hundred-year-old mansion. The concept came from Las Vegas businessman Larry Ruvo, and he and Sig Rogich helped identify donors to allow the house to have separated public and private areas. Sandy's high school classmate Tony Marnell, who had designed and built many Las Vegas hotels, assigned his assistant, Lee Cagley. By the time the Guinns moved in, it was remodeled. By then the population of Nevada was closing in on two million people, and much had changed since I took over almost a decade earlier—much less since 1955, when Ross Miller transplanted his family from Chicago.

In my final year as governor, with the remaining months of my term drawing short, I'd realized it would be strange leaving the job after ten years. I was still a young man when I became governor; now I was a father of three, with two children in college, and very much in middle age.

I began interviewing with law firms and sought one that would be flexible in my caseload and in giving me time to pursue outside interests. The firm I settled on was Jones Vargas, whose partners did, indeed, grant me the freedom I desired. Jones Vargas was headquartered in both Las Vegas and Reno and its atmosphere was relaxed. Ironically, Jones Vargas's president was an old familiar face to me: Joe Brown, my opponent in the bitter election for lieutenant governor fourteen years earlier. But politics is politics, and business is business. From my years as governor, I knew a great many people throughout the state, and was expected to bring clients to the firm.

In addition to Jones Vargas I also joined a national bipartisan public policy company. Dutko Worldwide had primary offices in Washington, D.C., while I ran a small office in Nevada. My focus was on state and local issues and interaction with the National Governors Association (NGA), where I had formed and chaired an association of past governors.

Serving on corporate boards also seemed to be a good fit. I accepted invitations to serve on the boards of a variety of companies, including America West Airlines, Newmont Mining Corp., Zenith National Insurance Co., International Game Technology, and Wynn Resorts.

The irony did not escape me. Ross Miller did everything he could to put his son on a career path that would not involve the business he had chosen. But not only had his son taken a job that put him in constant contact with the captains of that industry, he now was a de facto member of the gaming clan.

Less than a year and a half after I had returned to private life, I got a phone call from Dick Bryan. He told me he wasn't going to seek a third term in the U.S. Senate. He wanted me to be one of the first people to know, in case I was interested in tossing my hat in the ring for the election that fall. Ever the loyal party man, Dick wanted me to seek the seat he was leaving.

I could understand. The Senate in 2000 was fairly evenly divided between Democrats and Republicans, and that meant every election for a seat was important in the battle for a majority and the clout to shape national affairs. The Democrats needed a strong candidate to run in 2000. Because of my résumé, I fit the bill. And because it was a Senate seat, I started getting calls right away from people encouraging me to run.

Some of the callers knew of me by name only. These included representatives of constituency groups, and senators from other states. But within twenty-four hours of Dick's first call to me, Vice President Al Gore phoned from a plane over South America. Within forty-eight hours, I'd gotten calls from Tipper Gore, Hillary Clinton, and President Clinton. These were people whom I respected, and who had helped me over the years, who wanted me to run, and gave good reasons why. I certainly wasn't going to ignore requests from them. And I didn't. I gave it a lot of serious thought. I discussed it extensively with my family.

Nevada senator Harry Reid even called my son, Ross, at his dorm room at Stanford, explaining he believed I would win the campaign without much difficulty and wanting to put Ross at ease that it wouldn't be that hard to cope with negative attacks on our family during the campaign. Harry added that he and I could be a fantastic team on Capitol Hill, and that I, as a conservative Democrat, could be very effective in Congress in bridging the gap with the Republicans.

One morning during this time, my secretary walked into my office with a curious look on her face.

"Michael Douglas called you," she said. "He called from a movie set where he's filming. He's going to call you back."

Indeed, the famous actor and director did phone. His raspy voice, familiar to me from his movies, was full of sincerity and passion as he told me how the Democrats really needed me to run for the Senate, and that I could make a difference, and that he was going to support me and help raise money for my campaign and get others he knew in Hollywood to support me. It was hard for me not to feel flattered.

"Bob," he continued, in a tone that conveyed camaraderie, "it's obvious you're the man we need at this critical time."

"I appreciate this very much," I said. "And I'm just curious, have we ever met?"

"No," he said, "but I've been an admirer of yours for some time, and I know all about you."

After we hung up, I imagined him standing on a movie set between scenes, prepping for this call, and telling actress Sharon Stone, "Hold that, I have to read up more on Miller for a minute." What a great guy.

I decided someone high up in the Democratic Party or the Senate asked Douglas to call this guy Miller out in Nevada and talk him into running.

As I continued wrestling with whether to run for the Senate, my close friend and adviser Billy Vassiliadis put it all in perspective for me:

"You are a manager. You like to make decisions. You are not going to like going back there as a freshman member in the minority party, spending six to seven hours a day with your ever-famous hand-on-chin pose, listening to hours and hours of testimony. You're not going to be on the rock-star committees, something you're really going to care about, because, again, you'll be a freshman member. And you're going to be among more than four hundred other people in Congress who can say no to anything you propose. You could get a bill through the Nevada Legislature in sixty days, but Dick Bryan says it took four or five years to get car air-bag legislation through Congress. And you have less patience than he does!

"How in God's name are you going to be happy? You've given the last twenty years of your life to public service. You have a right to enjoy some part of your life. It's not like you'll love living in D.C. You love Nevada, you love the state. You could have moved any dozens of times for professional reasons if you wanted to. Why would you want to join the Senate? What are you going to fulfill?"

Sandy and I and the family discussed the possibility. For her it was desirable to have me in the Senate to pursue the values and issues we shared. However, it also meant, if successful, moving away from Nevada for six or more years, which was not as desirable. Ross and Corrine were pursuing higher education and Megan had yet to be a teenager. It seemed better to provide them the stability of parents in the private sector and in Nevada.

I called Dick Bryan and told him I wasn't going to run. I knew my life was going in a different direction now. I considered that, as governor, you make decisions and implement them. You're a chief executive. But as a U.S. senator, you're one of a hundred. One of the pitches I was getting to persuade me to run was that I'd shown in my dealings with the Nevada Legislature and as chairman of the National Governors Association that I worked well with Republicans, and that would be an invaluable skill in Congress. I thought about the contentious environment of Capitol Hill. Yeah, right, there was an incentive to run!

I'd come to the realization that I had no desire to spend the rest of my working days in politics. I loved living in Nevada, preferred living in Nevada, and believed I'd done a lot of public service and it was time to do something different. Spend six years of my life in Washington? Or twelve? Or, my gosh, eighteen? It didn't appeal to me. I issued a press release saying I wasn't going to run for Dick Bryan's seat. The phone calls ceased.

A month or two later, I was attending a boxing card at a Vegas hotel, and noticed that sitting in a row near ringside, about three seats in from the aisle, was none other than Michael Douglas, with his wife, actress Catherine Zeta-Jones. I couldn't resist. I walked down to the end of the aisle and casually stood there for several minutes.

My great admirer from Tinsel Town didn't even recognize me.

I have not thought much about returning to politics since Dick Bryan's call. My postgubernatorial life has not been boring and I have constantly found ways to keep myself stimulated. I also have visited places and met people that Ross Miller would never have dreamed of. I did return often to Mexico City along with my former assistant, Tony Sanchez, who had joined me at Jones Vargas. We explored on behalf of many of the Las Vegas casinos the prospect of legalized gaming in Mexico. Additionally I spent many years doing business in Bulgaria, of all places, after my former secretary of tourism and friend, Tom Tait, turned me on to the possibilities there. I accepted a request by the U.S. government to go to Bulgaria and discuss tourism potential. While there I became friends with a college president, Dr. Todor Radev, whose daughter Maria ended up coming to attend UNLV undergraduate and graduate schools while living with us for years. I was invited by Dr. Radev to return on vacation with my family, which I accepted and during that visit I met again with President Petar Stoyanov. He requested I ask President Clinton to come to Bulgaria, which no former U.S. president had ever done. I did mention it to President Clinton and ultimately accompanied him on his visit. This led to Tom Tait and me partnering with a Bulgarian, Maxim Behar, to do annual tourism conferences. During one such visit the deposed King of Bulgaria called Maxim and actually asked to meet with me. I thought, A king, me? King Simeon Saxe-Coburg-Gotha later formed his own party and became prime minister of Bulgaria. He is the first monarch to be elected to run a democracy. Eventually, the Bulgarian government named me as an honorary consul general. It also was through Tait and again the United States Aid to International Development (USAID) that I once spent some time with Mikhail Gorbachev. We discussed a tourism idea Tait had proposed called the Russian Heritage Highway. Ultimately Gorbachev and I were co-chairmen. At my invitation he came to Las Vegas to raise money for the foundation and to speak to one of the largest audiences ever at UNLV. I found Gorbachev to be a very interesting man. He understood English, but preferred speaking through a trusted interpreter. He proved to be charming and witty in person. I also admired him for his role in history. I can only smile thinking of what Ross Miller would have said.

I often wonder about that. I am not sure what my father, who traveled quite the literal and metaphorical distance from a bar in Chicago to the Las Vegas Strip, would have thought of his son, who went from a childhood spent in Sin City controlled by the mob to overseeing the modernization of a city and state as its longest-serving governor.

In one lifetime, Las Vegas went from being a little city far off in the Mojave that was a haven for organized crime and was scorned by mainstream

America, to a glittering, world-famous entertainment mecca and convention destination boasting multibillion-dollar properties funded by the foremost financial institutions. It went from disreputable to respectable, from pariah to pace-setting.

A Las Vegan no longer has to defend his or her hometown against disparaging remarks. Go anywhere in the world and say you're from Las Vegas today, and people's eyes will light up. Were my father to be transported to the present, the city's magnificent jump in stature, and its sheer growth, would have stunned him. Frankly, I can't help but marvel at the growth myself.

Flying into Las Vegas over the familiar interminable terrain of desolate desert, staring out the plane window at parched playas and jagged peaks, the sudden appearance of a grid of streets and houses and square green parks, the high-rise resorts on the Strip and downtown, the ribbons of freeway snaking through it all, the development stretching to the horizon, I'm constantly amazed at what's happened. I shake my head, remembering the modest town I'd first moved to in 1955.

Where our duplex stood on the outskirts is now lost in the midst of the city. You used to have to pack a lunch to drive out to Red Rock located on the mountains on the western side of the valley or other destinations outside town. Now residents live at Red Rock. Henderson, once separated by open space from the other populated parts of the valley, is no longer confined to the other side of Black Mountain; its development has stretched to meet Las Vegas. The whole valley has become populated.

In my childhood, no one took a walk along the Strip. The distance between hotels was great. Now, the three miles of sidewalks along the Strip are so packed with pedestrians visiting the megaresorts that locals avoid walking there.

And yet, the Las Vegas I found in the mid-twentieth century and the Las Vegas of the first decade of the twenty-first are alike in a lot of ways: growing fast, and dealing with the pains that come with that growth; powered by a tourist-based economy that promulgates a sexy image, and advertises it boldly; driven by several key players in charge.

In 1955, the population of Clark County was about 80,000 and the brand-new school district was on double sessions. Forty-five years later, Nevada's population was nearly 2 million, with some 1.3 million residents in Clark County. The Clark County School District had more than 300,000 students and was opening an average of one new school each month, and still was overcrowded.

The fact is, the mob's power in Vegas is a part of the city's history, but today it is only that. The relentless investigations and prosecutions of organized-crime figures by federal law-enforcement agencies, combined with the increasing vigilance of the Nevada Gaming Commission, finally crippled the underworld's control of various casinos in the 1970s and early '80s. The years-long campaign by the FBI, other federal agencies, and local law enforcement dealt lethal blows to organized crime in Vegas as key underground figures were identified, arrested, charged, and tried. The Nevada Gaming Commission's manual grew to several inches thick, outlining how to regulate the industry with everything from background checks of license applicants, to how resorts needed to handle casino takes.

The mob's last firm grip on Vegas casinos was broken amid hard-core federal investigations of organized crime and skimming, with an era-ending marker coming when the Stardust was sold to Boyd Gaming in 1985. Thought of as the swankiest resort on the Strip when I was growing up, and where I'd gotten canned from my first summer job as a snoozing busboy, the Stardust had symbolized the Chicago mob's presence on the Strip. No wonder it served as the model for "the Tangiers," the glittering gambling club depicted in the movie *Casino*. As if to add an exclamation point to the transition in time, the Stardust no longer exists, encased in the still-boarded-up Echelon Place, shuttered because of the Great Recession.

It is an era gone forever. The wise guys would be as out of place and ineffectual in today's corporatized and regulated casino industry as a pin-striped Bugsy Siegel would be on the trading floor of the New York Stock

Exchange. Scrutiny and security in the Nevada gaming industry are so stiff that casinos aren't even a good place for criminals to launder money.

The enduring mystique, and the public's fascination for crime, has spurred the creation of a repository for which the most fitting of all cities to host it is Las Vegas. The Mob Museum, which is located downtown, opened in 2010. Then-mayor Oscar Goodman (term-limited, he has now been succeeded by his wife, Carolyn) had pushed the idea of the nonprofit museum since his election, and negotiated the deal that let the city buy the old Federal Building for one dollar. A former FBI agent was recruited as a board member, and while the interactive exhibits will present the stories of the likes of Meyer Lansky and Moe Dalitz, and even Spilotro and Rosenthal, the vigorous and vigilant efforts of law enforcement to put the gangsters out of business will be highlighted, including displays on wiretaps.

While Las Vegas grows, so does the Strip, which generates most of the casino industry's take. Nevada's gross gaming winnings surpassed $2 billion in 1984, $3 billion in 1988, $4 billion in 1990, and have long since left the $10 billion-a-year mark in the rearview mirror. The Strip has changed greatly in appearance from when I was kid. Bellagio replaced the Dunes, Mandalay Bay replaced the Hacienda, the Venetian supplanted the Sands, Echelon Place will rise someday in place of the Stardust. The Greater Las Vegas Area as of 2012 has over 150,000 hotel rooms.

The industry has changed from what it was when my dad got involved in it. Instead of the intimate old showrooms, big stars appear in huge arenas, and highly computerized and stylized shows such as Cirque du Soleil and Broadway productions have for the most part replaced the old-fashioned production shows. While casinos still generate substantial profits, hotel corporations actually make more from nongaming operations such as food, rooms, entertainment, and shopping. They talked about luxury in Las Vegas in the 1950s, but now it's real luxury.

Take the Wynn Las Vegas. In 1998, Steve Wynn's Bellagio was the most expensive hotel ever built. In 2005, Steve Wynn topped it by opening a property with fewer rooms, 2,700 rooms in the $2.7 billion Wynn Las Vegas, with a full-service Ferrari and Maserati dealership, a huge art collection, a forty-five-story tower, and an eight-story mountain overlooking a three-acre lake. It's luxury in the extreme and simply gorgeous.

Some people lament the change. Some observers believe that Las Vegas has become incredibly expensive as a vacation destination, and they blame that on the departure of organized crime, whose operators kept rooms, meals, and entertainment cheap on the theory that the more guests in the house, the more gamblers, and the bigger win. When you adjust dollar prices for inflation, the premise that Vegas prices have skyrocketed is less true. But Nevada long since lost its national monopoly on legal gambling, and I don't mean just to Atlantic City, New Jersey. Today, forty-eight states have some form of gambling: bingo, card rooms, Indian casinos, lotteries, racetracks, riverboat casinos, or whatever else. Only Hawaii and Utah haven't joined that list.

With next-door California having Indian casinos and other gambling, Las Vegas properties can ill afford to concentrate exclusively on their casinos. So, yes, it is more expensive to visit there now, but you get a lot more different things for the dollar you spend. And those casinos do have stockholders to answer to, sometimes thousands of them, as opposed to the precorporate days when a few guys would get together and invest.

In fact, Wall Street influences have greatly affected Las Vegas. In 2000, Kirk Kerkorian's MGM took over Wynn's Mirage Resorts. In 2004, MGM Mirage swallowed Mandalay Resorts. Harrah's bought out the Rio, the Showboat, and Binion's. Caesars, the Hilton casinos, and Park Place were combined under one corporate umbrella. Locally, Boyd Gaming bought out Coast Casinos. It's been the age of the merger, and now private equity firms are stepping in.

The Las Vegas gaming industry has been in a constant state of evolution, and now the evolutionary wheels are spinning even faster. It's impossible for me to predict what the city will look like a decade from now. Going back two decades, who could have predicted the megaresort boom?

In his 2005 book, *Sharks in the Desert: The Founding Fathers and Current Kings of Las Vegas*, *Las Vegas Review-Journal* columnist John L. Smith pointed out that, in 1994, *Time* magazine designated Las Vegas "the All-American City." Smith also wrote how the rest of America's embrace of legalized gambling, and the pornography industry's spread to late-night television cable channels, finally rendered Las Vegas's image as a city of sin, with casinos and racy floor shows, as no longer that of "the outlaw city." Smith continued, "It had become a community that prospered because it remained intriguing and was able to constantly reinvent itself."

There is something seemingly indestructible about Las Vegas. Even the spread of legal casino gaming throughout the nation, and the emergence of glittering Vegas-like resort developments in various places around the world such as Macau, haven't interrupted the visitor count in Vegas from every year approaching or surpassing 40 million. Skeptics and critics saying the Vegas bubble will burst have so far been proved wrong. But there has hardly been complacency among Vegas business boosters.

In the early 2000s, the R&R Partners ad agency undertook, on behalf of its client, the Las Vegas Convention & Visitors Authority, a major project to rebrand Las Vegas as a tourist destination. Staffers spent about eighteen months surveying customers across the nation, in every demographic and in every geographic area that were markets for sending tourists to Vegas.

Two copywriters captured lightning in a bottle with five resonating words. The result was R&R's now famous campaign, begun in 2003, bearing the tagline, "What happens here, stays here." TV ads were full of suggestive innuendo about the carefree, and naughty, behavior that tourists engage in on Vegas trips.

But if it happens to be a place where you live and build a life for yourself and your family, it must be said that Las Vegas, and its state, Nevada, have offered my family, and thousands of others, a very special kind of freedom:

It's a freedom to make a new start, and to prosper in a way limited only by one's ambition, imagination, hard work, and, maybe, luck. Perhaps that's why Las Vegas has been the fastest-growing city, and Nevada the fastest-growing state, in the union during most of my children's lives.

Nevada's economy is more diversified today, and its standing among the fifty states is no longer that of a maverick or pariah. How can it be, with forty-eight of the states having some form of legalized gaming? And our rapid development proves our desirability as a place to call home. California equity migrants, retirees, young people seeking opportunities, and immigrants from beyond our borders continue to flock by the thousands not only to the booming Las Vegas metropolitan area but to the Reno-Carson–Lake Tahoe region. This has kept the Silver State at or near the top as the fastest growing in the union.

Nevada is much more respected than when I was growing up. There is recognition by the country at large that we've created a lot out of nothing. We may lack natural resources, but we've created a miracle in the desert.

A Nevadan, Harry Reid, is the U.S. Senate majority leader. In my children's generation, or the next, it is not inconceivable that a Nevadan may become president.

Wherever my parents are now, they must be assured that they made the right choice in moving our family out of Chicago to that little dusty and dry, sun-bleached desert town out West, more than a half century ago.

Epilogue

Ross Miller never told his son what to do with his life—although he may have given me a nudge or two toward law school. For my part, I was determined not to give his namesake a plan for what I wanted him to do. He would chart his own course.

As it happened, during college, my own son, Ross, explored politics on the national level as a White House intern over a summer and a semester of his junior year at Stanford. He worked under Thurgood Marshall Jr. (son of the famed Supreme Court justice) in the Office of Cabinet Affairs, which coordinated the president's policies.

Ross ended up pursuing two career courses. He enrolled at Loyola's law school, where I had gone, but he also pursued an MBA. He then returned to Las Vegas to work where his father had—the Clark County district attorney's office

Ross loved his job. But after five years in the DA's office, he questioned whether he should stay there for an entire career or move on to something new.

From time to time he'd thought about running for office, perhaps the Clark County Commission, or the Legislature, or even Congress. Two state constitutional offices especially appealed to him: attorney general and secretary of state. The latter would let him employ not only his legal background, but his business training. The secretary of state is charged with many functions, including overseeing voter registration, incorporation and business licensing, and the regulation of securities brokers. Ross saw the office as having great potential to be developed.

So Ross tossed his hat into the ring for the 2006 election for secretary of state. It seemed like the right race at the right time. The three-term incumbent, Dean Heller, was running for Congress. If any first-time candidate knew what he was getting into, it had to be Ross. He'd grown up in a political family. He'd watched his father endure six runs for office, from district attorney to governor. And since campaigning, as I've said, was a family affair, Ross himself had had to walk the walk and talk the talk.

He knew it would be grueling. But Ross also felt a very strong call to serve. Ross was a natural on the campaign trail, much more so than his father, and he would end up winning his first race against Danny Tarkanian, son of the legendary Runnin' Rebels coach Jerry Tarkanian. In 2010, despite a GOP surge across the country, Ross won reelection against a weak opponent. His name already is being floated for higher office and he thought about running for the Senate in 2012 before deciding against it. In July 2012, Ross was named president of the National Association of Secretaries of State.

Should he run for higher office one day, Ross won't be burdened by spurious attacks on his parents the way I had been, because of my dad's business background and my parents' ties to the gaming industry. My son was never alive to meet his grandfather, but he's heard a thing or two about him—and not just from me.

When Ross went to see Steve Wynn to ask for his help in his first campaign for secretary of state, the gaming mogul said, "So, Ross Miller is going to become a second-generation politician, huh? The first Ross Miller I knew is probably rolling over in his grave."

I doubt it. Ross Miller would be proud of what Ross Miller, the grandson of a gambling man, has chosen to do.

Index

Accardo, Tony ("Big Tuna"), 17, 18
accidents
  of Miller, Bob, 31
  of Miller, Ross, 10
accomplishments of, 130
acting governor, 151–63, 165–68, 198–99
  cabinet of, 153–54
  Craigie working with, 153–54, 157, 158,
    161, 166, 184
  transitional budget of, 153–54, 156–57
Advisory Commission on Sentencing,
  215
AFL-CIO, 177, 203
African-Americans, in Las Vegas
  community of, 181, 182, 186–89, 191,
    192
  as guests, 44
Air Force Reserve unit, 72
Aladdin, 63
All-American City, Las Vegas as, xiv,
  239
Ambassador Hotel, 73
America's Most Wanted, 130, 220
*The Anointed One: An Inside Look at Nevada
  Politics* (Ralston), 169
Argentina, ambassador to, 222
Armijo (photographer), 74
Army Reserve unit, 71

attorney, 95–96
  Clark County District Attorney, 2–3,
    106–10, 115, 127–29, 141
  deputy DA, 90, 91

bailiff, 87, 89
Bally's, 69
bar exam, 90
basic training, 71
basketball, 55–56
Becker, Patty, 204–5
Beckley, DeLanoy, Singleton and Jemison,
  141
Behar, Maxim, 234
Belafonte, Harry, 39, 46, 181
Bell, Rex, 118
Bellagio, 174, 237
Benedict, Al, 43
Bennett, Bill, 82
Berman, Davie, 19, 38
Berman, Susan, 38
Bible, Bill, 154
Bice, Todd, 198
Binion, Benny, 113–14
Binion, Ted, 114
Binion case, 137
Bishop, Joey, 46
Black Book, 51, 52, 95, 119, 125

243

Index

"Black Monday" stock market crash, 173
Blasko, Joe, 120, 123
Blevins, Rance, 114
blind date, 93–94
Blitzstein, Herbert ("Fat Herbie"), 123
Bluestein, Frank, 120
Bob Miller Middle School, 155
bosses, 44, 46
Bowles, Erskine, 222
Bowman, Dan, 114
Boyd Gaming, 238
Bray, Alan, 109
Bremer, Adrianna, 221
Bremer, Carlos, 221
brothel, 107
Brown, Joe, 134–39, 200, 230
Brown, Mahlon, III, 97
Brown, Seymour, 105–6
Bryan, Richard ("Dick")
  as governor, 131, 132–33, 139, 199
  senate campaign of, 1, 4, 5, 127–28,
    142–43, 145, 146
  senate seat of, 230, 232, 233
Buchanan, Bucky, 107–8, 109
budget
  transitional, 153–54, 156–57
  while governor, 174–78
building boom, in Las Vegas, 167, 173
Bulgaria, 233–34
busboy, at Stardust Resort & Casino,
  42–43

cabinet, of acting governor, 153–54
Caesar, Sid, 46
Caesars Palace, 79–80, 119, 174
Cafferata, Patty, 132
Cagley, Lee, 229
campaign
  of Bryan, 1, 4, 5, 127–28, 142–43, 145,
    146
  of Clinton, 195–96, 207
  for governor, 169–71, 203–13
  of Hecht, 142–43, 144, 145, 146
  of Jones, Jan, 199–202, 203, 204–11
  of Kennedy, Robert F., 73
  smear, 108, 109
  Vassiliadis during, 146, 205, 207, 208,
    210
Campbell, Ian James, 87–88

Campbell, Mike, 186
Carville, James, 196
Cashell, Bob, 131
Casino (Scorsese), 4, 120
casinos, 2, 20–21, 24. *See also specific casinos*
  customers in, 32
  lounge shows in, 32
  mega, 174
  Miller, Ross, in, 31–36, 37, 40
  security guards in, 49
  skimming in, 66–67, 111–13, 124
  on Strip, 17, 35, 40, 44
Chicago Outfit, 63
Chicago Syndicate, 17, 111
chief of staff, Craigie as, 153–54, 157, 158,
  161, 166, 184
childhood, 13–16
Circus Circus, 80–81, 103, 119, 174
Cirque du Soleil, 237
Citizens' Committee on Victim Rights,
  130
Civella, Carl, 112
Civella, Nick, 111, 112
Clark, Tony, 184
Clark County commissioners, 97–98
Clark County District Attorney, 2–3,
  106–10, 115, 141
  reelection for, 127–29
Clark County School District, 197, 236
Clark County Sheriff's Office, 49–50,
  86–87, 96, 168
class-size reduction proposal, 156–57, 161,
  196
Clinton, Bill, xiii–xiv, 219, 231, 234
  ambassador offer from, 221–22
  campaign of, 195–96, 207
Clinton, Hillary, 231
Coca, Imogene, 46
Cohen, Carl, 32
command center, during riots, 184, 185
Commission on Government
  Reorganization, 197
Conforte, Joe, 108
Corporate Gaming Act, 69
Coughlin, Paula, 216–18
Craigie, Scott, 161
  budget and, 176, 177
  as chief of staff, 153–54, 157, 158, 161,
    166, 184

during riots, 185
State of the State address and, 158
credentials, for governor, 168
Crime Victims Compensation Program, 130
crimes
  organized, 123
  of Spilotro, Tony, 123
Culinary Workers Union, 203–4
Cullotta, Frank, 123, 124
Cummings, John, 157
curfew, during riots, 186, 187, 189
customers, in casinos, 32
Cusumano, Joseph, 123
Cusumano, Samuel, 123

D Battery Army Reserve unit, 87
Dalitz, Moe, 237
Davino, Ernesto, 123
Davis, Sammy, Jr., 46, 181
Dawson, Richard, 39–40
death
  of Kennedy, Robert F., 74–75
  of Miller, Ross, 98–99
  of Spilotro, Tony, 125
  of Thomas, Carl, 113
Del Papa, Frankie Sue, 152, 199, 220
DeLuna, Carl, 111
democrats, 127, 128, 167–68
demonstrations, 178–79
Denton, Ralph, 52–54
Department of Justice's Organized Crime and Racketeering Section, 145
deputy DA, 90, 91
Desert Inn Country Club, 40, 41
destruction, during riots, 182–85
Dini, Joe, 160–61, 162
district attorney. See Clark County District Attorney
District Attorneys Association, 111
Dorfman, Allen, 3–4, 17, 80, 119–20
Dorfman, Paul ("Red"), 17, 19
Dors, Diana, 39–40
Douglas, Michael, 231–32, 233
Doyle, Coletta Jane ("the Irish Songbird"), 11–12, 13, 14, 110
Duckworth, George, 19
Dukakis, Michael, 143
Dull, Garth, 212

Duncan, Ruby, 44
Dunes, 51, 63, 237
Durst, Robert, 38
Dutko Worldwide, 230

education, 14, 26–27, 58
  bar exam, 90
  graduation, 90
  high school elections, 56–57
  law school, 70, 72, 85, 89, 90
  Law School Admission Test, 68
  Loyola Law School, 70, 79, 85–92
  Santa Clara University, 63–64, 65, 68, 70, 86, 87
Eisenhower, Dwight D., 77, 78
El Dorado Country Club, 76, 77
Elardi family, 203–4
electricity, restoration of, 191–92
eligibility, for governor, 195–202
Elliott, Walt, 204
Equal Rights Commission, 45
Europe on $5 a Day, 65–66
Europe trip, 65–66
Excalibur, 82, 174

Family Feud, 40
FBI's National Crime Information Center, 130
Fischer, Steve, 18
Fitzsimmons, Frank, 78
Flamingo, 18, 19, 39, 63, 69
Flanagan, Newman, 129
Foley, Roger, 67
Francine (dancer), 64
Franklin, George, 107, 109
Fremont, 112
Frontier Hotel & Casino, 203, 204

Gagnier, Bob, 177, 199
Gallaway, Jim, 170–71, 201
gambling, legalization of, 26
gaming, in Mexico, 233
Gaming Control Board, 28, 70, 127, 154, 205, 206
gaming industry, 1, 3, 52
  governor and, 215–20
  state's control of, 67
Garber, John, 59
Ghanem, Elias, 223–24, 225

Index

Gibbons, Dawn, 212–13
Gibbons, Jim, 211–13
Gibbons Tax Restraint Initiative, 212
Gold Rush Ltd., 123
golf, 82
Goodman, Oscar, 91–92, 111, 114, 120, 237
Gorbachev, Mikhail, 234
Gore, Al, 231
Gore, Tipper, 231
Gould, Elliott, 46
governor, xiii, 6, 147. *See also* acting
    governor
  Bryan as, 131, 132–33, 139, 199
  budgets and, 174–78
  campaign for, 169–71, 203–13
  credentials for, 168
  demonstrations and, 178–79
  eligibility for, 195–202
  gaming industry and, 215–20
  hiring freeze declared by, 178
  in legislative session, 177
  lieutenant, 131–39, 141, 142, 168
  support for, 167
Grable, Betty, 76
graduation, 90
Greenbaum, Gus, 18, 19, 29, 38–39
Greene, Shecky, 32–33
Greenspun, Brian, 207
Greenspun, Hank, 68
Greenspun, Myra, 207
growth, in Las Vegas, 154–56
Guinn, Kenny, 197, 213, 229

Hammargren, Lonnie, 222, 224
Harrah's, 238
Harris, Brian, 184, 185–86, 198
Harrison, Charlie, 75
Hart, Dan, 200, 204
Hawkins, Frank, 186, 187
Hecht, Jacob ("Chic"), 41, 223
  campaign of, 142–43, 144, 145, 146
  as senator, 1, 132, 133
Helldorado Days, 24
Heller, Dean, 242
Helms, Jesse, 132, 222–23
Hettinger, Karl, 88
Hickey, Dave, 64, 71
Hickory Room, in Riviera, 27, 28, 79
Hicks, John, 90–91

high school elections, 56–57
Hilton Hotels, 69, 238
hip surgery, 226–27
hippie movement, 65
hiring freeze, 178
Hoffa, Jimmy, 17, 37–38, 78, 80
Holden, Stuart ("Skip"), 225
Hole in the Wall Gang, 120, 123, 124
Holt, George, 106, 107, 115
honorable discharge, 72
Hoover, J. Edgar, 52
Hope, Bob, 76
Horn, Nicholas, 176
Horseshoe Casino, 113–14
Humphrey, Hubert, 45
Hunterton, Stan, 5, 145–46

illegal bookmaker, Miller, Ross, as, 2, 3, 6
indictment
  of Miller, Ross, 3, 66–67
  of Spilotro, Tony, 124
  of Thomas, Carl, 113
International Brotherhood of Teamsters,
    37, 78
International Hotel, 69

Jeffers, Ray, 117
Johnson, Lyndon, 77–78
Jones, Fletcher, 199–200
Jones, Jan
  campaign of, 199–202, 203, 204–11
  as Las Vegas mayor, 186, 192, 193
Jones, Ted, 200
Jones Vargas, 230, 233
Justices of the Peace (JP), 96–97, 101, 102,
    103, 105

Kelley, Virginia Cassidy, 207
Kennedy, John F., 52, 53–54
Kennedy, Robert F., 52, 63
  campaign of, 73
  death of, 74–75
Kennedy, Ted, 53, 54
Kerkorian, Kirk, 69, 174, 193, 238
King, Rodney, 181–82, 187
Korshak, Sidney, 33

La Cosa Nostra, 33
Lamb, Ralph, 49–51, 87, 95–96, 107, 115

Index

Lansky, Meyer, 91, 237
Las Vegas, xiii. *See also* casinos
  African-American community in, 181,
    182, 186–89, 191, 192
  as All-American City, xiv, 239
  building boom in, 167, 173
  Clark County Sheriff's Office in, 49–50,
    86–87, 96, 168
  decreased tourism in, 175
  growth in, 154–56
  institutional racism in, 181
  Jones, Jan, as mayor of, 186, 192, 193
  mega casinos in, 174
  Miller, Ross, in, 19–21, 23–30, 49–54
  as "Mississippi of the West," 181
  murder rate in, 122
  new era in, 151–52
  in 1960s, 37–47
  in 1970s, 93
  organized crime in, 123
  Organized Crime Strike Force in, 5
  past mob history of, 236–37
  population of, 26, 40
  riots in, 181–93
  Westside in, 181, 182, 183, 185–89, 192
  as world-famous entertainment mecca,
    235
Las Vegas Country Club, 28
Las Vegas Hilton, 216–17
Las Vegas Metropolitan Police
  Department, 96, 128, 168
  during riots, 182, 184–85, 186, 187, 191
Las Vegas Review-Journal, 158, 163, 168, 210
Las Vegas Shrine Club, 83, 112
Las Vegas Strike Force, 145
Las Vegas Sun, 162, 204, 206
Lau, Cheryl, 212
Laverty, Roger, 200
Law Enforcement Man of the Year, 138
law school, 70, 72, 85, 89, 90
Law School Admission Test, 68
Lawford, Peter, 46
lawmakers' compensation bill, 161–62
Laxalt, Paul, 67, 68–69, 135, 222
Legislative Counsel Bureau, 176, 198
legislative session, 141–42, 177
Lenzie, Chuck, 191
letter, about Thomas, Carl, 144
Levinson, Edward, 67

Leypoldt, Butch, 49
Liberace, 24, 34, 39, 45, 46
licensing hearing, for Riviera, 28–29
lieutenant governor, 131–39, 141, 142, 168
lifeguard, at Riviera, 43, 45, 47, 59–60
Lionel, Sawyer and Collins, 169, 198
List, Robert, ("Bob"), 2, 113, 127
lobbyist, Vassiliadis as, 218–19
lounge shows, 32
Loyola Law School, 70, 79, 85–92, 241
Luxor, 82

Mafia, 3, 4, 5, 17. *See also* La Cosa Nostra
Mallin, Stanley, 80, 82
Mandalay Bay, 82, 237
Marnell, Tony, 229
Martin, Dean, 46
Masto, Catherine Cortez, 204, 229
Matteucci, Judy, 154, 156
Maxey, Bob, 192
McCarran, Pat, 52
McCarran International Airport, 23, 104
McCarthy, John, 115, 120, 121–22
McKay, Brian, 169, 170
media news, of riots, 181–88, 189, 191
mega casinos, 174
Mercury News story, 3–4, 5
Mexico
  ambassador to, 221–22
  gaming in, 233
MGM Grand, 69, 174, 192–93, 238
military
  Air Force Reserve unit, 72
  Army Reserve unit, 71
  basic training, 71
  D Battery Army Reserve unit, 87
  honorable discharge, 72
  Private First Class, E-3, 71
  religious preference, 71–72
  ROTC, 71
Milken, Michael, 225
Miller, Bob. *See also specific topics*
  as "Boob," 31, 56
  as Miller, Robert, 103–4, 105
Miller, Corrine, 106, 137, 184, 232
Miller, Ed, 129
Miller, Herschel, 10, 11, 12, 14, 19, 41
Miller, Lou, 75
Miller, Megan, 167, 184, 232

Index

Miller, Ross, 2
  accident of, 10
  background of, 9–11
  Bob's fight with, 59–60
  Bob's graduation attended by, 58
  as casino big shot, 31–36, 37, 40
  death of, 98–99
  dream home of, 37
  expectations of, 34
  golf played by, 82
  as illegal bookmaker, 2, 3, 6
  indictment of, 3, 66–67
  integrity of, 82
  Kennedy election and, 53–54
  in Las Vegas, 19–21, 23–30, 49–54
  in Las Vegas Country Club, 28
  in 1960s, 37–47
  in Palm Springs, 76–78
  Riviera and, 18–19, 20, 23, 75–76
  Sarno as friend of, 79–83
  Silver Palm bar owned by, 11, 12, 14,
    19, 31
  Thomas, Carl, and, 111, 112–13, 143
Miller, Ross (son), 106, 221, 231, 232, 241–142
Miller, Sandy Searles, xiv, 93–94, 106, 133,
    155, 208, 212, 232
mining industry, 156, 159, 160
mining tax, 175
Mirage, 151, 165–67
Miranda Rights, 88
Missing Children Act, 130
"Mississippi of the West," 181
mob history, 236–37
The Mob Museum, 237
Moran, John, 5, 128, 138, 186, 187
Moulin Rouge, 182
Multi-Jurisdictional Community
    Empowerment Commission, 192
murder charges, of Spilotro, Tony, 124
murder rate, in Las Vegas, 122
Mustang Ranch, 108

National Association for the Advancement
    of Colored People, 186
National Association of Secretaries of
    State, 242
National District Attorneys Association
    (NDAA), xiv, 117–18, 128, 129–30,
    135, 219, 220, 233

National Governors Association (NGA),
    xiv, 195, 219, 230
NDAA. See National District Attorneys
    Association
Neal, Joe, 187
Nellis Air Force Base, 26, 72
Neumann, Lawrence ("Crazy Larry"), 123
Nevada
  democrats in, 127, 128, 167–68
  governor of, xiii, 6, 147
  lieutenant governor of, 131–39, 141, 142,
    168
  mining industry in, 156, 159, 160
  politics in, 1, 51
  school system improvements in, 155–57
  tax increase in, 156–57, 160, 161
Nevada Citizens Alliance, 202
Nevada Commission on Economic
    Development, 142
Nevada Commission on Tourism, 142
Nevada Department of Transportation, 143
Nevada Gaming Commission, 127, 236
Nevada Judges Association, 105
Nevada National Guard, 184, 187–91
Nevada Partners Program, 193
Nevada Power Co., 191
Nevada State Education Association, 157
Nevada Test Site, 26
news conference, 5
Newton, Wayne, 46
NGA. See National Governors Association
Nielsen, Brooke, 199
1960s
  Las Vegas in, 37–47
  Miller, Ross, in, 37–47
1970s, Las Vegas in, 93
Nixon, Richard, 53, 54
notoriety, of Spilotro, Tony, 122

O'Callaghan, Mike, 162, 168–69
Ocean's Eleven, 46
Onion Field (Wambaugh), 87
Oram, Kent, 133–37, 207–8
organized crime, 123
Organized Crime Strike Force,
    in Las Vegas, 5

Palm Springs, 76–78
Panetta, Leon, 219

Parents of Murdered Children, 115–16
Patrick, Bob, 136
Pennington, Bill, 82
Pesci, Joe, 91, 120
Pitches, Pete, 87
plea-bargaining policy, 130
political advisor, Vassiliadis as, 2, 3, 5, 157, 201
political career, 95–99
    as attorney, 95–96, 141
    as bailiff, 87, 89
    bar exam, 90
    with Beckley, DeLanoy, Singleton and Jemison, 141
    as Clark County district attorney, 2–3, 106–10, 115, 127–29, 141
    as deputy DA, 90, 91
    end of, 229–40
    as JP, 101–2, 103, 105
    in Las Vegas Metropolitan Police Department, 96
    Law Enforcement Man of the Year, 138
    law school, 70, 72, 85, 89, 90
    in legislative session, 141–42
    as lieutenant governor, 131–39, 141, 142, 168
    as Nevada governor, xiii, 6, 147
    smear campaign in, 108, 109
population, of Las Vegas, 26, 40
Porter, Gene, 208
Powell, Gregory Ulas, 87–88
Presidential Task Force on Victims of Crime, 116–17, 130, 136
President's Commission on Organized Crime, 145
press conference, 145–46
Prima, Louis, 32
Private First Class, E-3, 71
property, on Strip, 18, 23
prostate cancer, 224–26
Prostate Cancer Foundation, 225
public menace, Spilotro, Tony as, 120

Quaid, Dennis, 95
Quintana, Annette, 92

racism, institutional, 181
Radev, Todor, 234
Raggio, Bill, 141–42

Ralston, Jon, 159, 169, 171
Rape Crisis Center, 115
Raskin, Hy, 52
Rat Pack, 46
Reagan, Ronald, 116, 130, 135, 143
    reelection, 127–29
Reeves, David, 56
Reid, Harry, 147, 231, 240
relatives, 13. See also Miller, Ross
    Doyle, Coletta Jane ("the Irish Songbird"), 11–12, 13, 14, 110
    Miller, Corrine, 106, 137, 184, 232
    Miller, Herschel, 10, 11, 12, 14, 19, 41
    Miller, Megan, 167, 184, 232
    Miller, Ross (son), 106, 221, 231, 232, 241–42
    Miller, Sandy Searles, xiv, 93–94, 106, 133, 155, 208, 212, 232
religious preference, 71–72
Republican National Committeeman, 98
Rich, Charlie, 19
Rickles, Don, 32
Rio, 238
riots, in Las Vegas, 181–93
    command center during, 184, 185
    curfew during, 186, 187, 189
    destruction during, 182–85
    electricity restored after, 191–92
    King verdict and, 181–82, 187
    Las Vegas Metro Police during, 182, 184–85, 186, 187, 191
    media news of, 181–88, 189, 191
    Nevada National Guard during, 184, 187–91
    72nd Military Police Company during, 184, 191
    Vassiliadis during, 186, 187, 191
Rivers, Johnny, 32
Riviera, 119
    Chicago Outfit in, 63
    Hickory Room in, 27, 28, 79
    licensing hearing for, 28–29
    lifeguard at, 43, 45, 47, 59–60
    Miller, Ross, and, 18–19, 20, 23, 75–76
    sale of, 75–76
    Thomas, Carl, in, 113
Roemer, William, 33, 122
Rogich, Sig, 102, 133, 212, 229
Roselli, Johnny, 95

Rosenthal, Geri, 91, 125
Rosenthal, Frank ("Lefty"), 91, 123, 125, 237
ROTC, 71
Rozanski, Walter, 114
R&R Partners, 239
Ruffin, Phil, 204
Russell, Charles, 51
Russian Heritage Highway, 234
Ruvo, Larry, 229

Sahara Hotel, 94
sale, of Riviera, 75–76
Salinas (president), 221
Sanchez, Tony, 233
Sandoval, Brian, 213
Sandy Searles Miller Academy of
    International Studies, 155
Santa Clara University, 63–64, 65, 68, 70,
    86, 87
Santini, Jim, 135
Sarno, Jay
    Caesars Palace and, 79–80
    Circus Circus and, 80–81
    Miller, Ross, as friend of, 79–83
    in Strip, 80
Sawyer, Grant, 34, 44–45, 51–52, 63, 170
school system improvements, 155–57
Schreck, Frank, 168, 196, 198, 205–7
Scorsese, Martin, 4
Scott, Jesse, 186, 187
Scott, Randolph, 76
Searles, Jim, 184
security guards, in casinos, 49
senate campaign, of Bryan, 1, 4, 5, 127–28,
    142–43, 145, 146
Senate Finance Committee, 142, 176
senate seat, of Bryan, 230, 232, 233
Senate Select Committee in Improper
    Activities in the Labor or
    Management Field, 17
senator, Hecht as, 1, 132, 133
Sennett, William V., 29
Seven Lakes Country Club, 76
72nd Military Police Company, during
    riots, 184, 191
Sharks in the Desert: The Founding Fathers and
    Current Kings of Las Vegas (Smith), 239
Shattuck, Ellie, 34
Shattuck, Frank, 34

sheriff's office. See Clark County Sheriff's
    office
Siegel, Benjamin ("Bugsy"), 19, 38, 236
Silver, Jeff, 93
Silver Palm bar, 11, 12, 14, 19, 31
Silver Slipper, 35
Sinatra, Frank, 46
Skelton, Red, 46
skimming, 66–67, 111–13, 124, 143, 144
Sloan, Mike, 196
Slots-A-Fun Casino, 82–83, 107
smear campaign, 108, 109
Smith, Jimmy Lee, 87–89
Smith, John L., 239
Smith, Keely, 32
speed-reading class, 73, 74
Spilotro, Michael, 123, 125
Spilotro, Anthony ("Tony the Ant"), 4, 91,
    113, 119–25, 237
    Blasko and, 120, 123
    crimes of, 123
    death of, 125
    Dorfman, Allen, and, 119–20
    Hole in the Wall Gang of, 120, 123, 124
    indictment of, 124
    murder charges of, 124
    notoriety of, 122
    as public menace, 120
    Rosenthal, Lefty, and, 123
    as target, 120
    wiretapping operation of, 119, 120–21
Stanford, 241
Stardust Resort & Casino, 42–43, 112
State of Nevada Employees Association,
    177, 203
State of State address, 158–60, 216
Stevens, Joseph E., 3
Stoyanov, Petar, 234
Streisand, Barbra, 45–46
Strip, 6, 34, 37
    bosses and, 44
    as bustling tourist draw, 215
    casinos on, 17, 35, 40, 44
    neon on, 46
    property on, 18, 23
    Sarno in, 80

Tailhook Association, 216–18
Tailhook Bill, 217

Index

Tait, Tom, 116, 234
Tangiers, 236
Tanya (elephant), 81–82
Tarkanian, Danny, 242
tax increase, 156–57, 160, 161, 175
Teamsters, 80
Teamsters' Central States Pension Fund,
    17, 69, 119
Teamsters Union Pension Fund, 38, 80
Thomas, Carl, 2–4, 83
    death of, 113
    indictment of, 113
    letter about, 144
    Miller, Ross, and, 111, 112–13, 143
    in Riviera, 113
    skimming and, 111–13, 143, 144
Thomas, E. Parry, 32, 69
Thunderbird Hotel, 90
Tiberti, Tito, 56, 57, 65, 71, 75
tourism decrease, 175
tourist draw, Strip as, 215
Treasure Island, 173, 204
Tropicana, 112, 144
Twain, Mark, 142

United States Aid to International
    Development (USAID), 234
U.S. ambassador
    to Argentina, 222
    to Mexico, 221–22
USAID. See United States Aid to
    International Development

Vassiliadis, Billy, 232
    during campaign, 146, 205, 207, 208, 210
    as lobbyist, 218–19
    as political advisor, 2, 3, 5, 157, 201
    during riots, 186, 187, 191

Vegas, 95
Venetian, 237
Victim and Witness Protection Act, 130
victims, 115–16
Vietnam War, 65, 70
Vogel, Ed, 159

Wadsworth, Don, 121
Walsh, Adam, 129–30
Walsh, John, 129–31, 135–36, 138, 139,
    220
Wambaugh, Joseph, 87
The Washington Post, 5
Weatherford, Harvey, 185
Webster, Angelo, 179, 192, 223
Western Governors Association, 165,
    166
Westside, 181, 182, 183, 185–89, 192
When the Mob Ran Vegas: Stories of Money,
    Mayhem and Murder (Fischer), 18
Wiesner, Tom, 98
Williams, Claudine, 35
Williams, Wendell, 187
Winnemucca, 106
wiretapping, 119, 120–21, 146
witness, in trial, 88
Woofter, Roy, 96, 107, 108, 109
World Series of Poker, 114
Wynn, Steve, 6, 151, 201, 242
    Bellagio opened by, 174, 237
    Mirage opened by, 165
    Treasure Island built by, 173
Wynn Las Vegas, 237

Yucca Mountain, 143, 196

Zedillo (president), 221
Zeta-Jones, Catherine, 233